*Hope Is Not A Winning Strategy
… But Price To Win (PTW) Is!*

Hope Is Not A Winning Strategy … But Price To Win (PTW) Is!

An insider's guide to Price To Win (PTW) and why
it is needed to turn wishful thinking into a sure thing
when pursuing major competitive contracts.

Anthony C. Constable

© 2011 and 2014 CAI/SISCo

All rights reserved. No part of this book may be reproduced or transmitted in any form or by any means, electronic, mechanical, photocopying, recording, scanning or otherwise, without prior written permission of the author or the publisher.

Published by:
CAI/SISCo
6 West Third Street
Frederick, Maryland 21701 USA
www.caisisco.com

Limit of Liability: While the author and the publisher have used their best efforts in preparing this book, they make no representations or warranties with respect to the accuracy or completeness of the contents of this book. Neither the author nor the publisher shall have any liability to any person or entity with respect to any loss or damage caused or alleged to be caused directly or indirectly by the instructions contained in this book.

First Edition: September 2011

Second Printing: November 2014

ISBN 978-0-9893708-3-7

Editing: Susan Shealer
Design & Production: Kathy Carl
Indexing: Clive Pyne

Printed in the United States of America.

To paraphrase Winston Churchill:

*Business developers can always be counted on to do the right thing...
after they have exhausted all other possibilities.*

Acknowledgements

Dedicated to Capture Teams everywhere that strive long and hard to succeed for their employers in the highly competitive government services marketplace. I hope this book helps.

Special thanks to the employees and friends of CAI/SISCo who applied themselves cheerfully to the task of making this the best, if not the only, Price To Win (PTW) book there is.

Extra special thanks are due to the following friends and colleagues who took my final draft and helped turn it into the text you see before you:

> Larry Wiesen, bid pricing expert, educator, and President of American GSC, who devoured my rough draft and provided a thorough review and several important examples and insights, most of which have been gratefully incorporated.

> Dr. Mike Nash, competitive intelligence guru, educator, worldwide Air Traffic Control market watcher, and President of ATC Market Analysis, LLC who provided valuable comments and constructive criticisms.

> Dr. Alex Metcalf, transportation economist and President of TEMS, Inc., who provided insightful comments and observations.

> Ken Newland, worldwide business development consultant, educator and President of Newland Training & Consultancy, who showed me the way to do a book like this and also provided valuable suggestions, comments and constructive criticisms.

This book is also dedicated to:

> *Life, Liberty, and the Happiness of Pursuit.*

Table of Contents

Foreword		**xv**
Introduction		xv
About the Author		xvi
About This Book		xviii
Book Structure		xviii
The Next Edition		xix
Feedback and Comments Are Invited		xix
About CAI/SISCo		**xxi**
Section I	**An Introduction to Price To Win (PTW)**	**1**
	Opportunity Capture Process Similarities	3
	What Most Opportunity Capture Processes Leave to Chance	3
	How PTW Changes the Capture Process	4
	Shedding Light on the Competition	5
	PTW to Improve Win Probability (pWin)	6
	Who Uses PTW and Why?	7
	Some Key PTW Terms	7
	Price Target-Driven Solutions	10
	PTW and Game Theory	11
	PTW's Value Proposition	12
	PTW's Relationship to the Black Hat Review	12
	PTW's Role — Helping to Fully Inform Capture Teams	13
	The Information Dilemma	14
	PTW Serves All Stakeholders	16
	Ways of Employing PTW	16
	Who Commissions PTW Studies?	17
	PTW's Role in Helping Shape Successful Capture Campaigns	17
	Don't Forget — PTW Has to Tell a Story	18
	How PTW Should Be Funded	18
	PTW and Painting by the Numbers	19

	Business Development Models and PTW	19
	Strategic Bid Pricing 101	20
	The PTW Practitioner's View of Incumbency	21
	The "Best Value" Issue	22
	More Approach Advice for PTW Teams	22
	PTW — To Do or Not to Do	23
	Needed PTW Resources	23
	PTW and Ethics	24
	A PTW Case Study — Food for Thought	25
Section II	**CAI/SISCo's Price To Win (PTW) Framework**	**27**
	Relationship of PTW to the Overall Capture Process	28
	PTW as a Parametric Process	28
	CAI/SISCo's PTW Framework	29
	A. The Opportunity Defined	30
	B. The PTW Framework Phases Defined	31
	Partially Gamed vs. Fully Gamed PTW	31
	Other Views of CAI/SISCo's PTW Framework	32
	PTW Team/Capture Team Encounters	33
	Tasking to Support the PTW Framework	34
	The PTW Framework in a Nutshell	36
Section III	**Phase 1 of CAI/SISCo's PTW Framework** **Developing Situational Awareness and the Top Down PTW**	**37**
	Phase 1 of the PTW Framework	**37**
	What PTW Wants to Learn from Encounter 0	38
	PTW Phase 1 — A Road Map	39
	PTW Framework Phase 1, Step 1 — Developing Situational Awareness	40
	The Effectiveness of Lobbyists	40
	Acquiring Needed PTW Information	41
	Developing Opportunity Understanding	41
	A Lack of Understanding Can Really Hurt	42
	PTW and SOO-Based Acquisitions	42
	Understanding the Customer's Cast of Characters	43
	Understanding the Customer	43
	Grappling with Customer Requirements	44
	Understanding Competitors and the Home Team	44
	Teaming Issues to Bear in Mind	45
	PTW and the WBS for Top Down Analysis	46
	Back to PTW Framework Phase 1, Step 1	48

	Top Down Competitor PTW Analysis — Approach 2	48
	Budget Realities	49
	PTW Framework Phase 1, Step 2 — Evaluation Modeling	49
	The Phase 1, Step 2 Evaluation Modeling Process	51
	Competitor SWOT Summaries (b)	51
	Color Coding as a Basis for Non-Cost Evaluation Scoring (b)	52
	Provenance for Non-Cost Evaluation Scoring (c)	52
	Budget Projection (d)	52
	Top Down Competitor PTW Analysis — Approach 3	53
	Completing the Basic Evaluation Model (BEM) (e)	55
	A Word About Scoring Evaluation Models	55
	Defining an Opportunity's Strategic Strike Zone (SSZ)	56
	Encounter 1 — What PTW Needs to Impart to the Capture Team	57
	Phase 1 of the Progressive PTW Problem	**58**
Section IV	**Phase 2 of CAI/SISCo's PTW Framework Developing the Partially Gamed Bottoms Up PTW**	**59**
	Phase 2 of the PTW Framework	**59**
	PTW's Suite of Modeling Elements	60
	PTW Framework Phase 2, Step 3 — The WBS for Bottoms Up Analysis	61
	PTW Framework Phase 2, Step 4 — The Labor Model	62
	About Corporate Personality	63
	Labor Rate Build-Up Realities	63
	Developing Labor Rates for CY2 and Beyond	64
	Forward Pricing Healthcare Costs	65
	Why the Wrap Rate Build-Up Approach Should Be Favored	66
	Why Non-Wrap Rate Build-Up Approaches Should Be Avoided	66
	A Word about Uncompensated Overtime	67
	A Word about GWACs	67
	Off-Site Labor Opportunities	68
	Developing Blended Labor Rates to Lower Evaluated Prices	69
	The Labor Model in Perspective	70
	PTW Framework Phase 2, Step 5 — The ODC Model	70
	Change, the Only Constant	71
	ODC Discounts and Deflators	72
	Solution Development to Lower Costs	73
	Commoditization — The Signs	74
	Monitoring and Adjusting Pricing Curves	74
	PTW Framework Phase 2, Step 6 — The BOE Model	75
	Producing WBS-Based BOEs	76

    WBS-Level BOE Development 76
    The BOE Model in Perspective 77
    Additional Thoughts on BOEs & BOMs 78
    PTW Framework Phase 2, Step 7 — Evaluation Model 78
    Encounter 2 — What PTW Needs to Impart 78
    What Is/Is Not in the Partially Gamed PTW 79

Phase 2 of the Progressive PTW Problem **79**

Section V   Phase 3 of CAI/SISCo's PTW Framework Fully Gaming the Partially Gamed Bottoms Up PTW 81

Phase 3 of the PTW Framework **81**
    PTW Framework Phase 3, Step 8 — The Reality Model 82
    How Is a Reality Model Developed? 83
    Forecasting and Estimating Contract Potential 83
    Ways of Estimating the "Real" Opportunity 84
    Contrasting the Evaluated and Reality Cases 84
    A Word about Engineering Change Proposals (ECPs) 85
    Reality Modeling Information Sources and Examples 86
    PTW Framework Phase 3, Step 9 — Gaming the Partially Gamed PTW 87
    Delta Margin Gaming — The PTW Practitioner's Edge 87
    Delta Margin Gaming: Solve for Lower Price or Higher Profit? 88
    An Alternative Phase 3, Step 9 Price Gaming Approach 89
    PTW Framework Phase 3, Step 10 — Final Evaluation Model 91
    Encounter 3 — What PTW Needs to Impart 91

Conclusion **92**
    From Top Down PTW to the Partially and Fully Gamed Bottoms Up PTWs 92
    How the Fully Gamed PTW Is Related to pWin 93
    Setting the Home Team's Final, Fully Gamed PTW 93

Phase 3 of the Progressive PTW Problem **94**

Section VI   Food for PTW Thought 95
    Routes to the Government Labor Market 95
    The Landscape Is Always Changing 96
    Additional Thoughts on Developing a Top-Down PTW 96
    The U.S. Federal Government Staff Augmentation Marketplace 97
    The Public-Private Partnership 97
    The Other Big Bangs 98
    A Cautionary Incumbency Tale 98
    Additional Pricing Strategies for PTW Practitioners 99
    A Word about Unintended Consequences 101

	General Research Sources	101
	Finding Opportunity, Agency and Competitor Information	101
Section VII	**The Progressive Price To Win (PTW) Problem**	**103**
	Phase 1 of the Progressive PTW Problem	103
	Understanding the ITCON Opportunity	104
	The ITCON Competitors	104
	The Competitive Bid Teams	104
	Past Bid Behavior	105
	What Needs to Be Done	105
	Phase 2 of the Progressive PTW Problem	107
	Needed ITCON Capture Team Support	107
	More Intelligence	107
	What Needs to Be Done	108
	Phase 3 of the Progressive PTW Problem	112
	More Intelligence	112
	How to Game ITCON Prices	112
	Completed Phase 1 Tables	114
	Phase 1 Budget Table — Done	114
	Phase 1 PTW History Table — Done	114
	Phase 1 Evaluation Model — Done	115
	Completed Phase 2 Tables	116
	Phase 2 BOM Tables — Done	116
	Phase 2 Labor Tables — Done	117
	Phase 2 Price Tables — Done	118
	Phase 2 Evaluation Model — Done	119
	Completed Phase 3 Tables	120
	Phase 3 BOM Tables — Done	120
	Phase 3 Discount Tables — Done	120
	Phase 3 Labor Tables — Done	121
	Phase 3 Phase 3 Gamed, Bottoms Up Price Tables — Done	122
	Phase 3 Evaluation Model — Done	122
	Glossary of Terms & Acronyms	**125**
	Index	**131**

Foreword

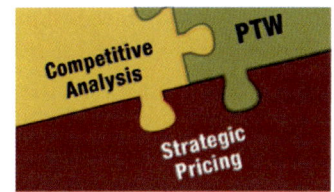

I, like many, was much impressed by the introduction to the well received management book *In Search of Excellence* that was co-authored by Tom Peters and Robert Waterman in 2003. You may recall that this well-written piece opened up by extolling the virtues of the Four Seasons Hotel in Washington, D.C.'s Georgetown section. This establishment was chosen based on its business model's ability to allegedly anticipate a client's every need.

A few years after I read that book, my wife and I checked into this hotel for an overnight. The room was on the upside of adequate but not exceptional. We decided to dine in that evening and went downstairs to their restaurant. We were seated and given menus. Realizing that I had left my reading glasses in the room, I summoned the waiter and asked for a pair of reading glasses. Evidently this basic client need—*you can buy cheap reading glasses by the bushel at your local dollar store*—had not been anticipated. I refuse to believe I was the first person in that hotel with that need.

But business-related oversight is not unusual. In my field, which is helping corporate clients win major government contracting opportunities, it is well documented that price, at the end of the day, is the major determinant for 85% of all competitive contract awards, assuming all else is acceptable. Notwithstanding, few companies have re-engineered their capture processes to embrace this reality.

Sensing that pieces were either missing from or under-utilized in our customers' contract capture processes, CAI/SISCo hung out a shingle in the early 1980s as a provider of independent Price To Win (PTW) services on a first come, first served, opportunity exclusive basis.

In a nutshell, the PTW concept is this: Support the Home Team's opportunity capture team with a detailed and incrementally developed, competitor-centric view of what it will take to win, all non-price and price issues considered.

Making a Capture Team aware of their competitors' ability to earn evaluation award points shows what the Home Team needs to do to win. It does so by providing the Capture Team with that proverbial "other hand against which to clap." Without an independent view of what it is most likely going to take to win, a bidder has only "the sound of one hand clapping."

Introduction

The introduction to a *Wall Street Journal* article about the abysmal track record of government agencies charged with predicting national budget deficits and surpluses had caught my eye. The problem, it seems, is not that we cannot accurately describe the input events such as tax cuts, natural disasters, and so forth—it is more that the models and assumptions we use to determine the outcomes are inadequate or just plain wrong. In a nutshell: The national budget modeling kings are wearing few opaque clothes.

To me, the significance of this piece is not that systems and processes lag behind what is really needed. What the article underscores is how difficult it is to change systems and processes, even when they have been proven to be sub-optimal.

Several years ago, I reached the opinion that the same sort of thing is true in business development—the processes and tools that are in place emphasize what their authors were promoting (e.g., proposal development), not what is needed to succeed. Perhaps this is a little harsh, but the fact is that for major opportunities, the competing bid teams are chasing a single award.

PTW, in seeking to shed more light on the competitive environment, must deal with all sorts of personalities—not just people, but companies, agencies, and so forth. Even government contracting opportunities, which range from mundane to highly complex sets of requirements, have "personalities." For instance, some acquisitions seek to buy or lease solutions, while others want a service and yet others want to acquire labor and/or various sorts of hardware. Other dimensions of opportunity personality can include Service Level Agreements (SLAs), evaluation schemes and criteria, security clearance requirements, and the customer environment and organization to be served and supported.

Similarly, bid teams that form to capture a specific opportunity also have unique personalities. Team personality is formed as a confluence of team members and their differing priorities, capabilities, structures and overhead elements.

At my firm, CAI/SISCo, a small yet highly-focused enterprise, we have for years developed and improved our information, methods, and tools by providing our PTW services to hundreds of major capture efforts involving all sorts of opportunity, corporate, and team personalities. As a result, we have been exposed to the good, the bad, and the ugly. Our mission, therefore, is to show how PTW can raise all Capture Team boats by increasing awareness that the key to success is developing good solutions that can profitably live within winning prices.

About the Author

I came to the United States from England on April 6, 1968, landing at Washington, DC's almost new Dulles International Airport the Sunday after Dr. Martin Luther King, Jr. had been shot. Washington, DC was on fire, but in the Rockville, Maryland suburb where I was to live and work, all was relative tranquility.

As a computer programmer, I had been recruited in the U.K. to work for then-government contractor CEIR, Inc. By the time I got to the U.S., CEIR had been acquired by Control Data Corporation (CDC), then the undisputed leading maker of supercomputers.

To start my first work day, I was given a 200-page document that turned out to be a proposal that CEIR had submitted to NASA. I was told to read it and to prepare questions. Evidently, a contract to do the proposed work had just been received and this job was to be my first assignment.

My first year at CEIR exposed me to several other government agencies and several more opportunities and contracts. I was impressed and overwhelmed at the diversity of problems and solutions that the government marketplace represented. I still am.

Almost before I had truly found my bearings at CEIR, my first boss contacted me and gave me an employment offer I could not refuse. He had left CEIR and formed his own firm developing packaged mainframe software applications. I pursued this line of work for several years until, in 1975, I became an independent contractor and moved to California to develop an IT scheduling and resource allocation system for the original Bank of America.

When this work was completed in late 1977, my family decided to move back to the East Coast. Casting around for work back in the National Capital Region (NCR), I found a job writing a procedures manual for the Environmental Protection Agency's (EPA) data center.

As always, one thing led to another. Soon I found myself in the role of hired gun developing technical solutions for Martin Marietta (now Lockheed Martin) and others as they pursued major opportunities in other federal agencies. It became evident to me fairly quickly that good technical solutions could only win if they were supported with equally competent management approaches. Accordingly, I began to focus on management aspects of bids that demonstrated how the offeror intended to manage their solution to success.

It was clear to me that a strong management focus improved success rates, but I was drawn, moth-to-flame-like, to price—still what I consider to be the final frontier for capture success. From that point forward I have been a student of pricing strategies and tactics, much as I had been a student of technical and management solutions before that.

My fascination with and growing knowledge of all aspects of bid pricing must have been obvious to some observers since, in 1978, I received a request to try to figure out what price a major competitive bid team would be likely to bid on a "must win" deal my customer was pursuing. My customer had some notion of what sort of solution the competitor would be offering, but wanted an independent assessment of their most likely bid price and gaming potential.

I had long-since learned that if you want to be an independent consultant, there is no such word as "No" when opportunity knocks. I contend to this day that life is governed by one's responses to hard questions like the one posed to me, so I agreed to develop the competitor's likely price for this rather complex bid. And I agreed to do it in a compressed timeframe.

Unbeknownst to me, this was my first Price To Win (PTW) engagement. And serendipitously, I ended up with a happy customer and my first price-related win. Not only that, but also… my phone began to ring. Thus, I discovered that there was a pent-up demand from contractors for independent assessments of competitor-likely bid pricing.

After my first full year of doing this, I had six high-profile competitive pricing analyses under my belt, and demand for my services was still hot. At this level of demand I needed help and, to get it, I hired a technical solution resource so that I could concentrate on marketing and the pricing and gaming aspects of the opportunities.

We continued to grow and hired more help. After five or so years of continued growth, we were doing over 20 of these analyses a year.

My first real employee was Nick Robertshaw, a borderline genius. Nick was a real fan of the Apple Macintosh, which was introduced in 1984. In response to my perceived desire to try to remember all of the personalities that we had come into contact with in past and present engagements, Nick created a client/server implementation of Apple's Hypercard PC database software. To do this, Nick created a simple polling program on a Macintosh that was designated to be the server, and a peer-to-peer communications utility that connected each client Mac to the server Mac. This was the beginning of the concept of *Infocentricity*, whereby information capture, pre-positioning, and sharing became the centerpiece of our corporate culture and of our business success. (You can obtain a copy of a short book I wrote on the subject of *Infocentricity* from Amazon. The book is called *Everything About Everything: If Information Is Power, Why Aren't We More Powerful?*)

The second major piece of our infostructure to receive attention was the creation of our models and analysis tool suites. We decided that, to the maximum extent possible, all models needed to accomplish a project would be developed by leveraging and improving what had gone before. The secret was to replace older, less sophisticated models with newer, improved ones. This has been and still is a constant process improvement story.

By 1987, I had to face up to the fact that I had created a firm whose main products were studies that independently derived estimates of competitive team bid prices. This is what has become known as Price To Win (PTW).

In 1988, to sustain manageable growth and maintain quality, I took the first tentative steps toward codifying the CAI/SISCo approach to single- and multi-target PTW analyses. This evolved over the next few years until it became the 3-Phase, 10-Step PTW Framework that this book describes.

It was all coming together. We now had the experience, the PTW Framework, the culture, an infocentric knowledge worker support system (we eventually abandoned our Hypercard-based infostructure in favor of Lotus Notes), and a complete suite of rapidly adaptable models and tools in place to support the growing number of concurrent PTW analyses that the world was bringing to our door. We also had that Holy Grail of efficiency—great leverage.

So, there you almost have it. The pieces that have been added more recently are:

- Our PTW and other business development training seminars that we started giving in 2004; and, more recently,
- The infostructure consulting services that we now offer to help clients support and develop their own infocentric cultures.

As far as I know, there still is no formal way to become a PTW practitioner, short of just doing it. Other alternatives would be to attend one of CAI/SISCo's regularly scheduled PTW training seminars or reading this book carefully, and *then* just doing it.

Anyway, that's how I became a PTW practitioner.

About This Book

I suppose, like nature, I abhor a vacuum, and it was the vacuum for the PTW Framework and processes that drew me in and compelled me to write this book to introduce PTW to a much wider audience. Along the way, I have shared many of the concepts and realities of *doing* PTW studies and the pitfalls of *not doing* them.

As successful as this and our other training seminars have become, the continued absence of any sort of "how to" book on the subject of PTW haunted me until, in late 2010, I resolved to write the best book I could about the need for and benefits of PTW. Halfway through 2011, with much help and encouragement from colleagues, customers and friends, a first edition of this book was finished.

The book's purpose is to provide a Price To Win (PTW) framework and process to help achieve win probabilities (pWins) of 100% for competitive opportunities. Not 73% or 87%, but 100%.

The book's ideal readers are:

- All who are involved with any aspect of business development involving the pursuit of competitive contract awards;
- Contracting business owners and their senior managers looking to take their businesses to the next level (i.e., small to mid-sized, mid-size to large-sized); and
- Anyone else who is curious enough to want to learn about the bigger picture.

Book Structure

As shown in the book structure roadmap graphic below, this book is comprised of seven major sections and a glossary of acronyms and terms.

Brief descriptions of the elements of this book follow:

- Section I, *An Introduction to Price To Win (PTW)*, sets the stage for the succeeding sections that deal with the "how to" aspects of PTW under the aegis of CAI/SISCo's tried and tested PTW Framework.
- Section II, *CAI/SISCo's 3-Phase, 10-Step Price To Win (PTW) Framework*, lays out the framework for conducting orderly, timely and compelling PTW studies.
- Section III, *Phase 1—Developing Situational Awareness and the Top Down PTW*, takes the reader through Phase 1 (Steps 1 and 2) of the PTW Framework.

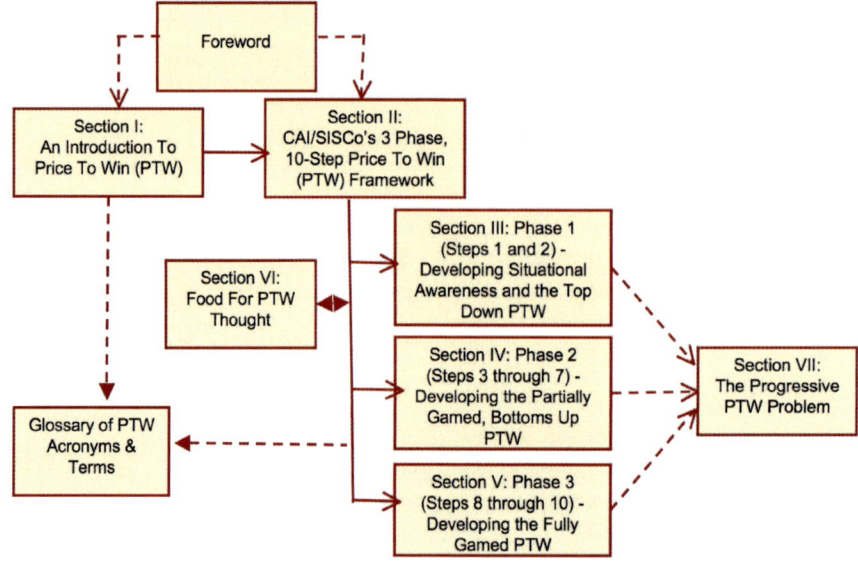

- Section IV, *Phase 2—Developing the Partially Gamed, Bottoms Up PTW*, covers Phase 2 (Steps 3 through 7) of the PTW Framework.

- Section V, *Phase 3—Developing the Fully Gamed PTW*, explains Phase 3 (Steps 8 through 10) of the PTW Framework.

- Section VI, *Food for PTW Thought*, presents several broader context issues that PTW practitioners should consider, explore and expand upon.

- Section VII, *The Progressive PTW Problem*, provides an animated and progressive view of how PTW might deal with a typical opportunity through the phases and steps of the PTW Framework.

The takeaway that this book strives to provide is that PTW should be embraced by firms that vie for competitive awards because:

- PTW can significantly improve opportunity pWins by focusing on the competition, providing the Home Team with timely information concerning what it needs to do to overcome competitors in terms of:
  - Aggregate evaluation award points (for team, approaches, solutions, past performance, etc.); and
  - Most likely gamed bid prices.

The bottom line for PTW is to help the Home Team focus on preparing *and* pricing a solution that can be bid at a profitable price that beats the fiercest competitor and wins!

The Next Edition

The next edition of this book is already in the planning stage. We expect to be adding "how to" sections on Strategic Pricing and Competitive Intelligence.

The centerpiece of the Strategic Pricing section will be a framework that will animate a novel approach to Strategic Pricing. This framework uses a solicitation's key characteristics (e.g., contract type, evaluation quantities, etc.) to rapidly identify which of about 200 pricing strategies are likely to be most effective in developing the Home Team's winning bid price. Detailed descriptions of scores of pricing strategies along with explanations of when they should or could be used will also be included, as will case studies that demonstrate the cumulative effect of multiple strategies in reducing an evaluated price while maintaining desired profit margins.

This next edition will also add a Competitive Intelligence section, the focus of which will be: You can't win using yesterday's data and price points; you have to learn how to predict tomorrow's.

Inquiries concerning the availability of the next and subsequent editions of this book should be emailed to **training@caisisco.com**.

Feedback and Comments Are Invited

Please use the comments page in the *PTW Book Comments* to provide your valuable feedback on this seminar—email to **training@caisisco.com**.

Also, please join the "Price To Win" group on LinkedIn.™

About CAI/SISCo

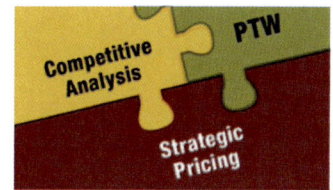

CAI/SISCo is a very experienced business development support services and training firm operating primarily in the national, international, and local government marketplaces. Our firm does not do or compete for government work ourselves—everything we do is done on an opportunity-exclusive basis to help a client capture a major complex competitive opportunity.

Since 1975, we have provided capture support to a veritable *Who's Who* of major corporations, covering well over 1,500 complex government programs with an aggregate value of more than $1 trillion. The majority of our work is derived from Price To Win (PTW) engagements. As we see it, our job is to provide *outside insights* for client business developers charged with retaining or capturing major government contracts and other business opportunities.

At time of writing, my company is supporting ~200 major PTW engagements per year (~20 concurrently at any point in time). Program subject matter covers a wide swath of activities including: base and range operations, weapon systems, border security, telecommunications, satellite systems, C4ISR, EW, software development, IT services, systems integration, training, embedded systems, intelligence systems, logistics, ERP, law enforcement, managed services, energy management, cloud computing, web portals, tax collection, case management, utility pricing, seat management, virtual reality, PKI, strategic and tactical systems, healthcare, vehicle maintenance, and many other activity areas.

To support the ever-expanding volume of work, we have developed a comprehensive PTW support environment and tool suite consisting of models, templates, and estimating tools. Supporting this is Infocenter, our "Corporate Memory," which contains pre-positioned information "snowflakes" that are exhaustively tagged and can be rapidly and dynamically organized into hundreds of views.

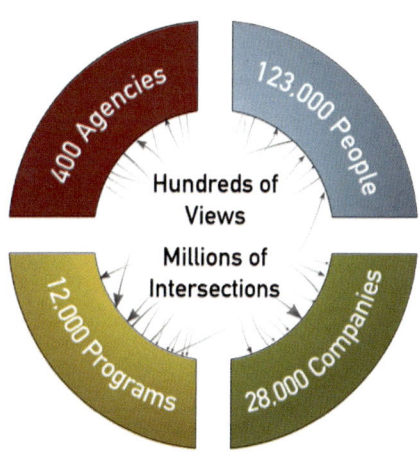

Our Infocenter also includes access to Subject Matter Experts (SMEs) of all sorts and "rules of thumb" for estimating and pricing scores of esoteric situations and activities.

Other opportunity capture services we provide include Pricing Strategies, Reality Models,* and Infostructure Consulting, whereby we assist clients to customize our processes, models, and database schema to develop their own infocentric cultures and environments.

---

*A Reality Model is a depiction of what evaluated items a bid team believes it will sell (hardware items, services, labor categories). Reality Models are developed to allow the deltas between the customer's evaluated case and the reality case to be exploited during PTW and Strategic Pricing. See Section V of this book for more detail on this subject.

Section I

An Introduction to Price To Win (PTW)

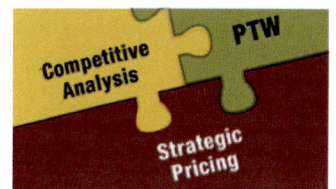

This book is all about how to do effective Price To Win (PTW) studies. More to the point, this book is about winning.

Here is the most common scenario for competitive contract competitions: Four bidders—one winner. Employing PTW is the best way there is of improving the odds of not being one of the three losers.

PTW is important because it helps people responsible for capturing new business for their company to confront, up front, the question of "How to Win?" using a rigorous process that delivers an accurate and timely target price based on competitor realities. Why is this so critical? Because, in 85% of all cases, when all is said and done, price is the most significant determinant of competitive awards. Not solutions, not proposals, not team—beyond a certain level of competency, it's all about price.

The critical difference that PTW brings to pursuits is setting bid price targets early, if not up front. If the Capture Team can't get to a winning price, don't bid.

That bidders risk considerable treasure mounting competitive opportunity capture campaigns without knowing who they are competing against *and* what bid price will most likely be needed to prevail, has long been a source of amazement to me. In good economic times it is possible for firms to thrive using a "nothing ventured, nothing gained" approach to business development. When customer budgets tighten, however, firms need to rethink the way in which they target winnable opportunities.

The brutal reality of a typical competition is that the government customer's job, it seems to me, is to maximize competition by keeping as many bidders in the game as possible. That is until the *denouement*, the final resolution of the intricacies of the acquisition plot. Short of a "no bid" decision, PTW is the best way that firms have of protecting against becoming one of the three losing teams.

PTW started off as a nostrum in the 1980s. In recent years, PTW has become fairly widely spoken of but, I fear, is still little understood. This book seeks to shine a light on this "art of the possible" by providing a soup to nuts treatment intended to inform and enlighten. As the foundation for the "how to" aspects of PTW, we have used CAI/SISCo's tried and tested 3-Phase, 10-Step PTW Framework. This framework provides both form and substance to what is a complex but not complicated subject. Onward!

Most government competitions are "winner take all" actions. In the commercial product world, a firm can make lots of money as the #2 beer seller or the #2 rental car company. Coming in second, however, for a government bid has only the negative reward of having chewed up resources, human energy, and hope, which, as we shall see, is no strategy at all.

Moreover, as collectors of coins, stamps, and so forth well know, acquiring rarities implies a cost that is inversely proportional to scarcity. Major contract opportunities are also relative rarities, but to acquire them generally requires the winning bidder to offer a high perceived value at a low apparent price. ("Apparent" is an interesting word because, as we shall see, it relates to gaming bid prices.)

When customer budgets shrink, price becomes ever more the key determinant for making competitive contract awards. This does not mean that price is the customer's only interest; he is, of course, also looking for value-for-money. That is, the balance of cost (purchase price), functionality, cost of ownership, time to the start of benefits and life of those benefits, and so on, all need to be taken into account. Also, the customer's own costs may be different for each solution that is offered and these, too, need to be factored in.

Traditional approaches to competition addressed just this perspective. The goal of the bid game was to convince the customer that you offered *better value* than the competition when all things were taken into account. This remains a key element of the successful bid. Its weakness is based on the assumption that the "best value" offer is determined only by the content and nuances of the offer. The actual cost of the offer is still based on the incurred costs + overheads, margin, etc.

A contemporary price-driven marketplace demands that solutions also be shaped by winning prices, not the other way around. As most bidders still focus competitive efforts on the inventive solution and the powerful impact of the well-written proposal—price remaining as a by-product of a cost+-derived solution—there is a competitive opportunity for those companies that build their solutions around a winning price.

> **PTW: It's all about the money.**

Recent experience is showing us that universally, competitive landscapes are changing: non-traditional players are shaking things up by offering better value solutions for less money, and competition within the marketplace has become brutal.

The majority of large firms that vie for major contracts in the U.S. have reacted by refocusing their capture processes on price. Most now use some form of PTW as a matter of course when pursuing incumbent recompetes… or new "must win" opportunities.

More recently, businesses operating in the European, Asian, and other major markets have also begun to recognize the value of PTW. They, too, are beginning to see that PTW is missing from their capture processes and that it needs to be the cornerstone of successful capture campaigns.

The purpose of this book is to address the philosophy, mechanics, and principles of the PTW-driven proposal. I have no doubt that many readers, at the start of this book, will argue that their organizations are already using price to drive design and cost base, and that they have been doing this for some time. This may, of course, be true, and this book may not offer them any greater insights until they realize that PTW develops its version of price from the Home Team's competitors and their most likely team, solution, and gaming abilities.

Readers should be aware that PTW, as described in this book, is only a part of overarching business development approaches. Some firms refer to PTW as being all or part of what they call *Positioning To Win,* or *Deal To Win,* or *Solution To Win.*

During the many years that CAI/SISCo has been conducting successful independent PTWs for our clients using the framework and processes explained in this book, we have also been studying how firms with internal PTW activities do their work. In summary, we have only come across a handful of these organizations that undertake PTWs with the rigor and consistency that can be practiced. Regardless, even the best internal PTW practitioners still call upon outside support for a second opinion for "must win" bids.

The big question for firms that compete against companies with robust internal PTW capabilities is "How should we combat the competitive firepower that is arrayed against us?" The answer is by using this book's framework, processes, and strategies to implement a PTW capability of your own.

As stated above, the subject matter presented in this book encapsulates 35-plus years of experience, derived from supporting the capture of hundreds of major complex opportunities. It is a tried and tested approach that is known to work. Some of what you will learn may not be easy to implement at first, but it does get easier, and it does work! You can, of course, simplify the approach, make it easier and less taxing to implement. In your current marketplace this may be good enough. In general, however, it is always wiser to simplify from the high ground of doing PTW fully than to simply avoid effort and end up not doing enough to win.

If you can, leave your day job outside the door while reading this book, and become a PTW practitioner in training. Immerse yourself in the journey of discovery. As the story unfolds, the relevance and justification of preceding steps become more apparent and, by the end, you will realize that PTW, as described herein, is a complete and self-correcting approach.

There is something else that you should take into account. This approach to PTW is based on a scope of the PTW practitioner's role that may be at odds with your current organizational structure and job roles. That is, some of the functions that are the job of the PTW practitioner in this book may be someone else's responsibility in your organization. This sometimes causes the PTW student to doubt that the approach can be successfully implemented in his organization or that perhaps an implementation is possible by bringing a team of different disciplines together to perform the PTW practitioner role. Suspend that thought until the end of the book. At this early stage, there is no point in trying to argue a point or to debate the principle. When you have formed a complete view, we shall return to how PTW can best be implemented.

Opportunity Capture Process Similarities

Customer Request For Proposals (RFPs) express customer needs while a company proposal matches a product, service, or solution that it wants to sell to the need expressed in the RFP. To meet this need, businesses have a means by which they respond to customer RFPs and Requests For Quotations (RFQs). There are many books and training seminars that set out the fundamentals of the capture process, and all organizations will have some internal procedures for this activity.

How bidders are organized differs according to the needs of their product suites, the marketplace, and the cultures of the organizations. For some bidders, the emphasis may be on the sales staff; for others it may be on the engineering team. Either group can take the lead in putting the proposal response together, or there may be another dedicated team that undertakes this on their behalf.

What Most Opportunity Capture Processes Leave to Chance

Regardless, as shown in the puzzle piece graphic, the three key elements that these approaches seem to leave to chance are:

1. **Competitive Analysis** to develop a deep understanding of the opportunity and the competing bid and Capture Teams, their likely solutions, and their relevant past performances.

2. **Price To Win (PTW)** to develop timely and well supported top down (see Section III of this book) and bottoms up competitor PTW estimates (Sections IV and V).

3. **Strategic Pricing** to meld Competitive Analysis and PTW results and probabilities with a Pricing Strategy (i.e., the agglomeration of tactics that are to be employed to develop a winning bid price) and a comprehensive cost basis, to develop a winning, yet profitable, solution-based bid price.

Although PTW is one component of this trio, the role of the PTW practitioner is to ensure the best combined and integrated relationship among these elements.

How PTW Changes the Capture Process

Figure I.1 depicts the typical government contract acquisition process. An acquisition comes into focus first as a Draft Statement Of Work (DSOW), a Draft RFP (DRFP), or Draft Performance Work Statement (DPWS), and later as a final RFP document. A Capture Team is formed and they set out to:

- Form a bid team;
- Develop a solution;
- Develop a proposal; and
- Develop artifacts that support the cost basis of the bid—Levels Of Effort (LOE), Basis Of Estimates (BOE), and Bills Of Materials (BOM).

The job of the Capture Team (comprising the sales, bid, and proposal development processes) is to promote that product or service as meeting, or exceeding, what the customer has said that he wants to buy. This solution is used to derive the cost basis for the bid.

The problem with this approach is that Capture Teams tend to eat up just about all of the time available to come up with their cost basis. This leaves very little time for pricing people to do much more than populate customer price models—certainly no window for Strategic Pricing, which is the process that uses gaming and other techniques to develop the Home Team's winning evaluated bid price.

Enter PTW. **Figure I.2** shows how PTW and Competitive Analysis (which determines who the competition is, and is part of any robust PTW process) are focused on the competition. PTW's task is to incrementally provide a Capture Team with a current and accurate assessment of their competitors.

If that were all PTW needed to accomplish, it would be enough. As shown in the figure, PTW's job is also to galvanize the Capture Team into being able to produce the bid's cost basis in time to ensure that Strategic Pricing has enough time to craft the Home Team's winning, yet profitable, price proposal that is focused on beating the fiercest competitor's most likely bid price.

Furthermore, for all contracting organizations, there is a requirement to respond to RFPs to protect their future profits (or meet strategic objectives) by ensuring that the prices quoted are sensitive to the realities of the tasking and inherent or perceived risks. To ensure appropriate rigor for this, there are usually management reviews, or "gates," to which the Capture Team must submit as the organization undertakes its due diligence. Percentage-based corporate uplifts add the required overheads for the business, the required margins, and contingency for the perceived business risks.

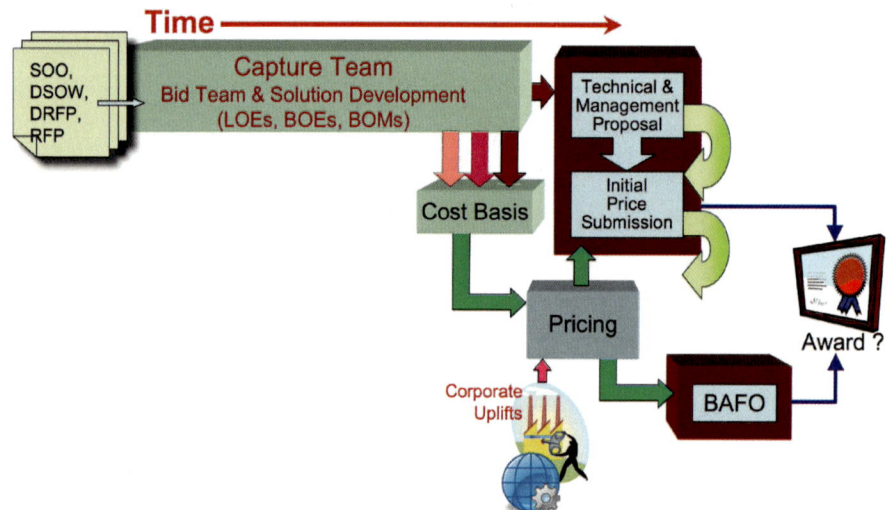

FIGURE I.1

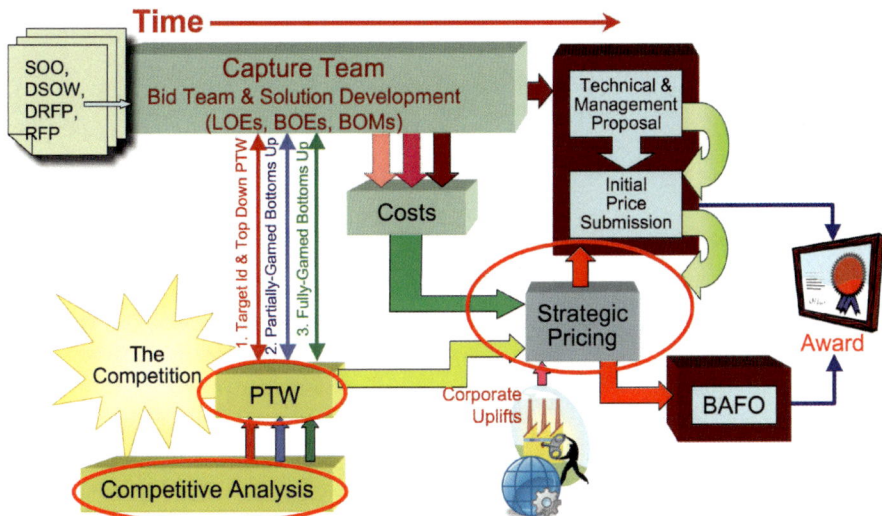

FIGURE I.2

Shedding Light on the Competition

The neat assumption is that the customer will determine the competitiveness of the offer by comparing it with those from other like-minded bidders. In the end, the decision as to which proposal best meets the customer's requirements, and which offers the best overall "value," is left to the customer.

The PTW practitioner knows this approach to bidding is too introspective: it is heavily focused on what we want to sell and insufficiently focused on how to beat the competition. The role of the Capture Team is to meet the opportunity's requirements with its proposed solution. The function of PTW, as shown in **Figure I.3**, is to illuminate and quantify the competitors' worlds—what can perhaps be termed the "dark side" of business development.

The role of the PTW practitioner is principally to present timely findings about the dark side that challenge and educate the Home Team's solution developers. This allows the Capture Team to focus their attention on their solution options that can be bid within the competitive price window. The additional information and insights can also empower bid strategists and those who price solutions to be innovative in how they approach their tasks with more certain knowledge of what they have to accomplish. The collective output of these understandings can then be used to guide Capture Teams and business development managers so that the decisions they make are better informed and more likely to be competitively astute.

Because of the addition of the competitor's perspective, it is appropriate to redefine the classic business development model to include the three puzzle pieces introduced earlier. By using these balancing activities, we can bring an understanding of the competitive dark side to the otherwise hollow center of the typical capture activity.

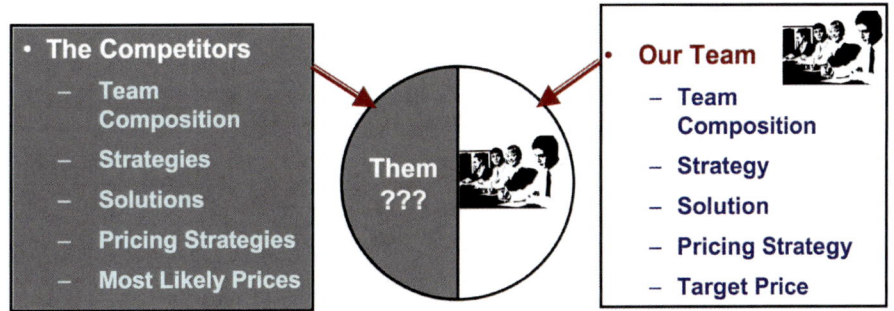

FIGURE I.3

PTW to Improve Win Probability (pWin)

pWin or "probability of a win" is a commonly used method of continually measuring the win plausibility of a job by using key weighted Capture Plan elements, by periodically rating each Capture Plan element and by aggregating the resulting element scores (weight x rating).

The principal job of business development is to target more winnable opportunities, book profitable wins, improve win rates, better manage business development investments, and expand the business. It is critical, therefore, to appreciate that more than 85% of all competitive awards are made to the lowest priced, acceptable bidder—technically, management-wise, and past performance-wise.

With price the most significant determinant underlying contract awards, major firms have begun to institutionalize or to mandate PTW to improve the price-related aspects of pWin. For instance, the pWin development table (**Figure I.4**) is representative of what major firms use to monitor pWin progress throughout the entire capture period.

A description of the parts of the table follows:

- Under the heading **Capture Plan Element** is a list of topics or characteristics of the capture activity that should be covered in a Capture Plan. The implication is that if you are perfect when addressing each element for a specific opportunity, then you would, assuming that your competitors are less than perfect, win the bid.

- The **Weight** column shows the weighting for each characteristic relative to the others, reflecting the relative importance of each characteristic to winning the bid. The lowest score is 10 and the highest is 40, suggesting that the highest is four times as important as the lowest. There is a subjective nature to these weightings that would need to be validated over many prospects to develop confidence in the relative weightings. In the table, the weightings are added to create a total, but there is no specific constraint on that value as the ratios used later on normalize the result.

- The scoring schema is based on five. Accordingly, the **Maximum Score** column is the weighting multiplied by five. The total of the maximum scores is the basis for the final ratio or percentage scores.

- Next is the judgment of the Capture Team that is used to populate the **Rating (0 through 5)** column. That is, the Capture Team decides on how near to perfection, or far from it, their progress to date is against each characteristic. Clearly, to score each of the items in this manner requires a deep understanding of the elements in order to exercise that judgment.

Capture Plan Element	Weight	Maximum Score	Rating (0 through 5)	Score (Weight * Rating)
Capture Organization	15	75	4	60
Assets/Resources	15	75	3	45
Time/Schedules	10	50	3	30
Program Understanding	10	50	4	40
Public Relations	15	75	5	75
Political/Government Affairs	15	75	3	45
Self Analysis	30	150	4	120
Competition Analysis	30	150	4	120
Customer Knowledge/Interaction	40	200	4	160
People	20	100	4	80
Offering	20	100	4	80
Price	20	100	4	80
Believability	10	50	5	50
Risk Exposure & Management	10	50	4	40
Win Strategy	40	200	4	160
Totals	**300**	**1,500**		**1,185**
			pWin	**79%**

FIGURE I.4

- The final column **Score (Weight * Rating)** is the product of the weight for each characteristic multiplied by the rating. The sum total of these scores is the overall weighted value of the state of the Capture Plan characteristics. This sum, divided by the total maximum score, gives the **pWin**—in this example 79%.

- An overall weighted value for the prospect can now be calculated. In this example, the contract value is $100M and so at a pWin of 79%, the pWin value (one supposes in terms of potential future revenues spread over the opportunity's term) is $79M.

Most organizations involved in competitive bidding have many prospects underway at any one time (a portfolio) and are usually challenged by scarce technical and financial resources. That is, it is difficult to service all the prospects to the best extent at the same time. Comparing the pWin for each prospect in the portfolio provides an objective means for determining which bids are to be fully pursued and which are not.

The staggering fact that the pWin table reveals is that, notwithstanding the fact that price is, 85% of the time, the determinant for the award of a competitive contract, this scheme that is being taught to budding capture personnel weighs in price at a scant 6.6% of the total. Take a moment to consider the table's elements and how their weights should, or could, be changed to better reflect allocation realities for:

- Talent
- Pursuit funds
- Pipeline value

Who Uses PTW and Why?

PTW is being successfully employed by a veritable *Who's Who* of major firms that vie for competitive contracts, one of the major reasons being that it is designed to *avoid* the ready-fire-aim approach to bid pricing! In addition, PTW is necessary to lead Capture Teams to develop compliant, competitive solutions that can be bid profitably within a winning price envelope.

The why of PTW is much easier to grasp when one contrasts the way in which government contracts are evaluated in good economic times with the evaluation reality when times get tough. In good times, governments tend to spell out non-cost evaluation criteria along with their relative award point weights, and award to the bidder that gets the highest number of overall award points at a reasonable or supportable price. The so-called "best value" approach.

In harder times, however, while the evaluation set is still in evidence, the brutal truth (from a mid-2011 U.S. Army RFP) is this:

> As a basis for award, trade-offs between cost and non-cost factors are not permitted. Award will be made on the basis of the lowest evaluated price of proposals meeting or exceeding the acceptability standards for non-cost factors.

Be warned! When budgets are constrained, beyond a certain level of acceptability, price *is* really all that matters. This has a tendency to lead to what is euphemistically called *margin compression*.

Some Key PTW Terms

Every form of human endeavor seems to need to invent its own jargon. PTW is by no means immune to this tendency. Accordingly, here are a few of the terms and concepts that PTW practitioners use, or should at least think about, when engaging in a PTW study.

Cost As an Independent Variable (CAIV) is an approach to solution design and development that is driven by cost targets that are set up front. The issue that CAIV seeks to solve is underscored by the sardonic observation that follows:

> At the rate we are going, in the year 2054, the entire defense budget will purchase just one aircraft. This aircraft will have to be shared by the Air Force and the Navy, who will each own it for 3.5 days each week except for Leap Year, when the Marines will have it for that year's extra day.

The CAIV mindset is presented in **Figure 1.5**. It depicts a hypothetical consumer product—think of an MPEG-2 Audio Layer III (MP3) player if you wish—whose price target has been set by market research that suggests that, if priced correctly, the item will sell in sufficient quantity to provide a desirable Return On Investment (ROI). Let's call that price $500.

If we can agree that 20% is an appropriate net margin, then the remaining 80% of our sale price (this is the overall cost target) is available to be allocated and decomposed appropriately across and down through all of the cost elements associated with managing, designing and developing, manufacturing, and merchandising the item (these become the cost element targets).

The other aspect of CAIV as it relates to a product we expect to sell in quantity over an extended period of time is that we should be aiming to improve our product's performance over time within the same, or a lower, cost envelope.

> Isn't a PTW study that sets price bid element targets for the Capture Team really *Price As an Independent Variable (PAIV)?* Of course it is!

Materiality is critical to PTW given the short timeframes that typify a PTW study. (Short timeframes usually apply to PTW studies because they focus on bringing solid research *plus* the PTW practitioner's typical order of magnitude more experience to a Capture Team. A PTW practitioner's job is to right mind or remind a Capture Team of their competition and what they will have to do to prevail.)

To accomplish this, PTW needs to concentrate on significant elements and issues (i.e., the material issues) that relate to price and not go down immaterial "rat holes." After all, PTW is not developing a working prototype of anything or writing a meticulously compliant proposal.

In addition, since PTW is focused on the competition, PTW should not be drawn into solving Home Team cultural problems related to overcoming a competitor's bid posture. PTW's job is to frame the competitive situation, not to be the Capture Team.

Provenance relates to the PTW practitioner's need to provide support for each and every contention or assumption that is made. If the opportunity is to build a two-track railroad connecting Denver International Airport to Aspen, Colorado, then we must consider the costs of drilling tunnels through the mountains that obstruct the planned route. Costing the needed tunneling may lead us to a civil engineering website that contains, as a rule of thumb, that, based on practical experience, $100M per mile is the appropriate cost metric.

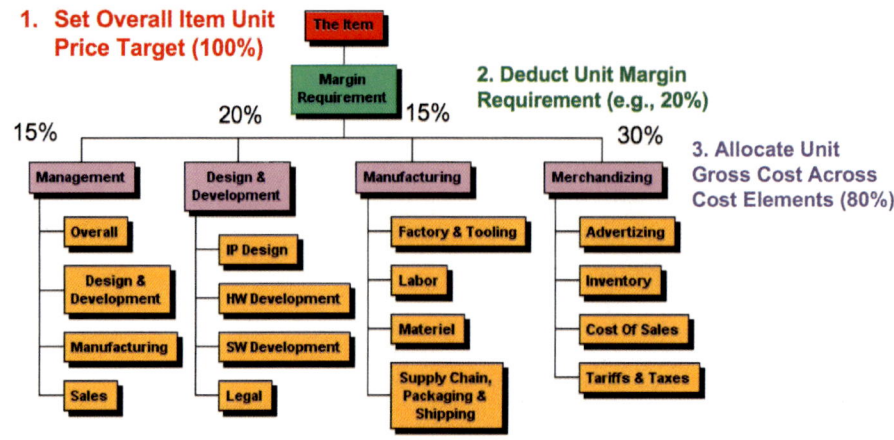

FIGURE I.5

The **Work Breakdown Structure (WBS)** is a hierarchical representation of a Statement Of Work (SOW), the purpose of which is to:

- Decompose the required activities into major, often time-phased and discretely managed areas of work; and
- Further decompose the major work areas into tree structures comprised of discrete work packages.

Snowflakes are units of information that can be used to develop understanding and build support for competitive positioning and PTW analyses. The fact is that every day, each one of us is driving into an information snowstorm. Incredibly, even in this day and age, most employees have job descriptions that do not require the information they are paid to learn be recorded, shared, or pre-positioned for possible reuse. PTW, as an ultra time-sensitive activity, cannot afford either the time or cost associated with learning the same information more than once. Accordingly, PTW relies heavily on ever-growing mountains of pre-positioned, rapidly accessible snowflakes that are conscientiously husbanded, reused, augmented, and mined.

Total Cost of Ownership (TCO) is never far from the PTW practitioner's mind. TCO relates the aggregate cost of a proposed capability to the sum of collateral savings benefits that accrue to a solution, both within and outside of the purview of the stated acquisition environment. A simple example may be showing how your solution requires significantly less energy over its life cycle than other putative solutions. Though the energy consumption issue was not raised in the acquisition documents, including an analysis in your proposal that highlights the TCO advantages of your solution can only enhance the desirability of your offering.

Figure I.6 shows how one might present a solution to an Operations & Maintenance (O&M) requirement that proposes to replace an "As Is" support system with a new "To Be" capability that significantly reduces overall costs over time.

The TCO aspects of such a proposal need to contrast the total cost of operating the "As Is" through the opportunity's life cycle with the lowered aggregate cost of:

- Developing and operating the "To Be" system; and
- Operating the "As Is" system during the "To Be" development period.

PTW practitioners are always on the lookout for TCO opportunities that can be reasonably attributed to targeted competitors.

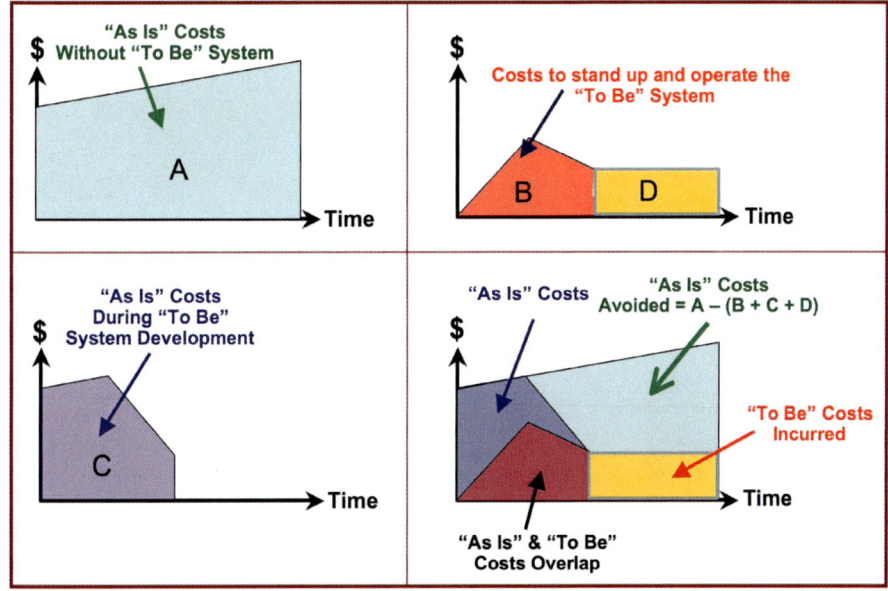

FIGURE I.6

Price Target-Driven Solutions

A typical PTW analysis determines the following major factors (in as much detail as possible) in the context of a specific opportunity:

- Who are the competitors?
- What are their most likely solution cost targets within the likely budget?
- What are their most likely solutions that meet or beat the cost targets?
- What is their most likely forward-priced (i.e., inclusive of expected inflationary or deflationary effects) evaluated price?

The results of this analysis are used to inform and influence the solution so that the cost, when uplifted by normal business overheads and margins, remains attractive to the customer when compared with the competition.

Many major, well-respected firms that vie for competitive contracts have a PTW-type process in use. The argument is that PTW is needed to lead Capture Teams to develop compliant, competitive solutions, and for the Pricing Team to bid them at profitable, winning prices. However, when the use of PTW is analyzed, it is found that there are different levels of implementation maturity which, in turn, cap PTW's effectiveness. These levels are shown in **Figure I.7**.

An organization's maturity progresses and ascends from left to right from a Level 0, through Levels 1 and 2, to a Level 3, where a firm that is a market leader in the subject area (e.g., service desk, cloud computing, etc.) has to strive to be. A Level 3 competitor is one that is able to determine its target price, or Bottom Line Up Front (BLUF), in advance and provide it to the Capture Team as the price envelope it needs to meet or beat. The in-between levels of sophistication relate to Late and/or Early PTW processes that focus on beating the bid prices that are likely to be offered by the competition.

Level 0 is the lowest maturity level, which is for companies that are not employing PTW techniques at all (e.g., Competitor D in the diagram) but who are engaged in wishful thinking as it relates to their ability to price a winning bid in a vacuum. The Level 0 approach is to design a solution to the requirement and to price that solution "bottom up." The resultant price to the customer can be described as pure cost+. These companies simply ignore the competitive situation and leave it to chance that they have a competitive price and solution.

Level 1 maturity includes a Late PTW analysis which is defined as one occurring after a DRFP or an RFP has been issued. A Late PTW (e.g., Competitor C in the diagram) is focused on the competitors and their likely solutions and prices but, as we shall see, its results do not affect much more than the Home

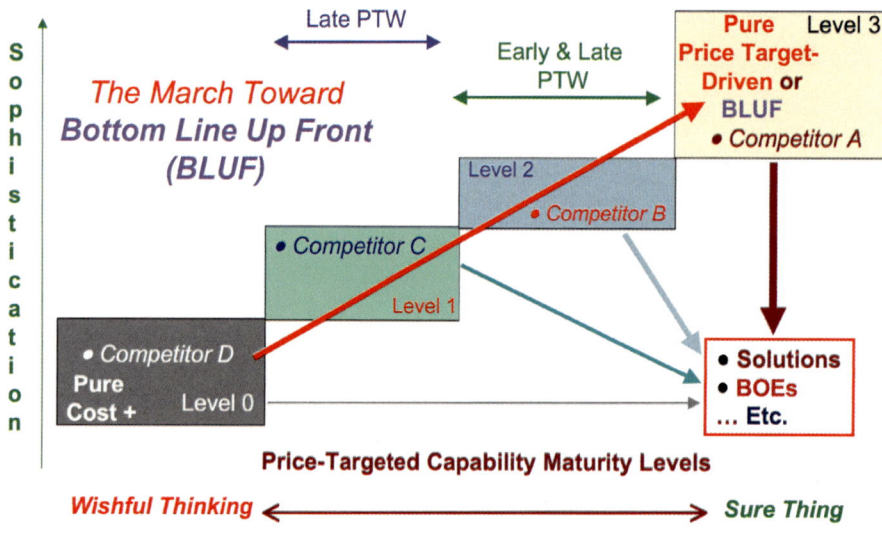

FIGURE I.7

Team's bid price. The Capture Team is then tasked with developing high level candidate solutions that are consistent with the preliminary PTW and that fit within cost targets. Changes in understanding of the requirement and/or competition trigger a repeat of this cycle.

Level 2 maturity includes both an Early and a Late PTW analysis. An Early PTW is one that defines the target price within which the Home Team's solution must live to be competitively viable. An Early PTW occurs as much as six months, or more, prior to an RFP being issued. It is based on very general requirements and is cyclic in nature. Based on what is known about the requirements, the Early PTW analysis first describes the likely competitive landscape, addressable budget or opportunity value, and potential competitive bidders. A preliminary PTW is then developed reflecting how competitors are likely to target costs for the same, or similar, requirements within available budget.

Based on the available acquisition document (e.g., a DRFP, an RFP, etc.), the PTW analysis will develop an overview of the opportunity and its pricing requirements, the firm, likely, and possible competition, and how the Home Team's characteristics compare within this overall competitive landscape. PTW will also sketch a generic solution that may be the same as the generic solution that would have been developed during an Early PTW analysis, if one was conducted.

Level 3 maturity (e.g., Competitor A in the diagram) suggests that the Home Team, as a regular dealer in the goods or services that are the subject of the opportunity, has to be able to dictate, early on, both the solution and the bid price target. These elements, suitably sized, priced, and forward-priced, are provided to the Capture Team as both the solution and the price target to be turned into a proposal. This is as close to a "sure thing" bid as any bidder is likely to come.

To recap, Early PTW can help solution developers by establishing competitor CAIV-like cost targets for the major WBS elements. Solution developers, for their part, need to be constantly focused on working to meet *and beat* cost targets both at the subsystem level and in the aggregate.

To be most effective, cost targets need to be baked into a winning, price-driven solution development process—not developed in a retrospective pruning exercise! Price should never be a by-product or an afterthought of a solution development process!

Without PTW, solution developers have little propensity to go beyond the cost-plus approach. In addition, price aside, sometimes solution developers without adult supervision have a tendency to be too clever. Here is a case in point:

> A pharmaceutical company responded to an Army RFP seeking a vaccine solution against Adenovirus (a type of Rhinovirus). The solicitation called for a two-pill solution. Because the company's solution developers were clever, they devised and bid a one-pill solution, presumably because it was more elegant and cheaper. Of course, as so often happens when you give a customer a solution they have not asked for, this bidder lost.

The moral of this story is that the time to change what the customer is asking for is after award, not before! Most often, but not always, the winning approach is to bid what the RFP asks for but price the bid as if the lower cost, one-pill solution had been bid and strive to change the solution post-award. This, of course, is a variation on Reality Model-Based Price Gaming spoken of in this book's *About CAI/SISCo* section.

PTW and Game Theory

One of the principles of Game Theory is that you must view the game through your opponents' eyes, not just your own. That is precisely what PTW does.

As shown in **Figure I.8**, the PTW Team uses acquisition documents from the ultimate customer to focus on the competitors to determine their most

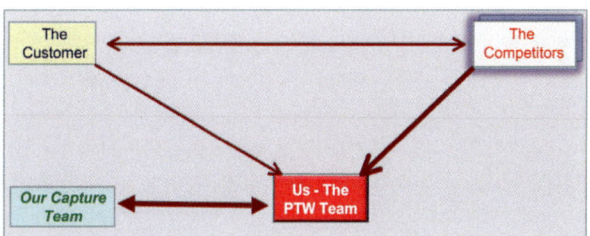

FIGURE I.8

likely teams, solutions, and bid prices and bring this understanding to the Home Team.

PTW's Value Proposition

Because most PTW study periods are 30 days in duration and most capture activities are three months and longer, PTW practitioners can be expected to bring a wide swath of contemporary opportunity experience to the capture table. As a consequence, the journeyman PTW practitioner is likely to have been exposed to an order of magnitude more pursuits than the average capture person. For this reason, and because PTW practitioners are, of necessity, highly experienced and continually exposed to the changing rules of the game, they represent an indispensable "success multiplier" to the average Capture Team.

PTW's role is to provide the Capture Team with unbiased, non-political, accurate, timely and detailed comparative assessments of targeted competitors' teams, likely solutions, acquisition approaches, and likely pricing. PTW must also reveal the hard truths about the competition and the Home Team and continually challenge Capture Team assumptions about competitor capabilities and their likely costs and cost avoidance potential. PTW also needs to reveal how competitors, post-award, are likely to be able to manage the customer, contract sales performance and bottomline risk as part of their quest to be the lowest-priced, otherwise acceptable bidder.

> **PTW practitioners should always assume that competitors will**
> ***Bid and Price it to Win* and then be able to *Manage to that Price*!**

PTW analysis is based on repeatable and rapidly adaptable processes, experience, time-tested methods and tools, activity templates, and pre-positioned information and intelligence. For firms that provide a wide variety of capabilities and services, the PTW Team may, from time to time, need to engage Subject Matter Experts (SMEs) to augment their knowledge databases.

The other part of PTW's value is to support Capture Teams and the overall business development organization by capturing, organizing, pre-positioning, and making available for reuse all of the known information related to a pursuit. Capture Teams do not record, analyze, compare, or publish competitive information but the PTW practitioner must. Moreover, not only is the PTW practitioner concerned with the knowns of a competitive situation, he or she needs to also be interested in identifying the situation's known unknowns and even its unknown unknowns. In short, while PTW's job requires mastery of the first two knowledge groupings, it also includes being prepared for the third group—the unknown unknowns.

PTW's Relationship to the Black Hat Review

An integral part of a typical capture process is an event called a "Black Hat" review. (In some parts of the world, this may be referred to as "war gaming.") Its purpose is to spend a day or so to develop an understanding of the competitive bid teams and present the results to the Capture Team to show them what they are up against and how the competitors are likely to try to beat the Home Team.

A facilitator is chosen and charged with:

1. Developing the Black Hat session review materials and organizing the participants into competitor Review Teams.

2. Facilitating the Black Hat review session, presenting the review materials, and assisting competitor Review Teams to focus on the essential elements of information.

3. Synthesizing each competitor reviewing team's findings and having them presented to the Capture Team.

Figure I.9 depicts the process for the Black Hat review. The material developed in Black Hat Step 1 is designed to act as the grain of sand that stimulates the oyster—the Review Team—to produce the pearls of wisdom in the Black Hat session.

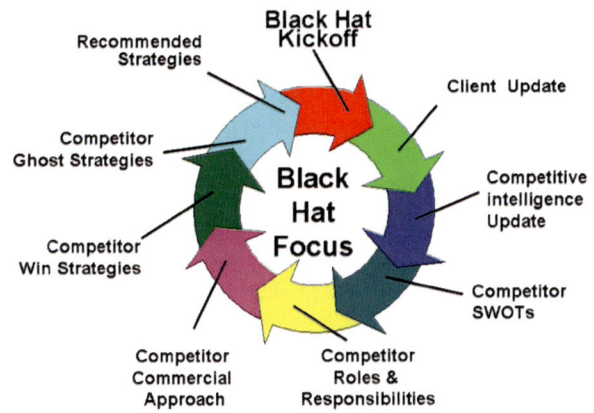

FIGURE I.9

On the day of the review, the facilitator leads all participants through a review of the opportunity and the rules of the road for participating in the competition-specific parts of the proceedings.

Participants form pre-organized groups to represent competing bid teams and develop the Black Hat readouts (i.e., a set of slides or a narrative) for each targeted competitive team consisting of some, or all, of the following:

- Corporate Profile
- Corporate Personality
- Black Hat Statement of Strategic Objectives
- Black Hat Strategic Platform
- Statement of Strategic Approach
- Statement of Solution
- Strengths, Weaknesses, Opportunities and Threats (SWOTs)
- Statement of Technical Approach
- Statement of Business Solution
- Statement of Pricing Solution
- Capture Tactical Plan
- Post-Award Operational Plan
- Post-Award Marketing Plan

From the PTW practitioner's point of view, a Black Hat review is a beginning, not an end. Too often, the outputs of a Black Hat review are a Capture Team's only consideration of its competition. Almost always, these outputs provide nothing of value related to competitor pricing.

What PTW strives to provide is what can be thought of as the running Black Hat that identifies the innovations, pricing strategies and tactics that competitors can, and are likely to, use to change the game and/or expand the opportunity. Moreover, PTW is focused on competitor pricing.

Over the years, we have encountered something that we have begun to call the "Black Hat Syndrome." This is a situation where the results of a Black Hat review take on a gospel-like aura and, as a consequence, are not dynamically updated. Incredibly, in some situations, this even includes crucial information contained in newer acquisition documents.

PTW's Role — Helping to Fully Inform Capture Teams

PTW's job is to stimulate the Capture Team (the oyster) into producing a win (the pearl). Because pricing a bid without knowing the most likely win price wastes capture funds, time, and human energy, PTW is also the "other hand against which to clap" a Capture Team's view of the pricing issue.

Anecdotally, a senior executive was being briefed by a Capture Team on the proposal they were about to submit for a major competitive acquisition. The briefing went into team, solution, implementation approach and ended up with the Capture Team asking for permission to bid a certain price. The executive, without missing a beat, asked "Compared to what?"

"What do you mean, compared to what?" the Capture Manager asked.

"Put yourself in my position," the executive replied. "Your team has spent a large amount of money developing what looks to be a great team, a great solution and an excellent proposal. And now you are asking me to bless a price without providing any indication that the price you are asking for will beat our competition, which, frankly, you don't seem to know too much about. Did you do a PTW?"

"Well, not exactly," the Capture Manager replied, "but we are fairly certain that our price is aggressive and, at that level, we hope to have a better than even chance of being successful."

Really? How do you know that?

Individual Capture Managers are each marinated in different past realities. PTW's role is to be the common environmental denominator that brings market and competitor realities to the table.

Ignore PTW, and the customer and your competition are the only—and *final*—arbiters of the value of your bid price. Without PTW (or something like it), you will only have the pitiful sound of one hand clapping.

The Information Dilemma

Today, there's an enormous and growing demand for competitive intelligence in the global economy. Capture Teams want to find out what their competitors are doing; everybody does. Any Capture Team that says they don't want to know is not being truthful.

A collection of random facts isn't worth much unless you can put it together so as to understand what the data tells you about the real world. How do you know what's important and what's not? Which information is going to help or hinder competitors, or affect the competitive picture? PTW practitioners gather information and weave it together to produce "actionable intelligence." PTW practitioners need enough data points confirming a thesis before they can recommend any action.

It's not enough to have one source telling you something. Ideally, you want to hear it over and over again from people in the know before you act on it. Notwithstanding, PTW practitioners often have to prioritize information and be able to reach conclusions based on less than complete information.

Today, Information Technology (IT) is much more about technology and a lot less about information. In a hyper-competitive world, this is most unhelpful and has to change—and fast! Information is central to just about everything that people in the business development world do. Therefore, it makes eminent sense to collect, ingest, husband, and pre-position any and all information that relates to customers, competitors, potential primes, and subcontractors. In fact, every relevant snowflake that hits the windshields of all of your customer facing operatives needs to be collected, ingested, husbanded, and pre-positioned for possible reuse by all involved with business development.

It is, however, pointless to collect and store data without the means to mine it, fusing together topic-based views (e.g., by company, opportunity, etc.) to produce timely, coherent and actionable sets of information for analysts to analyze and decision makers to act upon. PTW relies on the next level of collective intelligence to combat enterprise amnesia—CAI/SISCo calls it *Infocentricity*! **Figure I.10** depicts an infocentric infostructure. This infostructure supports *Infocentricity*, information acquisition, and knowledge development.

To the right, the figure shows knowledge workers (Capture Managers, proposal developers, PTW practitioners, etc.) who should be seated in front of the best technology that money can buy. Why? Because while technology is cheap, people are not. In the fast moving world of PTW, you don't want to have expensive people waiting for cheap technology.

To the left, we have all of our pre-positioned information that is under the aegis of an enabling technology such as IBM's Lotus Notes, Microsoft's Sharepoint or just about any modern SQL-based RDBMS. The entirety of our information holdings needs to be at the fingertips of our knowledge worker community. The information should be organized and tagged to provide any and all useful views (e.g., by products, by person, by opportunity, etc.) ready for them to use, modify, augment, and supplement. As shown, this database needs to be proactively fed from the

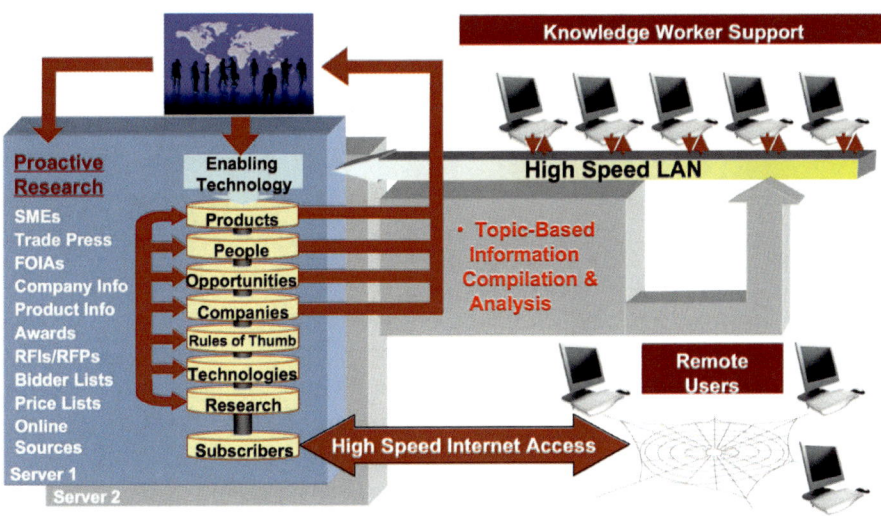

FIGURE I.10

sources shown (SMEs, trade press, etc.) and reactively fed as knowledge workers pick up snowflakes from encounters, canvassing, and other interviews.

While *Infocentricity* relies on foundation software, its success is very much dependent on a cultural change. The required culture is one that values information, requires learned items to be pre-positioned on the corporate *infocenter*, and frowns upon paying in time and money to learn the same information twice. Perhaps job descriptions of the future need to include this requirement.

For more information on *Infocentricity*, please refer to an earlier book by this author that is also available on *Amazon*.

> **If Information Is Power, Why Aren't We More Powerful? or
> "Everything About Everything"**
>
> ★ ★ ★ ★ ★
>
> A futuristic tale about *Infocentricity* and a young man with a nose for information and an inquiring mind
>
> ★ ★ ★ ★ ★
>
> An inspirational text about information recycling and reuse

The idea is to bring the collective corpus of information to the knowledge workers so that they can leverage what is available rather than having to discover what has already been discovered. The fact is, however, without a receptive and nurturing culture, IT is always going to be 99% about technology and only 1% about information.

To those who believe that everything that can be known is knowable through the Googles and Bings of the world, I say: Knowing what everyone else knows or can know from these sources just isn't enough. Other relevant information needs to be learned, captured, and organized for the infocenter to reach its full potential.

Once you have a critical mass of information in your corporate information landfill, how does the PTW practitioner go about digging out treasures *on demand*? The key is having a capability so that PTW can use those morsels of information that can be summoned from memory to latch on to the required information from your InfoCenter.

For example, trying to remember the name of a specific project that involved a particular firm (XYZ) who has a top secret facility in a particular state (NC) repairing SATCOM terminals might be found with a query string of search terms along these lines:

"XYZ & SATCOM & Top Secret & NC"

Often, all we can incrementally remember is search terms such as these, and as we summon others, the information seeker can zero in much better on the needed information.

PTW Serves All Stakeholders

As shown in **Figure I.11**, successful PTW has to support the interests of *all* business development stakeholders, not just the Capture Team whose job it is to capture the opportunity.

All stakeholders need PTW to help them understand early on what competitors can and/or are likely to do to try to capture the subject opportunity.

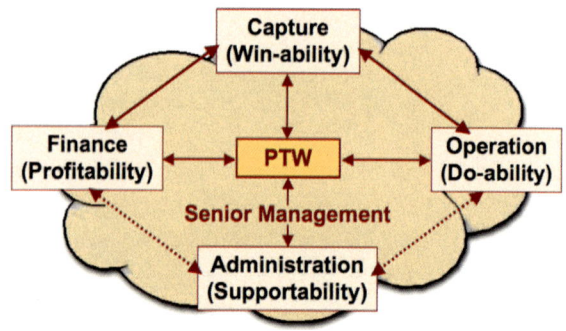

FIGURE I.11

Therefore, PTW must focus on serving all of those who can be affected by the competitive situation and consider, up front, the pros and cons of winning or not winning. For instance:

- Senior management needs to be involved to arbitrate between the Capture Team's view and the PTW Team's view.

- Operations, whose responsibility includes managing and doing the work after award, has to understand and support the risks of both winning the job (and having to do it) *and* not winning the job (possibly having to lay off staff).

- Administration, whose job it will be to support the project post-award with staffing services and other resources.

- Finance, whose responsibility it is to maintain and improve revenue streams and profitability.

PTW studies need to be developed using standard products that include presentation formats, graphics, tables, and other artifacts that are familiar to all PTW readout participants, pre-positioned templates and information, knowledge and experience, credible and accurate analysis, rapid prototyping, persuasive presentations and continuous, incremental improvement.

Ways of Employing PTW

Even though most major firms that vie for major competitive contracts employ some form of PTW support for their pursuits, the manner in which this support is utilized, and by whom, varies widely. **Figure I.12** presents five ways that PTW support can be employed, though there are surely others.

1. In this circumstance, a Capture Team commissions a PTW study to gain competitive insight for a specific opportunity. This presumes that the capture budget includes the ability to fund either an internal PTW activity or to buy an external PTW study.

2. Here, business development mandates the use of PTW to assist/monitor/guide multiple capture activities as a means of improving overall win rates.

3. Finance, having shouldered the blame for price-related losses, uses PTW to birddog Capture Teams to gain early insights into the competition and the competitive pricing realities to support Strategic Pricing activities.

4. An internal PTW capability is stood up to institutionalize and apply standardized, quasi-independent qualification/quantification processes that assure due diligence is done and that statutory requirements (e.g., Sarbanes-Oxley in the U.S.) are met when bidding for competitively-awarded contracts.

5. The last instance involves top management employing its own instance of PTW when faced with a "must win" or "bet the company" opportunity.

Who Commissions PTW Studies?

Many companies leave the decision to conduct a formal PTW study, or not, to the individual Capture Manager. Such decisions are predicated on whether the Capture Manager has the budget to support a PTW study.

Even when PTW studies are undertaken, however, it is often unclear how the results are to be used and what effect they are intended to have on the teaming, solution development, and pricing processes and associated decisions.

Even among firms that recognize the value of a rigorous PTW study as a means of improving win rates, there is still great disparity concerning:

- Whether a Capture Manager should commission and consider PTW inputs.
- How differences between the Capture Team's view and the PTW view are to be resolved or escalated to management for resolution.

Management needs to recognize the need to address the issue of how to reconcile the Capture Team and PTW views of solution element sizing and promulgate guidelines in order to address it. Above all, management needs to get involved and make judgments concerning issues of scale (e.g., PTW's breadbox-sized element versus the Capture Team's refrigerator), and so forth, whenever opinions diverge.

PTW's Role in Helping Shape Successful Capture Campaigns

Among PTW's tasks are helping business developers in general and Capture Teams in particular:

- Understand not just each competitor's most likely bid price, but what drives it;
- To think both inside and outside of the box formed by the RFP's requirements, if there is one; and
- With the solution development and (sometimes) the proposalmanship needed to get the Home Team into the competitive range.

Since price is the key to success, PTW is an essential Capture Process and Strategic Pricing ingredient. Much like a Black Hat review, PTW's brief is to prepare and present a sort of *contrarian's* view of each pursuit from the point of view of the competitors and their positioning. Showing the Home Team how competitors are likely to position themselves to win makes the outcome of the capture process more certain, or less controversial.

Contrary to some elements of popular opinion, PTW is not just about *low price*. PTW is about the *winning price* and how the solution underlying that winning price can be successfully delivered.

Stated differently, PTW is not price to win *at all costs*, it is price to win *all things considered*. By developing competitor-likely bid prices and supporting rationale, PTW provides results that are necessarily developed incrementally and shared with the Capture Team by means of "encounters." To support an Early PTW, these incremental PTW deliveries are made *well in advance* of the Capture Team's ability to develop firm solutions and set in stone its own bid-based quantification.

(There is much more to be said about Capture Team encounters in Section III of this book.)

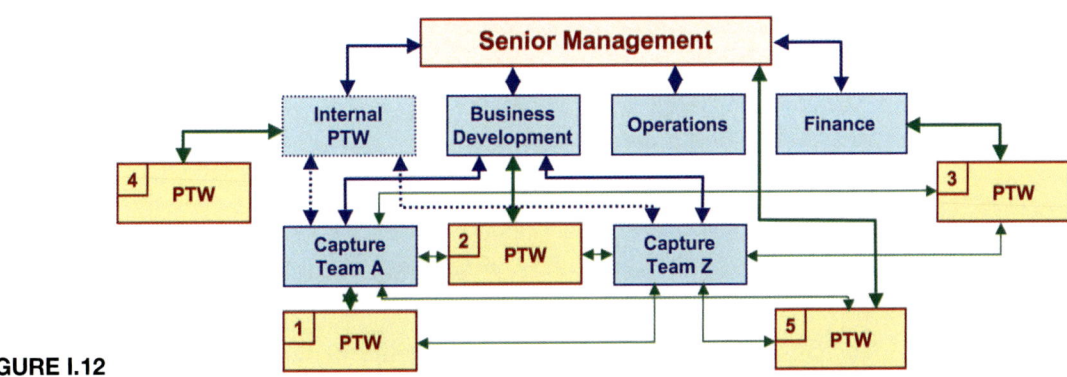

FIGURE I.12

Don't Forget—PTW Has to Tell a Story

Collecting information, performing analyses and conducting readouts is not likely to change many minds in a Capture Team unless these results are presented as part of a compelling story. That story needs to be the highest and best abstraction of what has been learned to date. For instance, the story, at its highest level, may go something like this:

> Team B, a well-placed insurgent, is likely to aim for a low evaluated bid price to counteract and overcome incumbent Team A's perceived ability to avoid costs by leveraging existing software modules under their expected Service Oriented Architecture (SOA) solution.

Typically, a PTW practitioner will learn more and more about a given competition as time passes. As new information is learned that changes the story, then the story must change. The better the story gets, the easier it becomes to win adherents and change minds.

Lest we forget, PTW success also relies on:

- A framework and process for approaching PTW studies;
- Pre-positioned information and aggressive acquisition of other needed and potentially influential information;
- Leverageable processes and models;
- Experienced PTW practitioners; and
- Thorough and accurate analysis encapsulated in persuasive presentations.

A successful PTW study will describe the extent to which each of the Home Team's competitors:

- Understands the customer and the problem that needs to be solved;
- Can develop and present a credible team, supportive past performance, a desirable solution, and sound processes that support successful solution implementation; and
- Is likely to be able to *price his bid to win!*

How PTW Should Be Funded

Capture Teams should always be aware that non-price proposals (e.g., technical and management volumes) rarely win bids outright. Yet, most Capture Managers tend to overspend, preparing introspectively acceptable proposals.

When all is said and done, however, 85% of the time it is a competent bidder's price that seals the deal! Too often, insufficient pursuit funds are applied to identifying and understanding the competition (Competitive Analysis), developing their likely bid prices (Early and/or Late PTW), and countering these prices with the Home Team's winning price (Strategic Pricing).

Given that most firms are unlikely to be willing or able to allocate more funds to business development's pursuit budget, from where should the money to fund PTW and the other price defining activities come? Here is a suggestion:

> The way in which firms allocate pursuit funds to projects is often archaic and static. As shown in **Figure I.13**, the "As Is" pursuit fund allocations barely consider price's role in determining competition's outcome. Yet, most of the time, proposal development usually gets the lion's share of available pursuit funds.

Capture Activity	Pursuit Fund Allocation	
	As Is	To Be
Positioning/Teaming	~20%	~20%
Competitive Analysis/PTW	Mostly 0%	10%, at least
Engineering/Solutioning	~15%	~15%
Proposal Development	~60%	~45%, or less
(Strategic) Pricing	~5%	~10%

FIGURE I.13

During the time that CAI/SISCo has been in business (we were incorporated in 1975), the only major changes I have seen in proposal development circles are these:

- Proposal developers, through organizations such as the Association of Proposal Management Professionals (APMP), are well on their way to becoming *conspiracies against society* in the mold of attorneys and accountants; and
- Productivity improvements have been glacial at best.

Under the "To Be" scenario, pursuit funding allocations need to be better aligned with the reality of how most major awards are made. This probably means that Competitive Analysis/PTW and Strategic Pricing need to be seriously funded, most likely at the expense of proposal development funding.

Activities such as proposal development need to find better and cheaper ways of templating, reusing and repurposing their products. There is a tendency to treat every proposal as a sacred product, supported by a sea of cubicles populated with replaceable parts, many of which have little or nothing of consequence to add to the product except their hourly billings.

Senior management and Capture Managers should employ a CAIV-like approach to capture fund allocations to ensure that funds meet a given opportunity's specific needs. For example, some capture activities may require less engineering/solution development funding, while others may require more Strategic Pricing funding.

PTW and Painting by the Numbers

As children, most of us were exposed to the concept of painting by numbers. We started out with a palette of numbered paints that were to be applied to a black on white image. Shapes within the image contained numbers corresponding to numbered colors. As colors were appropriately applied, a colorful image took shape, eventually revealing a completed childish masterpiece (see the graphic).

PTW (and proposal development and pricing) are rather like painting by numbers. The fact is that in business development, there is rarely time to complete masterpieces. While time remains, masterpieces can be improved. When time runs out, the masterpiece must be abandoned.

PTW, when combined with and supported by pre-positioned information and an infocentric culture, always seeks to reuse the parts of relevant unfinished PTW masterpieces in subsequent analyses.

Business Development Models and PTW

PTW practitioners need to develop a keen sense of all aspects of the competitive environment. One such aspect is whether a competitor adheres to the Integrator or the Aerospace business development model.

The **Integrator Model** involves two discrete groups—the "catch 'ems" and the "skin 'ems"—that interact to develop, win, and successfully execute profitable business opportunities.

The catch 'ems' task is to WIN the job while the skin 'ems' role is to DO the job once it has been won. As you may imagine, this often creates significant tension between these groups, since their respective motivations and roles conflict somewhat—especially as this relates to issues such as levels of effort and price.

Typically, Integrator Model adherents take the risk and try to lay it off on their subcontractors. Their solution development mantra is "better, faster, and cheaper." In support of the Integrator Model, PTW tends to start when a DRFP is issued.

Contrast this with the **Aerospace Model** wherein the catch 'ems *are* the skin 'ems. Another way of saying this is that Aerospace Model adherents have to build what they bid. This sometimes involves lots of "walking into the future backwards," (i.e., this is how we have done it in the past, versus this is how it could be done cheaper, faster, *and* better).

This situation can lead to large doses of risk mitigation and padded levels of effort being included in bid prices. In addition, when Aerospace Model adherents compete with Integrator Model firms, they often bring with them inappropriate corporate cultures such as:

- Only 1,600 billable hours per year versus the Integrator Model adherent's more like 1,920 hours per year;
- No use of uncompensated overtime (UOT); and
- Uplifts (e.g., to cover marketing, the corporate jet, etc.) that may bring no value to the customer or the work to be accomplished.

In support of the Aerospace Model, PTW tends to start well in advance of a DRFP being issued.

Strategic Bid Pricing 101

For each competitive opportunity, bidders can be expected to develop an appropriate pricing strategy that PTW practitioners must approximate.

Section VI of this book describes and discusses the many strategies and tactics that can be used to lower a bidder's evaluated price, yet guarantee a profitable contract execution. This includes Delta Margin Gaming (DMG), which is often used by PTW practitioners to approximate the magnitude of gaming potential for bids that involve evaluation quantities and Reality Models.

A Reality Model is a depiction of what a bid team believes it will be able to sell of each evaluated item (e.g., hardware and software items, services, specific labor categories, etc.). PTW practitioners develop Reality Models on behalf of the targeted competitors to allow the deltas between the customer's Evaluated Case and the Reality Case attributed to a competitor to be exploited during PTW by means of Strategic Pricing. The desired effect of this juxta-positioning of views of contract potential is shown in the **Figure I.14**.

As shown by the curve labeled "Evaluation Model Cumulative Profit Margin," when a bid's unit prices are developed using the quantity differences or deltas between what is being evaluated and what a contractor expects to actually sell (i.e., reality), the evaluation quantities may, overall, appear to put the contractor into an Apparent Loss position. This, however, is illusory, since the bidder's strategy is to sell against the "Reality Model Cumulative Profit Margin" curve at the same reality-based unit prices that sent us into the Evaluated Case's loss position.

It is worth mentioning that any Pricing Strategy, whether devised by the Home Team or attributed by PTW to a competitor, has to be designed to deliver the desired margin on the way in. Why? Because if we can't make money on the deal, why would we be bidding?

Do not confuse a Pricing Strategy with a "get well" plan, the purpose of which is usually to re-baseline, broaden or change the scope of a contract. All bid prices have to be developed within a strategy that includes making money. Pricing a job such that a get well plan is required before contract award implies an element of suicide.

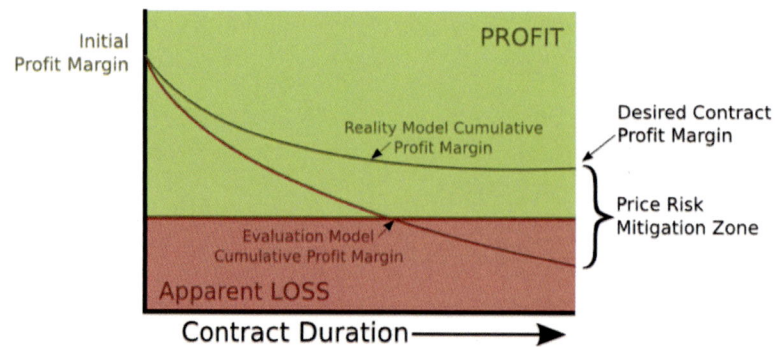

FIGURE I.14

The PTW Practitioner's View of Incumbency

While incumbency is almost always going to be a significant factor in a PTW study, how much should an incumbency be worth? Because of what is known about the incumbent's contract from when it was awarded, and the limited options it has for the recompete, the incumbent can be said to be walking around with a target on its back.

Some incumbents turn in excellent performances, others not so. To unseat a well-performing incumbent, an insurgent bidder may have to bid as much as 15% below the incumbent's bid to get an award. To unseat even a poorly performing incumbent, an insurgent may also have to be the low-priced bidder. Why?

Most often these days, contractors are the government's arm's-length workforce. As such, they often represent the government's institutional knowledge of the function that they perform and, therefore, the government is incapable of training a new contractor because only the incumbent knows what actually needs to be done.

Accordingly, government customers are unlikely to want to replace incumbents and to train an insurgent, unless the insurgent offers a significant reduction.

In addition to the well-performing incumbent's price advantage, here are some of the other issues that usually benefit an incumbent contractor:

- **Page Constraints**—fewer pages allowed for the proposal make it more difficult for competitors to demonstrate their qualifications.
- **RFP Content**—the less specificity (e.g., in a SOW) and background information provided, the better it is for the incumbent.
- **Sample Tasks**—detailed, current, and numerous sample tasks.
- **Technical Approach**—detailed responses and approaches required, incumbent approaches currently in use.
- **Management Approach**—a way of managing work that is familiar to the customer.
- **Draft Plans**—required to be submitted with the proposal, particularly important when the incumbent has already developed and implemented these plans (it is added cost for other bidders).
- **Phase-In**—a strong feature which favors the incumbent and a performance risk for other bidders.
- **Key Personnel**—more resumes required, stringent and detailed requisite qualifications, large numbers of key personnel requirements that are very detailed or signed commitments, letters of intent, and using current employees.
- **Specific Experience**—more specific experience required, especially experience tied to proposed personnel, limited number of projects to be cited, and strong emphasis on experience to SOW correlation.

PTW practitioners need to understand that astute insurgents have their own advantages. Chief among them is this driver of pricey bids: Firms that understand what the customer wants best—lose! Clearly, the incumbent should know precisely what the customer wants. If that understanding, however, is not reflected in the RFP . . .

Here are some other issues that PTW practitioners working for a non-incumbent prime have to consider:

- Is the incumbent *making money* on the present deal? If the answer is NO, then the incumbent is unlikely to price the recompete at, or below, their present price points. Not all primes are able to "get well" on contracts that have been underbid.
- Is the incumbent (aided and abetted by the customer) able to string out the competition or get a contract extension (which is sole source) or otherwise delay the opportunity's procurement schedule?

Research has to find answers to these sorts of issues, since they are very material to effective PTW analyses.

The "Best Value" Issue

In the terminology of a U.S. federal government business bid, a non-protestable "best value" award has been determined to mean a procurement where two conditions apply:

- The winner is chosen on factors beyond, but including, bid price; while
- The weighting between price and non-price factors (e.g., technical and management issues) is left subjective.

For example, the U.S. Court of Appeals, Federal Circuit's referenced finding is that the non-price part of a federal proposal which is:

> one evaluation point better than zero which is equal to another bid but costs millions of dollars more may be selected if the agency can demonstrate within reasonable certainty that the added value of the proposal is worth the higher price.

What may seem like a small difference (e.g., as small as one evaluation point) in quality of staff, or in mission suitability, or in past contract performance, can translate what is otherwise a losing bid into a winner, or vice versa.

This means that our pursuit and capture efforts for this procurement, which certainly has the potential for being "best value," must focus on:

- The customer's perception of value;
- Potential competitors' value arguments;
- Your value arguments;
- The mechanics of how the above will affect the selection process; and
- The danger that what should be "best value" actually turns out to be lowest-price-wins, and vice versa.

Earlier in this section we touched on the subject of Total Cost of Ownership (TCO). TCO advantages can be the centerpiece of a favorable "best value" assessment. For instance, consider the following example. Let's say that there are two Optical Character Recognition (OCR) technology solutions that could be bid to meet a requirement. The least expensive solution only has a 98.9% effective character recognition rate. The other solution has a 99.2% recognition rate, but is more expensive.

Using the differences in recognition rates, we could easily build a TCO model that would prove that the more capable solution avoids a significant need for corrective human intervention. Over a five-year contractual period, the cost savings associated with the more expensive solution can easily be shown to have a far lower TCO. Points like this need to be thoroughly analyzed, documented, and pressed home with the customer in the proposal *even though the RFP may not have explicitly considered this factor.*

More Approach Advice for PTW Teams

The lessons learned from many years of doing PTW studies on major complex opportunities are legion. Here are a few:

- Don't assume anyone's "best value" characteristics are necessarily worth anything, but always advise the Home Team to play their own to the maximum anyway.
- Don't "walk into the pricing future backwards." Basing bids on history may be helpful, but it is *not* a guarantee of success. Remember, major bids don't relate directly to either past or present pricing realities; they relate to the period that is framed by the opportunity's start and end dates.
- Don't assume the competition is either stupid or like the Home Team in terms of either approach or world view.
- Remember Warren Buffet's "Innovator–Imitator–Idiot" cycle. Innovative strategies and products that once worked or sold well and were, for a time, successfully copied, eventually make idiots out of those who don't know when to quit. Think of the iPod. Apple innovated with that device and some others successfully imitated the iPod concept by bringing other MP3 players to market. Today, if another MP3 player were brought to market, the firm that introduced it might well be the idiot on wheels.

- Model reality *realistically*. As an example, if a bid evaluates 500 desktop computers and 500 laptop computers, our Reality Model may well suggest that, because of the relatively greater desirability of laptops over desktops, the Reality Model needs to indicate, say, 300 desktop computers and 700 laptop computers. An unrealistic Reality Model could be that zero desktop computers and 1,000 laptop computers will be sold.

PTW—To Do or Not to Do

If your firm believes price targeting using PTW is critical to success, these are some of your options:

1. Stand up an internal PTW capability to support both the Competitive Intelligence (CI) gathering and PTW analyses for all major pursuits.

   Doing so will require cultural change and an initial and sustaining investment; not be a task for novices; and, have significant potential shortcomings (e.g., CI development is never easy for a firm that is bidding on a specific opportunity).

2. Routinely hire outside PTW contractors to develop CI and perform a PTW analysis for each major pursuit.

   Doing this will have costs; should benefit from the external and independent perspective; lack leverage because it will only yield project-specific analyses rather than the capability to conduct future PTW studies; and can raise "Not Invented Here" (NIH) issues with internal Capture Teams.

3. Hire an outside firm to collect CI and do the PTW analysis in house.

   This will have some costs but can solve the difficult parts of Option 1.

4. Pursue all three options.

   This is recommended when pursuing "must win" opportunities.

Firms not convinced of the value of any of these PTW options will have to continue listening to the sound of one hand clapping. This, while playing Russian Roulette with their contract pipeline.

> *"Defensive strategy never has produced ultimate victory."*
> –General Douglas MacArthur

Needed PTW Resources

A major firm's internal PTW capability is likely to have to support scores of major opportunity capture efforts every year. These pursuits may cover a wide range of technologies, complexities, and program types that require PTW to have, or acquire, specialized knowledge, diverse skills, and deep understanding.

In addition, PTW study projects typically range from a normal 30-day duration, to sometimes 60 days, but very rarely a 90-day duration. Experience shows that the bulk of engagements are 30-day affairs. This 30-day period need not be contiguous since there is a tendency for opportunity capture timetables to slip to the right in time.

Another reality is that there may be many concurrent and quasi-concurrent engagements at any given point in time. Therefore, to support this often hectic workload, internal PTW activities need:

- Repeatable processes and model prototypes;
- A corporate memory;
- A continually refreshed repository of snowflakes and "rules of thumb;"
- A library of past PTW analyses and PTW post-mortem studies;
- Pre-positioned information that feeds and is fed by business development, marketing, sales, the Capture Teams, and PTW. We need to be headed toward what can be thought of as an *information democracy*.
- An employee base consisting of seasoned PTW study leaders well versed in the processes, models and pre-positioned information assets supported by junior and senior analysts and modelers.

As has already been stated, internal PTW activities require serious and sustained investment.

To fully support the full range of PTW activities, several skill sets will be needed. As a practical matter, CAI/SISCo has found that PTW practitioners fall into one or the other of two main types. There are those who are centered on information and there are those who are analysis-centric. Regardless, the needed skill sets, or personalities, include:

- **Information Hounds and Leveragers**—people who are driven to discover essential snowflakes of information from all sorts of sources.
- **Bid Analysts**—who can look at acquisition documents and rapidly determine the nature of the opportunity.
- **Solution Sketchers and Developers**—who are able to adapt pre-positioned templates to complex sets of requirements. Some refer to this type of person as an "Enginerd."
- **Bid Modelers**—who can rapidly adapt generic labor, bases of estimates, and other models of all sorts to reflect a specific situation.
- **Bid Strategists**—who can lay out in appropriate detail how bid teams are likely to approach their bid pricing and gaming.
- **Presenters**—who are experienced, articulate and persuasive.
- **Post-mortemists**—who can discover what each PTW engagement did right, what it did wrong, what it could have done better, and how the underlying processes and models could be improved to support future PTW studies.

Corporate PTW practitioners are a relatively rare breed of professionals who are usually very senior or are bright, quick studies on a corporate management "fast track." The core group of internal PTW practitioners should be supplemented with Subject Matter Experts (SMEs) and consultants from a "virtual" resource that represents a *Who's Who* of independent talent.

PTW and Ethics

The last subject that this introduction to PTW needs to cover is perhaps as important as any other, and that is ethics. Over the years, firms of all sorts have been jolted by acts and allegations of ethical wrongdoing. Sometimes the costs have been enormous, resulting in sand being thrown into the gears of even normal competitive activities.

In the U.S., the 1988 Procurement Integrity Act defines the limits of legal behavior in federal government contracting. An employee of a government contractor who comes close to stepping over the line needs to realize that his firm has a lot more to lose in the long run than his unethical behavior can possibly gain in the short term.

The Strategic & Competitive Intelligence Professionals (SCIP) organization (*www.scip.org*) was founded in 1986. SCIP serves professionals engaged in the collection, analysis and management of information on competitive and business strategies—SCIP is the focal point of a global community of CI professionals.

SCIP's Code of Ethics is a great general guide to appropriate behavior for PTW practitioners and all others who strive to curry competitive advantage for their employers. Its tenets are as follows:

- To continually strive to increase the recognition of and respect for the profession.
- To comply with all applicable laws, domestic and international.
- To accurately disclose all relevant information, including one's identity and organization, prior to all interviews.
- To fully respect all requests for confidentiality of information.
- To avoid conflicts of interest in fulfilling one's duties.
- To provide honest and realistic recommendations and conclusions in the execution of one's duties.
- To promote this code of ethics within one's company, with third party contractors and within the entire profession.
- To faithfully adhere to and abide by one's company policies, objectives, and guidelines.

A PTW Case Study — Food for Thought

PTW has its share of heartaches, too. Here is a case study wherein the PTW Team called the situation almost perfectly, yet it was ignored by the Capture Team.

The subject opportunity concerned a major server consolidation (some may say re-centralization) requirement. Since bidders could propose the use of existing hardware, there were two fundamentally different solution approaches:

1. Bid today's technology and price points and make it last; or

2. Bid tomorrow's technology and price points and make it work.

The PTW Team, having studied the competitive situation, determined that their customer was up against a single competitor—a team led by a major systems integrator. (The PTW Team's Home Team was a hardware manufacturer.) Further study led the PTW Team to conclude that the competitive bidder's solution would be based on a low-risk, existing technology (approach #1) solution and would be priced at ~$350M life cycle.

For several reasons, the Home Team had dubbed this opportunity as their #1 "must win" pursuit in the government market. The reaction of the Capture Team to the PTW Team's conclusions was that the results were too conservative, and the price attributed to the competitor was too high. In other words, the PTW results were thus set up to be marginalized and mostly ignored.

The Home Team (recall they are a hardware manufacturer with access to long-range product roadmaps), fearful of losing on price, took every conceivable risk associated with implementing tomorrow's technology timetable today (approach #2). This led the Capture Team to propose a solution that forward priced at around $250M life cycle.

The outcome was that the government customer accepted the Home Team's ~$250M bid and the Home Team left ~$100M on the table *and* kept all of the risk of making tomorrow's technology work! Many months into the project, the Home Team was still struggling to make their win successful and profitable.

The only competitor's bid was ~$350M.

> **PTW needs to be able to convince the Capture Team and management that its analysis and results are valid and worthy of very serious consideration.**

Section II

CAI/SISCo's Price To Win (PTW) Framework

Price To Win (PTW) is a process of discovery, analysis and revelation that seeks to shed light on the darkness of how your competitors are likely to propose and price their offerings.

Section II lays out an overarching framework to accomplish a PTW study within a tight time period and for a reasonable cost. CAI/SISCo's 3-Phase, 10-Step PTW Framework was developed to enable us to conduct upwards of 100 major PTW studies each year in an orderly, timely, and manageable manner. This section takes the reader through the framework at a general level.

Subsequent sections provide the detailed guides through the phases, steps, and supporting processes that comprise the framework, as follows:

- Section III takes the reader through the details of Phase 1 of the PTW Framework—*Developing Situational Awareness and the Top Down PTW*.
- Section IV covers Phase 2 of the framework—*Developing the Partially Gamed, Bottoms Up PTW* which should be thought of as the Price *To Do* the job.
- Section V, *Developing the Fully Gamed PTW*, explains Phase 3 of the PTW Framework that culminates in the production of both a Fully Gamed PTW and a Final Gamed PTW recommendation for the Home Team. This is the Price *To Win* the job.
- Section VI, *Food for PTW Thought*, presents several broader context issues that PTW practitioners should consider and expand upon.
- Section VII, *The Progressive PTW Problem*, provides an animated and progressive view of how PTW might deal with a typical opportunity through each of the phases.

Before we go any further, however, readers need to recall that PTW is the process that provides Capture Teams with the following information:

- A detailed definition of their competition;
- An explanation of how the competitors are most likely to approach acquisition of the business; and
- A well-supported assessment of where the competitors are likely to price their offerings.

This information, which is provided to the Capture Team incrementally through a series of PTW Team-led encounters, coincides with the conclusion of each PTW phase. Each encounter is focused on what the PTW Team believes the Home Team needs to do to overcome its competitors.

Relationship of PTW to the Overall Capture Process

Figure II.1 lays out across time some of the critical capture flow elements. From bottom to top we have:

- The **Phases and Key Activities** of a typical capture process;
- **Decision Gates,** whereby an opportunity's pWin is re-examined by management and, if muster is passed, capture funding is escalated;
- **Price Definition**, the ultimate focus of PTW, seeks to initially establish and continually refine all targeted competitors' most likely bid prices, which is used to develop both the Home Team's winning price and, beyond award, to reduce the cost basis of the Home Team's bid (e.g., by means of CAIV) to ensure margin is maintained and/or improved;
- **Internal Reviews**, which subject the fruits of the capture process to management and peer reviews; and
- The **Customer Process** that governs the acquisition timetable.

Each of these flow elements needs to be understood and appreciated by the PTW activity since, like everyone else involved with a pursuit, time waits for no one. To underscore this, always remember that progress toward developing a proposal, a strategically derived price, or a PTW study ends when time runs out and show time begins.

PTW as a Parametric Process

The parametric process that underlies CAI/SISCo's approach to PTW seeks to converge on competitive bid teams' most likely fully gamed bid prices. The word *converge* is important, since our framework is designed to incrementally determine and reveal competitor and opportunity details.

As shown in **Figure II.2** and as described earlier in this section, PTW needs to learn, determine, divine, or estimate what the available budget is and what portion of that budget, if any, will not be available to the contractor (i.e., it is intended to cover other costs such as support for the customer's Project Management Office (PMO)).

This yields the Addressable Budget. As our competitive analysis endeavors that are part of Phase 1 of the PTW Framework discover the identity of the competitors, the PTW practitioner must then determine where these competitors are likely to target their bids in a top down sense within the Addressable Budget.

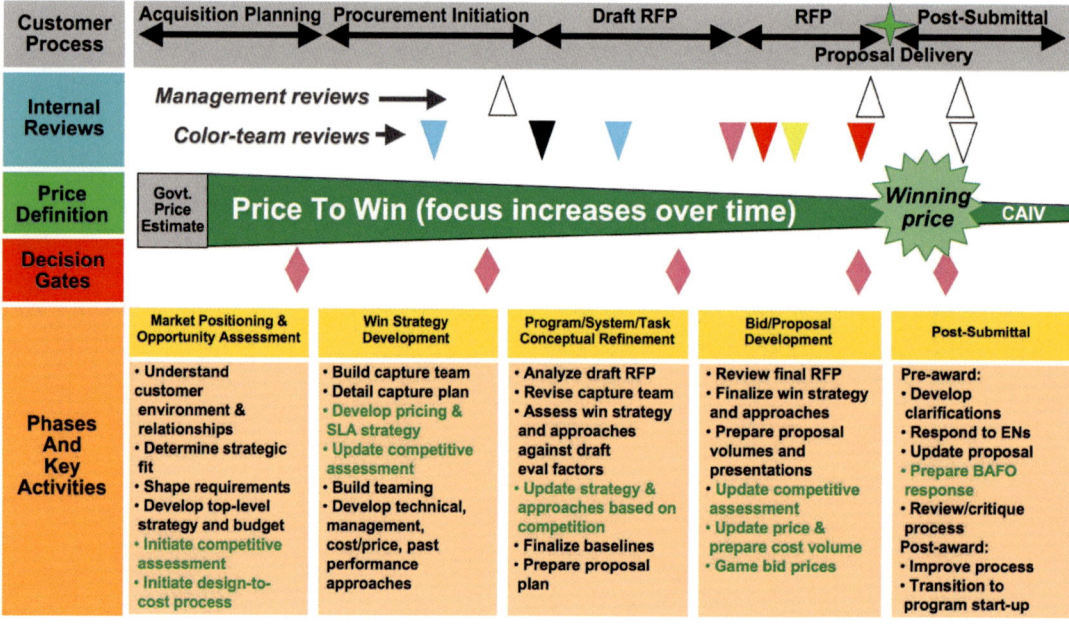

FIGURE II.1

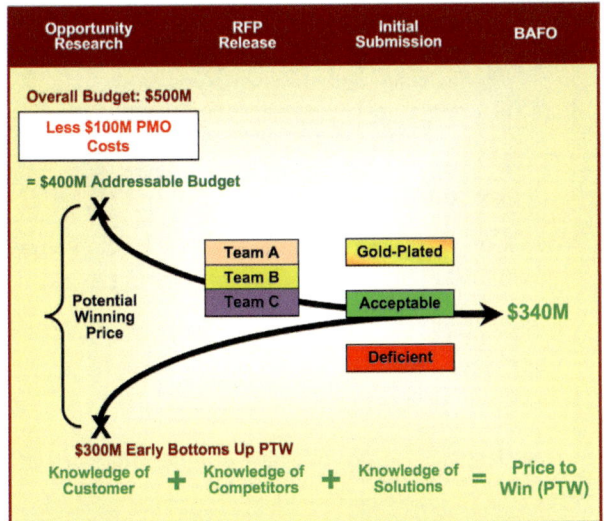

FIGURE II.2

(Phase 1 also assesses the competitors' and the Home Team's ability to earn non-cost award point scores—but this has us getting ahead of ourselves.)

The lower part of our graphic will, as Phase 2 of the PTW Framework, develop detailed Bottoms Up estimates of likely competitor solution bid prices (using bid element unit costs and prices that PTW must develop—but we get ahead of ourselves once more). PTW then refines these competitor price estimates, ultimately into a gamed version of the Phase 2 results during Phase 3 of the PTW Framework.

In summary, PTW considers three critical factors:

- Customer budget realities;
- Competitor past pricing behaviors; and
- A Bottoms Up "should price" estimate that is ultimately "gamed."

The PTW process, by means of convergence, drives toward predicting the lowest priced "otherwise acceptable" bid that can be reasonably achieved by each competitor, given each bidder's unique position and the desire of all participants to win a profitable contract.

CAI/SISCo's PTW Framework

Figure II.3 shows how the PTW Framework, over time, incrementally develops a PTW for a specific opportunity. The graphic shows:

- The elements of the opportunity that the government must or may define or supply;
- The 3 phases and 10 steps that comprise the PTW Framework; and
- How these elements work together over time to incrementally produce the PTW results and deliver them, by means of encounters to the Capture Team.

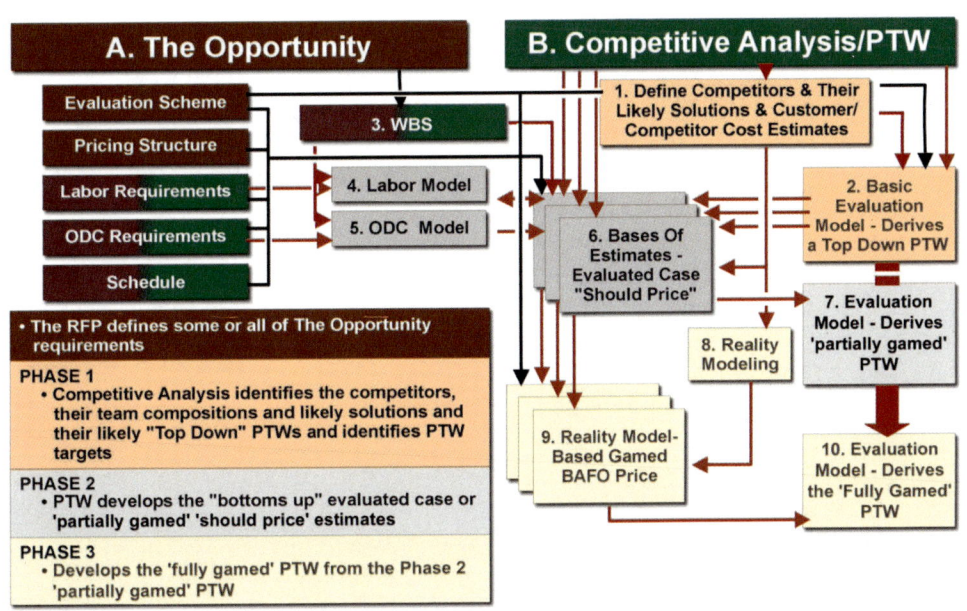

FIGURE II.3

A. The Opportunity Defined

The government must provide an **Evaluation Scheme** in its draft and final RFP that informs bidders what is going to be evaluated (non-cost issues, quantities, price, etc.) and the relative weight of each evaluation criterion. Also, the government needs to define its **Pricing Structure** in order for bidders to submit price proposals that can be compared on an apples-to-apples basis.

The areas of opportunity definition that are likely to be less than concrete relate to one, or more, of the remaining elements: **Labor, Other Direct Costs (ODCs), Schedule** and **Work Breakdown Structure (WBS).**

The U.S. government and other governments, by and large, are moving away from producing detailed Statements Of Work (SOWs) and toward Statements Of Objectives (SOOs), so there will be less and less definition of Labor Categories, ODCs, and other bid elements. What this means is that whatever PTW is *not* told in the acquisition documents, it has to create. But that's not so bad, because that's exactly what the Home Team and its competitors have to do also.

The same goes for Schedule, which may mandate delivery of a Fully Operational Capability (FOC) within 24 months of contract award, but which may state "if you want to propose an earlier FOC delivery, tell us how you intend to do it."

Nowadays, detailed Work Breakdown Structures (WBSs) are so rarely included in solicitations, it is hardly worth a discussion. (As shown in **Figure II.3**, the WBS is both an artifact that may be included, in part, in an opportunity solicitation but, at the same time, it is always also Phase 2, Step 3 of the PTW Framework.) Suffice it say that any opportunity that requires any sort of a Basis Of Estimates (BOE) is going to need a WBS. If the PTW Team has to create one, then so do the Home Team and its competitors.

A government RFP usually defines requirements in terms of:

- Program scope and subcontracting requirements.
- Program duration—usually from five to 15 years, with base and option periods.
- The Contract Line Item (CLIN) structure, evaluation quantities and units of what needs to be priced.
- The evaluation scheme (structure and relative importance) that the government intends to use to evaluate offers.

The eventual RFP may or may not define, but will imply:

- The labor categories (category descriptions) and evaluation quantities needed to meet requirements. Often the bidder must assess what labor categories are required and estimate the Levels Of Effort (LOE) that will be required.
- The location/s where the work is to be performed and the Cost Of Living Adjustments (COLAs), security clearance premiums, and danger pay that may or may not relate to these locations.
- The non-labor (other direct) costs (hardware, services, supplies, travel, etc.) and evaluation quantities needed to meet requirements. Bid elements may need to be developed and built, bought and adapted, or bought and integrated.
- The overall schedule and the major milestones, overall timing, and key events.

The fact is that the less structure the opportunity has, the more crucial and rigorous the process supporting PTW needs to be. This rigor also needs to include issues such as Service Level Agreements (SLAs) that are either required or that have to be proposed, leveraging of existing customer assets, and "best value" considerations, if any.

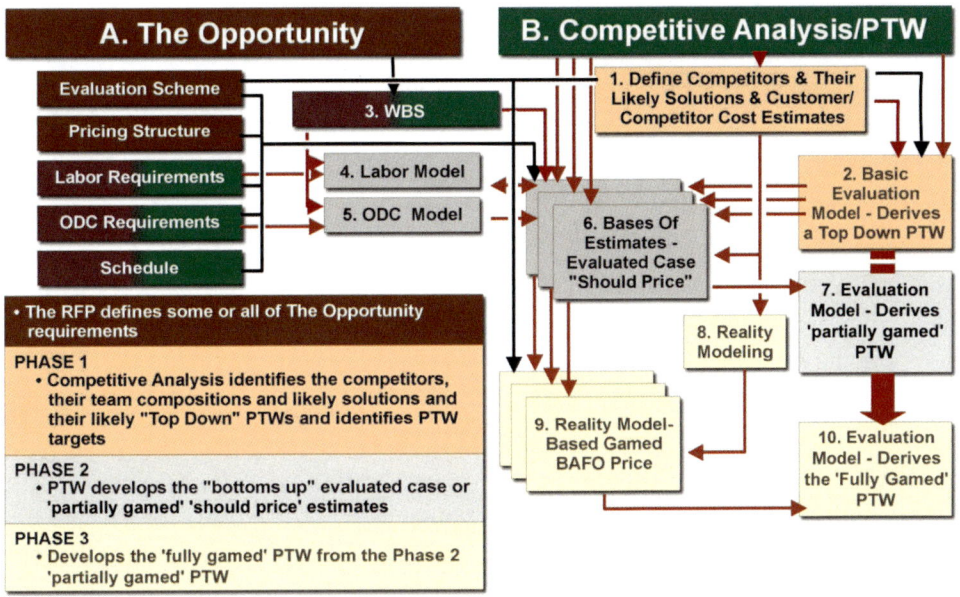

FIGURE II.3

B. The PTW Framework Phases Defined

The three phases of the PTW Framework and the steps they involve are:

- Phase 1, which develops *Situational Awareness and the Top Down PTW*, consists of Steps 1 and 2 and culminates in the Phase 1 readout encounter (Encounter 1) with the Capture Team.

- Phase 2, which develops *The Partially Gamed, Bottoms Up PTW*, consists of Steps 3 through 7 and culminates in the Phase 2 readout encounter (Encounter 2) with the Capture Team. For PTW purposes, this is the Price *To Do* the work.

- Phase 3, which develops *The Fully Gamed PTW*, consists of Steps 8 through 10, and culminates in the Phase 3 readout encounter (Encounter 3) with management, pricing and elements of the Capture Team. This can be thought of as the Best And Final Offer (BAFO) price or, as PTW tends to think of it, the Price *To Win* the job.

The box inset in **Figure II.3** (which is a repeat from page 29) provides a summary of what each phase produces. More detail is provided later in this section.

Partially Gamed vs. Fully Gamed PTW

PTW analysis always focuses on developing each *targeted* competitor's Partially and Fully Gamed Price To Win (PTW). As shown in **Figure II.4**, the way in which the framework distinguishes between the partially and fully gamed PTWs is as follows:

- The partially gamed price is what PTW develops during Phase 2 to estimate what a specific competitor is likely to develop as their **Price To Do** the job.

- In contrast, the fully gamed price is PTW's Phase 3 price that targeted competitors are likely to bid as their **Price To Win** the job.

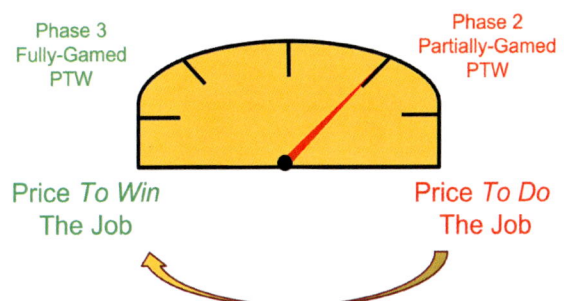

FIGURE II.4

In the context of the Section I discussion in this book concerning *Early* versus *Late* PTW studies, an Early PTW, because it focuses on providing the Capture Team with their solution price envelope, should go a long way toward otherwise reducing the gap between the **Price To Do** the job and the **Price To Win** the job.

The Home Team's partially or fully gamed price that PTW presents is always that which earns enough cost award points which, when added to the Home Team's non-cost point scores, wins overall.

The Partially Gamed PTW is typically a Basis Of Estimates (BOE) that is SOW-based, whereas a Fully Gamed PTW is a Partially Gamed PTW modified by strategic considerations unique to the requirement, the competition and the solution.

CAI/SISCo always adds an additional PTW element—we call it the Final, Fully Gamed PTW. This is a final adjustment to the Home Team's Fully Gamed PTW that widens the overall scoring margin over the strongest overall targeted competitor to, for instance, compensate for the perceived need to beat a well-performing incumbent's likely bid price by a suitable margin. (See Section V of this book for a detailed discussion of the Final, Fully Gamed PTW.)

Other Views of CAI/SISCo's PTW Framework

Figure II.5 shows how the three phases within the PTW Framework produce the Final Gamed PTW. The phases are driven by the latest available acquisition documents and, all the time, interact with pre-positioned and freshly acquired information that is added to the Home Team's Infocenter as it is acquired.

Each phase concludes with a PTW readout to, or encounter with, the Capture Team. During these encounters, information is exchanged and dialogues are joined. PTW will take copious notes and add any new items to the opportunity database: a corpus of opportunity, competitor, or individual information. And so it goes.

Figure II.6 shows a different view of the phases of the PTW Framework. The vertical bars in the graphic, when read from right to left, represent how a typical 3-phased PTW study progresses for a particular competitor from an Addressable Budget, to a Phase 1 Top Down Target Price, to a Bottoms Up, Partially Gamed PTW, to a Fully Gamed PTW.

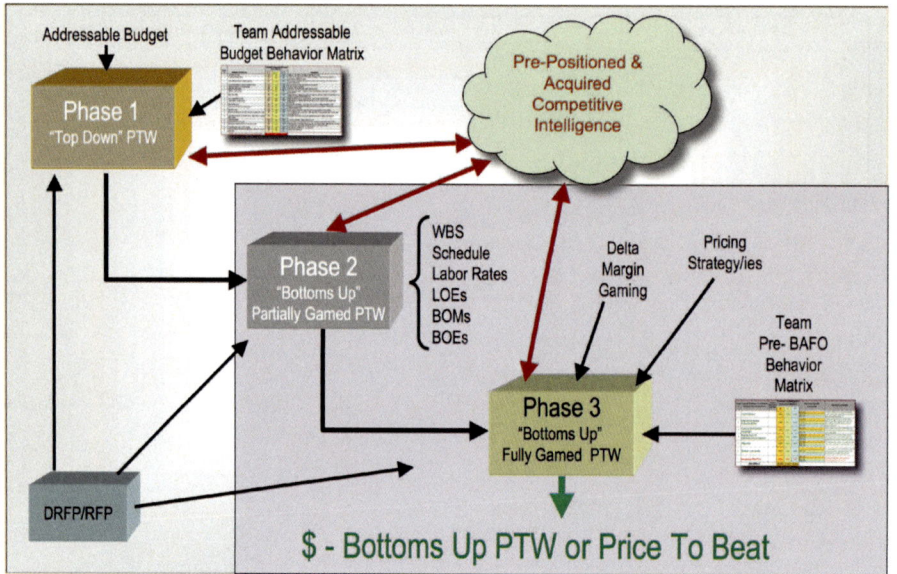

FIGURE II.5

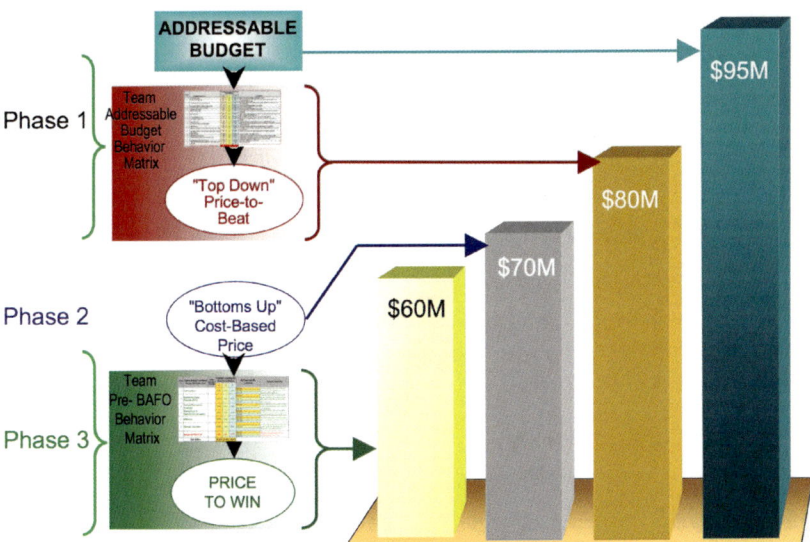

FIGURE II.6

Over the years, CAI/SISCo has observed that most PTW studies follow the downward stair-step (right to left) progression shown. Once in a while, for a host of possible reasons, this pattern is violated, and it becomes incumbent on the PTW Team to explain to the Capture Team what is behind the lack of orthogonal (i.e., having perpendicular slopes at the point of intersection) behavior. This could be, for instance, because all or a portion of a bid has to be Firm Fixed Price (FFP), or because the fully gamed price exceeds the partially gamed price when a bidder's corporate risk pool is funded.

PTW Team/Capture Team Encounters

While the PTW Framework suggests that, for a particular opportunity, there are three encounters with a Capture Team, there are actually four:

1. Encounter 0 is the Phase 1 Kick-Off. At this encounter, the Capture Team reveals to the PTW Team what they have in terms of competitive knowledge. The idea is for the Capture Team to share what they know to allow the PTW Team to hit the ground running. More on this in a moment.

2. Encounter 1 is the Phase 1 Readout wherein the PTW Team will qualify the opportunity, provide situational awareness, identify the competition and create their Strengths, Weaknesses, Opportunities, and Threats (SWOTs), score their ability to earn non-cost award points, peg competitor likely Top Down price targets, and reveal the price that the Capture Team will need to be thinking about beating.

3. Encounter 2 is the Phase 2 Readout which reveals Bottoms Up quantification of the opportunity's targeted competitors to include a WBS leaf position driven Basis Of Estimates (BOE) that includes Levels Of Effort (LOEs) by labor category and a Bill Of Materials (BOM), plus other outputs at the Partially Gamed PTW level. The PTW-developed prices for the targeted competitors, together with a refresh of their assessed ability to earn non-cost award points, revises the price that the Home Team now needs to beat in order to prevail overall.

4. Encounter 3 is the Phase 3 Readout. Please note that, while earlier encounters most likely will have been in front of the Capture Team, this final encounter may be with the management, the capture lead, and the Pricing Team. The reason for this change is that most Capture Team participants have been focused on estimates to support the Price *To Do* the job. For this encounter, the Phase 2 quantification developed for the targeted competitors is likely to be discounted to provide the Fully Gamed PTW and yield the gamed price that the Home Team will need to bid to prevail overall.

Tasking to Support the PTW Framework

Figure II.7 shows all four of PTW's encounters with the Capture Team and other Home Team elements.

Preceding Encounter 0, PTW, upon hearing of an opportunity that may be pursued by the Home firm, will embark on what we could call Phase 0 of the PTW Framework, which is a voyage of discovery to:

- Tap all available sources to understand the opportunity environment and compile a canvass hit list; and
- Ingest and tag new and existing contacts into the database in preparation for a possible canvass.

If Encounter 0 occurs, then the PTW Team will interview the Capture Team to learn what they have to share. (More on this in Section III of this book.)

It is important for PTW to remind the Capture Team that PTW is not trying to borrow the Capture Team's watch to tell them what the time is; PTW generally borrows the Capture Team's watch face, second hand, and half a watch strap which they will use to rapidly build a watch so that the entire Home Team can know what the time is.

Of course, Capture Teams come in all competency levels. A few are great, many are OK, and some are none of the above. PTW's job is to provide a level of competitor-focused support that lifts all Capture Teams a lot or a little.

Referring again to **Figure II.7**, once Encounter 0 has occurred, Phase 1 is live and its associated tasks, as outlined in the table, are executed to produce elements of the Phase 1 deliverable. The deliverable is read out at Capture Team Encounter 1 and the PTW Phase 2 targeted bid teams are identified as Bottoms Up PTW targets.

What is a targeted competitive bid team? In Phase 1, all competitive bid teams are identified and rank ordered to determine which ones are likely to be the fiercest Home Team competitors. If Phase 1 identifies 10 competitors (most often there are three or four), then it is most unlikely that more than the top two or three of the 10 will become subjects of detailed, bottoms up PTW analysis. Those competitive teams selected for Bottoms Up analysis are the *targeted* competitive bid teams.

After Encounter 1, the Phase 2 tasks are executed to produce elements of the Phase 2 deliverable. Similarly, after Encounter 2, the Phase 3 tasks are executed to produce elements of the Phase 3, and final, deliverable.

Please note that where the table indicates Update or Sketch rather than Develop, Determine, Float, Update, or Update/Replace, this implies that research precedes the development of a phase deliverable artifact or that updates based on newer information continue.

SECTION II — CAI/SISCo's Price To Win (PTW) Framework

Task #	Competitive Analysis & PTW Development – Phased Activities & Encounters	CAI/SISCo's PTW Framework Phases			
		Phase 0	Phase 1	Phase 2	Phase 3
-2	Tap all available sources to understand opportunity environment and compile a canvass hit list	Compile			
-1	Ingest and Tag new contacts and Tag existing contacts in preparation for the canvass	Ingest			
	Phase 0 "Make Ready" Activity Ends With "Kick Off" (Encounter #0)	Ask/Receive			
1	Opportunity Analysis		Develop	Update	Update
2	Customer Understanding		Develop	Update	Update
3	Contract Overview (IDIQ, SBs, CMM, etc.)		Develop	Update	Update
4	Overall & Addressable Budget (by CY)		Determine	Update	Update
5	Competitive Team Composition & Locations		Develop	Update	Update
6	Competitive Team Likely Solutions		Develop	Update	Update
7	Competitive Team SWOTs		Develop	Update	Update
8	Conduct Canvass & Compile Street Talk		Compile	Update	Update
9	Competitive Team Likely Top Down Budget Targets		Develop	Update	Update
10	Completed Evaluation Model		Develop		
11	Drafts of both Schedule and WBS		Float		
	Phase 1 Ends With Bid Team Encounter #1		Deliver	Update	Update
12	Final WBS		Sketch	Develop	Update
13	Final Schedule		Sketch	Develop	Update
14	Concept of Operations		Sketch	Develop	Update
15	Labor Categories (on site & off site)		Sketch	Develop	Update
16	Software Development Labor LOE (if any)		Sketch	Develop	Update
17	Other Labor LOE		Sketch	Develop	Update
18	BOM (Systems, Quantities/Schedule, Components)		Sketch	Develop	Update
19	Labor Model		Sketch	Develop	Update
20	BOM Model		Sketch	Develop	Update
21	BOE Model		Sketch	Develop	Update
22	Competitive Team Fees & Uplifts		Sketch	Develop	Update
23	Update (or Replace) Task 10 Evaluation Model			Update/Replace	
	Phase 2 Ends With Bid Team Encounter #2			Deliver	Update
24	Reality Model			Sketch	Develop
25	Competitive Team Likely Strategic Pricing Approach			Sketch	Develop
26	Gaming Model			Sketch	Develop
27	Update (or Replace) Task 23 Evaluation Model				Update/Replace
	Phase 3 Ends With (Pricing?) Team Encounter #3				Deliver

FIGURE II.7

The PTW Framework in a Nutshell

PTW Framework			Framework Element Description	Framework Element Desired Outcome
Phase	Step	Capture Team Encounter		
1			Determine the addressable budget and identify the competitive teams (composition, solutions) and develop their SWOTs. Rank order all competitors against all evaluation model elements.	Provides the Capture Team with opportunity and competitor information and determine which competitors should be targeted as the subjects of the Phase 2 Bottoms Up PTW analysis. Provide the Home Team with a Top Down PTW.
		0	PTW Team learns what the Capture Team knows about the opportunity, the customer, the budget, and the competition.	To learn Capture Team opportunity knowledge and use it to kick start the Phase 1 analysis.
	1		Identify the opportunity's addressable budget and all competitive teams, their compositions, and likely solutions, **plus** develop their detailed SWOTs.	To help the Capture Team to know and better understand the Home Team's competitors.
	2		Develops an Evaluation Model with which to rank order all identified competitors against evaluation elements (including likely Top Down target prices).	To show the Capture Team what it has to do to overcome all of its opportunity competitors.
		1	PTW Team qualifies the opportunity, provides situational awareness, identifies the competition and creates their SWOTs and uses the latter to score their ability to earn non-cost award points. Uses addressable budget to determine competitor likely Top Down price targets. Reveals the price that the Capture Team will need to bid to out-earn competitors in terms of Award Points.	Shares identification of all competitive bid teams and the targeted competitors for Phase 2. Seeks to learn any additional Capture Team information.
2			Quantifies the opportunity through the eyes of the targeted competitors and identifies what the Home Team now needs to do to prevail	Provides the Capture Team with opportunity quantification details supporting the Phase 2 Bottoms Up PTW analysis. Provides the Home Team with the targeted competitor's Price To DO the job.
	3		Develops a common Work Breakdown Structure (WBS)	Sets a common baseline of the work to be performed.
	4		Develops and populates a Labor Model to calculate targeted competitor team and team member labor rates.	Provides competitive team and team member labor rates for each year of the contract's duration
	5		Develops and populates an Other Direct Cost (ODC) Model to calculate targeted competitor team ODC prices.	Provides competitive team discounted and deflated/inflated ODC prices for each year of the contract's duration.
	6		Develops and populates a Basis Of Estimates (BOE) Model to estimate, by WBS element, labor Levels Of Estimates (LOEs) and ODC quantities using targeted competitor team labor rates and ODC prices developed by Steps 4 and 5.	Provides "bottoms up" details of each competitor's WBS-driven PTW with the Capture Team.
	7		Redevelops an Evaluation Model with which to re-rank targeted competitors against potentially revised evaluation model elements (including their Bottoms Up prices).	Reveals what the Capture Team has to do to beat the targeted competitors' Prices To Do the job.
		2	Reveals targeted competitor's "bottoms up, partially gamed" opportunity solutions and Prices To DO the job by CLIN and by WBS by means of a Basis Of Estimates (BOE) that includes labor category Levels Of Effort (LOEs) and a Bill Of Materials (BOM). The award points that these prices earn, together with a refresh of each team's assessed ability to earn non-cost award points, revises the price that the Home Team now needs to beat to prevail overall.	Shares the Phase 2 details and results with the Capture Team and learns any additional information that the Capture Team has.
3			Quantifies the "gamed" Price To WIN the job that the targeted competitors are likely to bid and identifies what the Home Team now needs to do to prevail.	Provides the targeted competitor's Prices To WIN the job and reveals the Home Team's final, fully-gamed PTW.
	8		Develops a detailed Reality Model for the opportunity and populates it with well-reasoned CLIN-level reality quantities.	Determines what the targeted competitive bid teams are likely to try to sell to the customer and when they are likely to try to sell it.
	9		Performs bid gaming based on Step 8 inputs and/or other criteria.	Uses the delta between Evaluated case and Reality case and other issues to game targeted competitor bid prices.
	10		Redevelops the Evaluation Model to rank order the targeted competitors against evaluation model elements (including their gamed Prices To WIN the job).	To know what the Capture Team has to do to beat the targeted competitors' fully-gamed Prices To WIN the job.
		3	Reveals how the Phase 2 "partially gamed" results for the targeted competitors are likely to be discounted to provide their "fully gamed" PTWs and what price that the Home Team will need to bid to prevail overall.	Shares the Phase 3 fully gamed results with the Senior Management, Pricing and the Capture Team leaders; learns any additional information that this encounter's participants have to share; and reveal the Home Team's final, fully gamed PTW.

FIGURE II.8

Section III

Phase 1 of CAI/SISCo's PTW Framework

Developing Situational Awareness and the Top Down PTW

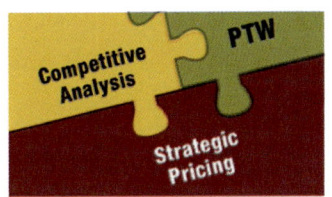

Section III lays out the overall process and takes the reader through the details of Phase 1 of the framework—*Developing Situational Awareness and the Top Down PTW*.

Phase 1 of the PTW Framework

As shown in **Figure III.1**, Phase 1 of the PTW Framework involves Steps 1 and 2.

This first phase of the PTW Framework is designed to determine each competitor's team details, their likely solution approaches and their likely Top Down PTW. In addition to the valuable analysis and information that a Phase 1 PTW study readout has to impart, it also determines which competitive teams should become the subjects of detailed Phase 2 Bottoms Up "should price" analysis.

Information to support Phase 1 is derived during Step 1 from pre-positioned information and other open source snowflakes acquired, for instance, by canvassing the field of *cognoscenti* to determine:

- The likely prime contractors, their teammates and relevant past performance/behavior; and

- The government's budget and the customer's likely Program Management Office (PMO) costs.

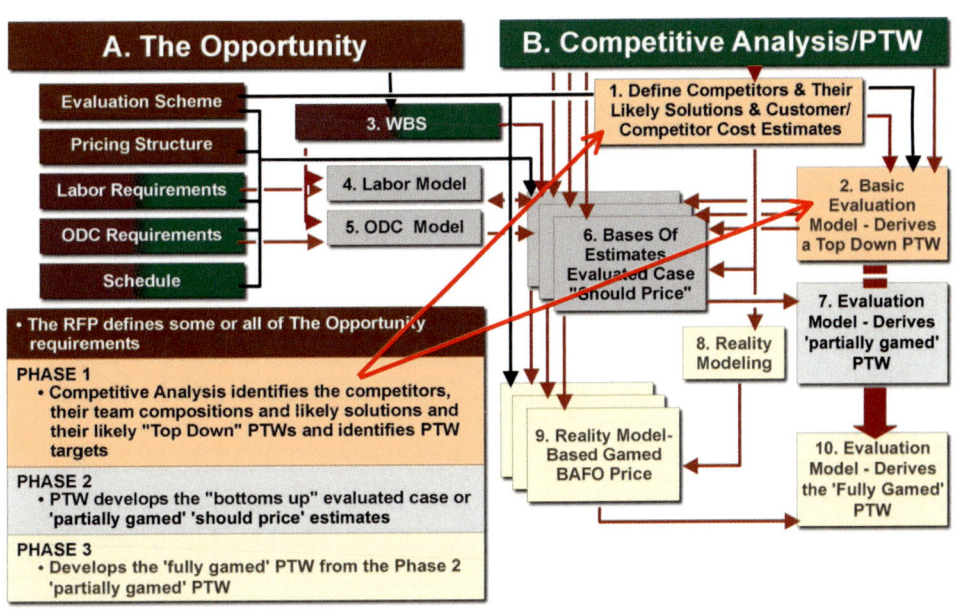

FIGURE III.1

Phase 1 research often yields PTW input detail that is needed later for Phase II's Steps 3 through 6, to include:

- Refinement of targeted bid team details that will vie for the/an award;
- Deeper relevant (team) past performance;
- Subcontractors and their likely revenue shares and roles on the team; and
- Teamed suppliers and their products.

It also develops scuttlebutt, or "street talk," concerning:

- The customer, its historic and projected spend rates/budgets and personalities;
- The competitive teams and their SWOTs (strengths, weaknesses, opportunities, threats); and
- Two of the three needed PTW parametric elements—Customer Addressable Budget Estimates (i.e., projected actual budget minus customer PMO overhead costs) and Competitor Target Pricing Estimates (i.e., where, historically, each competitor's relevant bids have been relative to a known addressable budget).

The Step 2 Basic Evaluation Model (BEM) is developed to aggregate and rank order each identified team's overall evaluation point scoring potential and provide the Capture Team with an early range of competitive PTW estimates. PTW estimates for the Step 2 BEM are derived by analyzing Step 1 information.

Phase 1 culminates in Encounter 1 with the Capture Team, wherein the PTW Team takes copious notes and, in the full spirit of *Infocentricity*, ingests those non-Home Team items gleaned from the encounter that are clearly not marked proprietary *and* are not subject to a Non Disclosure Agreement (NDA) and pre-positions them as an integral and reusable part of the opportunity and overall database.

What PTW Wants to Learn from Encounter 0

Phase 1 actually starts at Encounter 0. This is where the PTW Team and the Capture Team are introduced. This is PTW's opportunity to learn what the Capture Team knows about the opportunity and competitive environments.

The PTW study will be based on extant acquisition documents and other opportunity information. PTW should have already begun to collect and analyze this information and, using the knowledge thus garnered, should have compiled a canvass list of contacts consisting of companies and individuals with direct or indirect connections to the opportunity and other existing or planned customer initiatives. The purpose of the canvass will be to confirm or determine potential canvassee involvement with the opportunity and to poll these cognoscenti to document and analyze their understanding and assessment of the competitive landscape.

PTW should assess where the competing teams are likely to target their bid prices as a percentage of a customer's overall and addressable budgeted funds:

- In general; and
- For the subject opportunity in particular.

To best focus Capture Team and PTW Team efforts, the Encounter 0 Kick Off meeting should be convened to develop a baseline understanding of whatever the Capture Team has to share with PTW. Prior to Encounter 0, the PTW Team should present the Capture Team with a questionnaire that spells out their specific areas of interest. Sometimes a Capture Team may respond with a formal response at or before Encounter 0; other times the encounter is an interview. Needless to say, a lot of time and energy can be saved if the Capture Team can pre-prepare its questionnaire response.

The following list of major areas and topics within those areas can be used to develop a template for questionnaire development:

Opportunity Environment

- Program objectives;
- Customer's business environment and its "hard" requirements;
- Key government personalities, likes, and dislikes; and
- Known customer hot (and cold) buttons and other issues.

Procurement Background

- Schedule;
- Rough Order of Magnitude (ROM) cost or Independent Cost Estimate;
- Budget and contractor-addressable budget; and
- The customer's Source Selection Evaluation Board (SSEB) composition and their known preferences, if any.

Incumbent Contractors

- Primes, subcontractors, and suppliers—contact names and information, if available; and
- How well-liked the incumbent/s are and by whom.

Competitors (Incumbents and Insurgents)

- Incumbent prime/s, subcontractors, and suppliers (including those on the Home Team if they are the incumbent prime)—contact names and information, if available;
- Confirmed/likely/possible primes, subcontractors, and suppliers—contact names and information, if available; and
- Previous incumbent contract bidders—contact names and information, if available.

In addition, the PTW Team should request any Home Team internal Black Hat and Gate, Step, or Milestone review readouts.

PTW can lead the initial meeting or just take notes and ask questions. The meeting's purpose is to rapidly develop a basic understanding of the opportunity environment that can be both validated and augmented. Validation and augmentation are accomplished by means of the exhaustive canvass that PTW should undertake of the universe of interested parties surrounding the opportunity.

As always, at all encounters, PTW practitioners should take copious notes and practice *Infocentricity* by ingesting and pre-positioning within the opportunity database all issues, additional snowflakes, concerns, questions, and needs for illumination, etc. Remember, information *is* the life blood of PTW (and, we suspect, all business development activities).

PTW Phase 1—A Road Map

Figure III.2 provides a road map to Phase 1 activities that PTW should follow. The three major events in the red boxes are:

1. The point at which PTW first came across the subject opportunity or the time that PTW proactively initiated data gathering in its support.

2. Encounter 0, or the opportunity Kick Off meeting between PTW and the opportunity Capture Team.

3. Encounter 1, or the Phase 1 PTW readout.

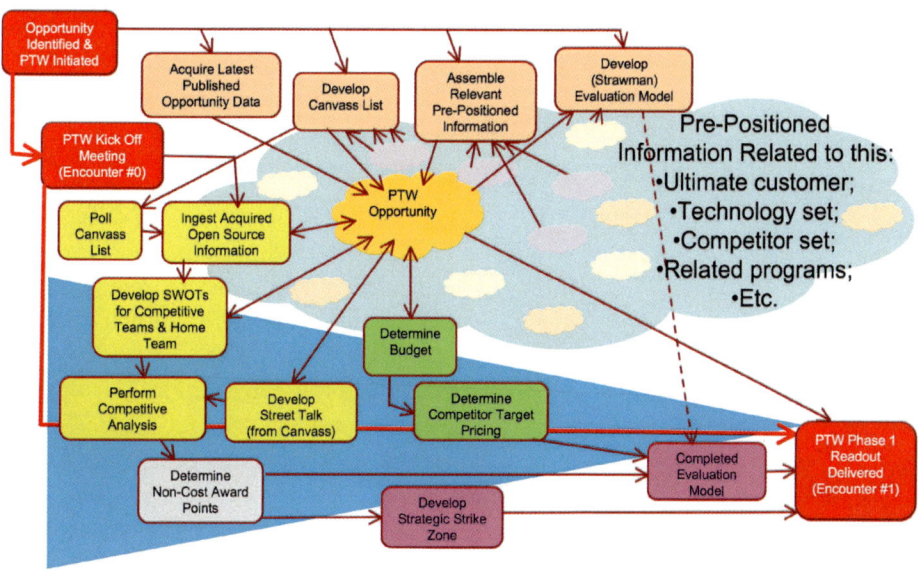

FIGURE III.2

As discussed, **Event 1** is a voyage of discovery that:

- Taps all available sources to understand opportunity environment and compile a canvass hit list; and
- Ingests and tags new and existing contacts in preparation for a possible canvass.

How does this happen? The major cloud in the previous graphic represents the entirety of the Home Firm's pre-positioned information. Within this major cloud are minor clouds related to:

- This customer and other customer opportunities;
- This technology set;
- This competitor or competitor set; and
- Other related opportunities.

If the new opportunity does not exist as a minor cloud already, PTW creates a new minor cloud for the new opportunity. In either event:

- New information concerning the opportunity is ingested and tagged to attach it to the opportunity cloud; and
- Existing information is tagged to point to the new opportunity in addition to all other tags it may already have.

Event 2 kicks off all of the Phase 1 steps and tasks to augment and interact with the new project's minor cloud and create the Phase 1 readout artifacts in preparation for Event 3, or Encounter 1 with the Capture Team. Each of the activities between Events 2 and 3 are described in subsequent parts of this section of the book.

PTW Framework Phase 1, Step 1— Developing Situational Awareness

Figure III.3 outlines how situational awareness information is developed in support of the Phase 1 deliverable which is to be presented at Bid Team Encounter 1. As discussed, development of Phase 1 readout ingredients begins prior to the Kick Off encounter.

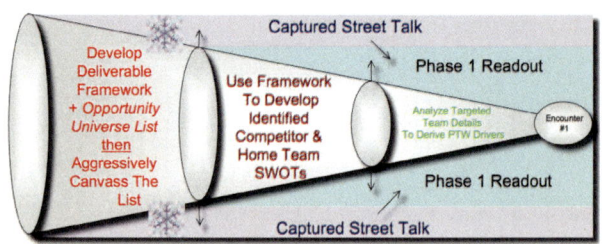

FIGURE III.3

Canvass sources include:

- Industry Day and bidder conference attendees;
- Interested party lists; and
- Contacts from related opportunities and personalities.

As shown in the left segment of the graphic, the resulting contact list has to be aggressively canvassed. PTW needs to capture and use information gleaned from the canvass in addition to leveraging all available pre-positioned information to determine who the confirmed, likely and possible competitors are.

Moving to the middle segment, we need to utilize a presentation framework within which to develop and/or complete the competitive team Strengths, Weaknesses, Opportunities, and Threats (SWOTs). The key, as always, is to use and augment with newly acquired information what is already known and deemed to be relevant.

In the right segment, to synthesize what PTW has learned, we now use that information to analyze competitive team details, derive the Phase 1 PTW drivers, and complete the Phase 1 readout package in preparation for Bid Team Encounter 1.

The Effectiveness of Lobbyists

Business developers usually have a limited purview of what it takes to win major competitive awards. Some focus on telling their story in a proposal, others on pricing games, and yet others on understanding the competition and their likely solutions, teams, and pricing, i.e., Price To Win (PTW). In short, most business development practitioners tend to be relatively insular, and one of the most often ignored avenues for helping to position a bidder or Capture Team for a win is lobbying.

Reading Eamon Javer's 2010 book **Broker, Trader, Lawyer, Spy**, sub-titled *The Secret World of Corporate Espionage,* one is reminded that lobbying is a high-yield activity. This book should be required reading for all who are engaged in developing products or business, including PTW practitioners. The following excerpt related to lobbying activities says it all:

> Getting government help can be vastly more rewarding than anything many companies can do in the private sector. That's one reason, for example, why they spend so much money lobbying the U.S. Congress for earmarks—those special, targeted, spending provisions often stuck into legislation moving through the Capitol. In 2005, on average, companies received as much as $28 in earmark revenue for every single dollar they spent on lobbying expenses. That's a much better rate of return than many could get producing and selling products.

> Some see politics and lobbying as relatively benign forms of organized crime.

Acquiring Needed PTW Information

PTW is a time-sensitive activity that provides opportunity qualification information and quantification inputs well in advance of most Capture Team's ability to so do. PTW lives in a 30-, sometimes 60-, but rarely a 90-day world.

Detailed and actionable information is needed on the following major elements of any PTW study:

- The Opportunity
- The Customer
- The Competition
- The Home Team

To fully describe a competitive situation, PTW needs to know *on the way in* what information and knowledge:

- Will be needed to understand the totality of the competitive landscape;
- Is already known (i.e., pre-positioned for re-use, or otherwise available); and
- Needs to be rapidly and aggressively acquired to bridge the gap between what we know and what we need to know.

Open Source information is everywhere! For PTW purposes, the major categories of need are:

- Competitor-related;
- Customer-related; and
- Opportunity-related.

For a comprehensive set of sources of available Open Source information, please consult the paragraphs entitled *General Research Sources: Finding Opportunity, Agency and Competitor Information* at the end of Section VI of this book.

Developing Opportunity Understanding

As the first step toward understanding the subject opportunity, PTW has to determine and/or confirm what the opportunity is and isn't.

As part of the canvass, PTW must seek understanding and/or confirmation of the customer's thinking from canvassees to help confirm or advance the Capture Team's thinking.

PTW also has to determine the level of leverage that exists to previous studies, since the requirement may be:

- A follow-on to an existing contract—i.e., the new opportunity covers the same old stuff;
- The same, or similar, to another opportunity from the same or a different customer. This may imply that leveragable templates exist; or,
- A unique one—i.e., one for which no overall template exists, but templates describing parts of the overall solution exist and are leveragable.

PTW also needs to understand which competitors have specific experience and lessons learned related to the subject opportunity. To ascertain this, PTW has to determine each competitor's relationship to both the customer and the opportunity.

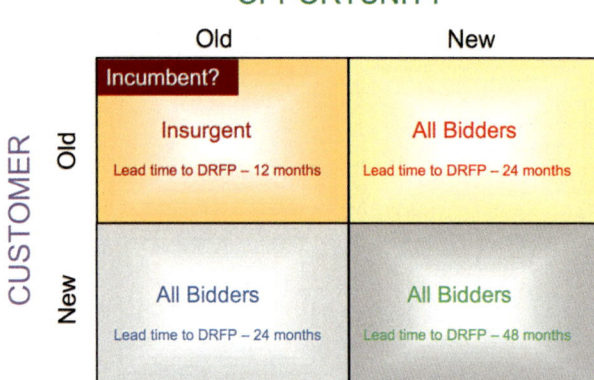

FIGURE III.4

The positioning graphic (**Figure III.4**) does just this. A bid team that is an insurgent (and even a partial incumbent) will be placed on the graphic relative to their respective bid posture—the strongest bidders appearing in the top left quadrant and the weakest in the bottom right quadrant. Note that the lead times vary depending on quadrant, implying that the weaker bidders will need more customer positioning time to gain credibility.

A Lack of Understanding Can Really Hurt

Here is cautionary tale of what can happen if one doesn't develop situational awareness and understanding:

> In the early 1970s, I was part of a team delivering a seminar for some major mainframe computer-using companies. The event was held in a conference room with a panoramic view of the Pacific Ocean at the fabulous Highlands Inn in Carmel Heights, California.
>
> After one particular attendee checked in—he represented a major oil company—the grumbling began about the room rate which was about $175 per night. In this person's mind this room rate, coupled with the undoubtedly high cost of meals at the hotel, would blow his expense account. So off to town he went in search of a McDonalds, or some such.
>
> The rest of the attendees enjoyed sumptuous meals for two full days at this little bit of heaven by the sea. What this person found out at check-out time was that all meals were included in the room rate.

For PTW purposes, information is the basis of meaningful analysis. Ask questions, develop insights, and use the understanding thus garnered to build your opportunity foundation.

PTW and SOO-Based Acquisitions

Statement Of Objectives (SOO)-based acquisitions are usually aimed at acquiring a solution that is shaped over time by largely evolving customer needs and requirements.

In RFPs that include a detailed Performance Work Statement (PWS) or Statement Of Work (SOW), bidders and PTW Teams typically use these documents to develop their opportunity Work Breakdown Structures (WBS). In the case of a SOO, bidders and PTW Teams are forced to create a SOW or PWS from which to develop their WBS.

Beyond that, price estimates developed using SOO-based RFPs reflect a bidder's and PTW's view of:

- Each bid team's perception of the requirements underlying the SOO;
- Their likely SOO-based SOW;
- Each bid team's past experience with programs of similar scope and size; and
- The customer's underlying budget, which is usually a supportable "worst case," Not To Exceed (NTE) amount for 100% of the SOO's purview, including provision for Engineering Change Proposals (ECPs).

The relationship of SOO-based contractor bid prices to budgets is often tenuous because:

- Bidders tend to cost out and price their bids based on a tangible set of bedrock needs and template-able requirements; and
- Evolving needs and requirements (i.e., add-ons) are expected to be ECP fodder.

Understanding the Customer's Cast of Characters

While PTW strives to know the background information on everyone involved in managing, buying, and operating the subject of the acquisition, it is not always the case that Capture Teams have this as a priority. Even if a Capture Team does compile and use this level of information, once the capture has run its course, this sort of information is no longer deemed to be useful.

PTW's role, therefore, among other things, is to be the historian for all pursuits and related information. PTW routinely collects and uses this sort of information and always ensures that it is added to the overall body of competitive knowledge by pre-positioning it on the enterprise's Infocenter for possible future use. This will include information on agency:

- Management;
- Acquisition community; and
- User community/ies.

This may strike someone who has never been infocentrically inclined as being a little over the top. Consider this though: Whether the PTW capability is an internal organization or a firm like CAI/SISCo that specializes in PTW studies, the question is: Do we intend to do another PTW with this customer? If the answer is yes, or even maybe, then why would we not capture and pre-position what we learn about these characters and augment it as we come across them on other opportunities, at other agencies, or eventually, in the private sector? *If you never start being infocentric, you can never hope to reap the rewards of information leverage.*

As shown in the following Venn-like graphic (**Figure III.5**), PTW must also strive to learn these folk's roles and authority in:

- Deciding program strategy;
- Defining requirements; and
- Deciding selection strategy.

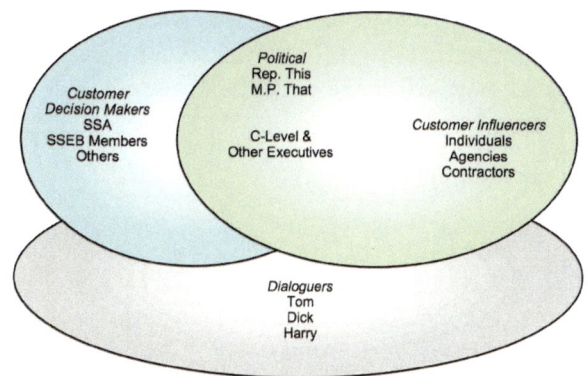

FIGURE III.5

Among the customer decision makers are the **SSA**—the Source Selection Authority; and the **SSEB**—the Source Selection Evaluation Board.

PTW also needs to understand how well the competitors have been able to understand and influence these customer personalities.

Understanding the Customer

PTW always leverages pre-positioned information and collects additional Competitive Intelligence to determine as much as possible about the customer's:

- Chain of command;
- Overall contracting history;
- Critical success factors;
- Business processes; and
- Goals.

PTW also needs to determine how the opportunity supports and/or drives the customer's goals. For instance, is the opportunity strategic or tactical?

In addition, PTW must determine who the key incumbents and insurgents are, and whether they are deemed by the customer to be part of the problem or part of the desired solution. Recall that government customers are unlikely to *want* to train a new contractor, especially if the incumbent contractor represents the customer's institutional knowledge. But understand, especially in tough economic times, that customers have a hard time avoiding this if a competent insurgent's price is substantially lower than the incumbent's.

Of great concern to Phase 1 is arriving at the customer's opportunity budget. To do this, PTW has to find out, estimate, or divine what the customer has in terms of an:

- Overall budget; and
- Addressable budget.

PTW also needs to know the customer's likely and/or historical overall budget hold back level to cover Project Management Office (PMO) costs, and the like. An addressable budget is that portion of a job's actual overall budget that is likely to be available to the contractor. The government's PMO may or may not have significant costs that it needs to cover (contractors for SETA or IV&V work, etc.) out of the allocated budget. Usually, the only way to determine the extent of this budgetary take-down is based on agency personality, type of job (e.g., developmental, highly technical, etc.), agency knowledge, and other aspects of the customer environment.

Other interesting pieces of information that PTW should try to obtain are why the:

- Particular evaluation scheme was chosen; and
- Contract type is considered appropriate or advantageous.

That brings PTW to what the opportunity-related pain threshold regarding risk and trust issues are likely to be. It is somewhat obvious that a new requirement involves the most potential for risk, whereas a re-compete presents the least. But, what does this customer think about risk, and what is the worst that could happen if the customer makes the wrong decision?

Alternatively, what is the best that could happen if she/he makes the right decision, and what, in the eyes of the customer, represents the right decision in terms of team composition, solution, experience, past performance, and price?

Who does the customer perceive to be most trustworthy?

- The incumbent (the Home Team, or not); or
- An insurgent (the Home Team, or not).

PTW may be able to weigh in on how the Home Team's Capture Team can convince the customer that they are more trustworthy than the competitors, and how these issues are likely to color customer proposal evaluations, especially in the areas of:

- Proposal risk; and
- Price risk.

Grappling with Customer Requirements

All customer requirements are assumed to be real, but do they have the same level of importance, especially to PTW? To answer this question, PTW has to rank order customer requirements to determine their Most Important Requirements (MIRs) and concentrate analysis on these *material* issues. Remember, materiality is a basic tenet of PTW.

While compliance is necessary when writing a proposal response, it is not often going to be a winning attribute. After all, requirements that all offerors must comply with are unlikely to produce discriminators or any sort of differentiator among competing offers. This is because discriminators only exist when a team exceeds requirements and/or lowers risks to the customer.

At CAI/SISCo, we have observed that requirements that can produce discriminators often become obvious as the result of a MIR analysis.

Understanding Competitors and the Home Team

For PTW practitioners to be able to effectively grade each of the competitors (including the Home Team) against the evaluation criteria, the PTW Team needs to assess each bidder's abilities to have developed customer awareness by means of research and quality face time.

During Phase 1, PTW has to leverage pre-positioned information and collect additional Competitive Intelligence on *each* competitive team, and prepare supporting provenance, to support the following four issue areas:

1. Their customer understanding in terms of critical success factors, business processes, and goals;

2. Their acquisition approach as it relates to corporate personality, past performance, teaming, likely capture strategy, solution development, and likely pricing strategy;

3. Their ability to earn non-cost evaluation award points for past performance, tools, and techniques that they can bring to the table such as Earned Value Management Systems (EVMS); and

4. Their most likely Top Down target prices, developed using one of several possible approaches for assessing each competitor's most likely discount to the addressable budget.

Determine, target price included, in descending order by aggregated award points, the identified competitors who are, all things considered, best positioned to win the opportunity. THEN examine issue areas 1, 2, and 3 on behalf of the Home Team. Issue area 4 uses the fiercest competitor's aggregate non-cost and cost/price point score to determine the target price the Home Team is going to need to win the competition overall by a small margin (Item 4).

The competitors' non-cost evaluation point scores and prices are used, in conjunction with competitor likely price targets, to shape the Home Team's winning price.

As described later in this section, the results are pictorialized in CAI/SISCo's Strategic Strike Zone (SSZ) which presents an "at a glance" graphic of the high-level results.

This process of collecting these sorts of data continues during Phases 2 and 3, where the focus turns mostly to the *targeted* competitive bid teams. Of course, to the infocentrically inclined, no information lacks potential value.

Teaming Issues to Bear in Mind

With respect to teaming, PTW practitioners need to appreciate some of the more global issues that pertain to the posture of competitive bid teams.

Clearly, if a major contractor were able to bid and win an opportunity with few or no teaming partners (i.e., few constraints on their post-award subcontracting), they would retain the most flexibility to go for an aggressive price. Their post-award strategy may be to propose post-award teaming, which could allow them to dictate aggressive subcontractor prices. This type of approach would have to be supported by an Evaluation Model that does not consider team composition.

On the other hand, competitive bidders sporting large teams or teams consisting of major teammates may be trying for higher non-cost evaluation scores. If, for instance, relevant past performance is deemed to be a prominent feature of the evaluation set, and the prime lacks in some past performance areas, then subcontractors with the requisite experience will probably be required.

Home Teams that sport this characteristic often fight PTW practitioners with respect to the relative value of non-cost and cost/price award points in an evaluation scheme. For instance, the DRFP/RFP may state that "non-cost issues are collectively more important than cost/price issues." PTW may interpret this to mean a 60/40 split, whereas the Home Team's capture folk may pray that it means 75/25, because their ability to price aggressively has been undermined by teaming decisions and therefore they hope that price is less likely to be the, or even a, primary issue.

PTW practitioners need to be aware that large aggregators (i.e., those that enter a competition when an opportunity's critical mass—due to consolidation— is too large to ignore), integrators or other players tend to do both. They:

- Use teaming partners for non-price scoring; and
- Try to renegotiate/set teaming partner price points post-award.

There are many examples of situations where this large company strategy has worked but, as cautionary tales, there are a few instances where this strategy has failed spectacularly, too. The Warren Buffet Innovator-Imitator-Idiot cycle is alive and well in competitive bidding circles.

PTW and the WBS for Top Down Analysis

To arrive at an apples-to-apples basis of comparison as early as possible in the PTW process, PTW must develop and present its initial Work Breakdown Structure (WBS) as part of the Phase 1 readout at Encounter 1. The WBS is rarely provided in an acquisition document and must be developed as a hierarchical representation of a Statement Of Work (SOW) or Performance Work Statement (PWS), the purpose of which is:

- To decompose the required activities into major, often time-phased and discretely managed areas of work; and

- To further decompose the major work areas into tree structures comprised of discrete work packages.

The initial WBS is used in the PTW process:

- To develop a common basis of understanding with the Capture Team at Encounter 1; and

- As the basis for setting cost targets for major elements of the overall work to be used by, for instance, Integrated Product Teams (IPTs).

The WBS can also be used as the framework for setting CAIV-like WBS element cost targets. The WBS shown in **Figure III.6** is a Top Down decomposition of the totality of the work that needs to be performed to accomplish *Job X*.

Thinking of a WBS in this manner, however, can be misleading since traditionally, costing is a "bottoms up" activity and that is not what PTW or pricing should be or is all about.

Second, to approximate CAIV-like targets, PTW will need to generically decompose the overall cost/price of the job down through the WBS structure. Using our *Job X* WBS, we determine how a hypothetical budget, addressable budget, target price, or bid price (which are all mostly unknowns at this point) should be allocated down through the WBS's hierarchy. The idea is to determine, regardless of the amount of money to be allocated, where the money needs to go (in a weighted allocation sense) to make the overall job realistically doable.

As an example, let's say that we have decided and documented that, at the IPT level, regardless of the amount of money available:

- Program Management should get 15% of available funds (this would be defined based on customer norms and expectations, job difficulties, etc.);

- Design, Development and Test (DD&T) should receive 50%; and that the

- The Operation & Maintenance (O&M) tail will get the remaining 35%.

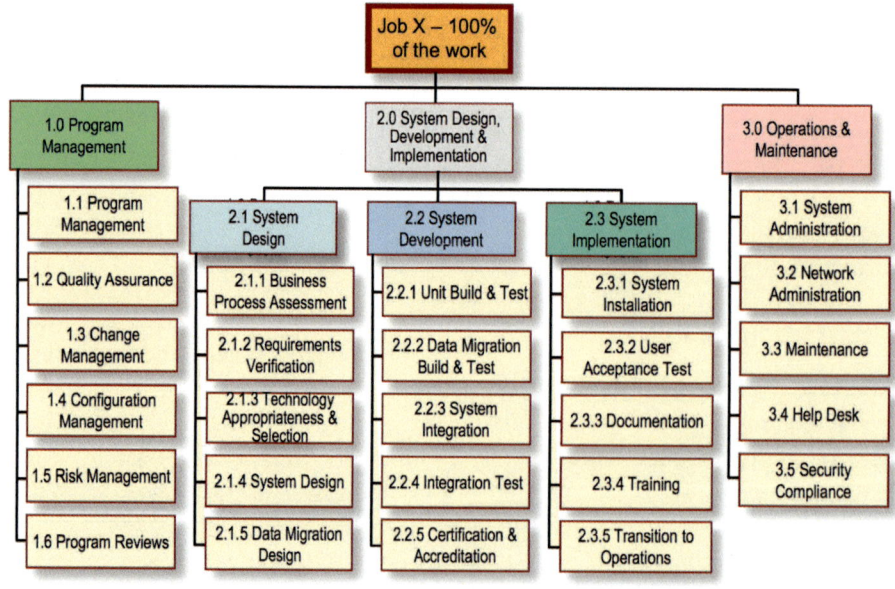

FIGURE III.6

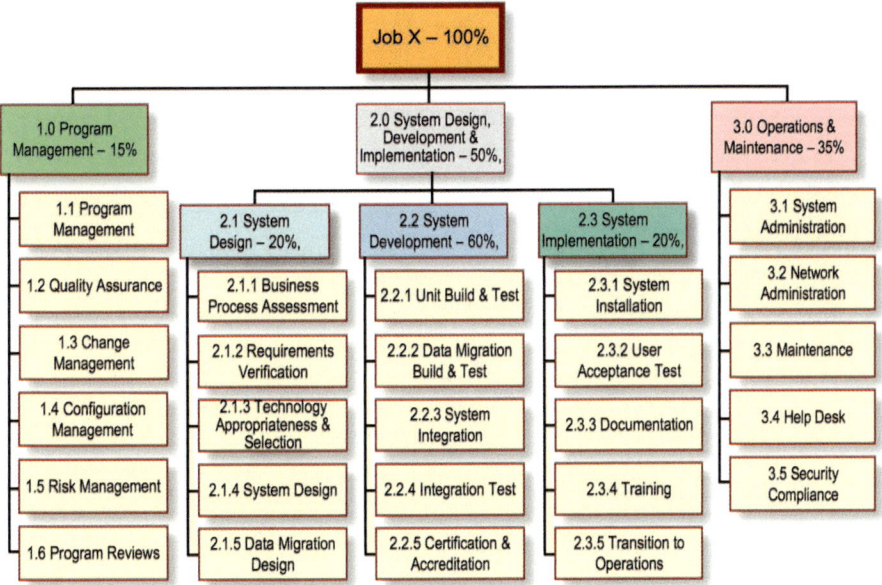

FIGURE III.7

In **Figure III.7**, this decomposition has been added to our WBS, at least at the highest levels, which should relate to IPTs, those multidisciplinary groups of people who are collectively responsible for delivering a defined product or process. Note that decomposition can also include labor and materiel as well as work designated for the prime contractor and/or its subcontractors.

Third, we will need to allocate an amount of money down through the weighted hierarchy shown in the previous graphic. For this purpose, let us use the fiercest competitor's likely target price to set our WBS-based targets as in **Figure III.8**.

Let us assume that *Job X* has an overall budget of $200M, and further that 25% of that budget (i.e., $50M) is typically needed to support this customer's PMO for a project of the subject opportunity's type and complexity. Thus, we are facing a contractor-addressable budget of $150M. If PTW analysis expects a specific competitive bid team to target their

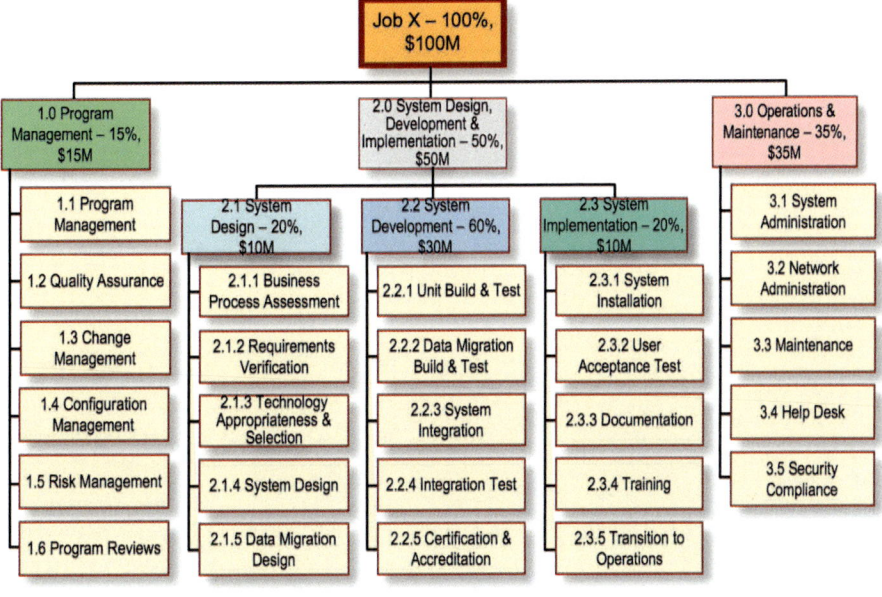

FIGURE III.8

bid price at 66% of the $100M contractor-addressable budget, then this competitor's target price would be $66M and this amount would be allocated, as shown in the previous graphic, down through the WBS to set Home Team IPT cost targets. The result would be something like the target numbers shown.

Stepping outside of the realm of PTW just a bit further, this is hardly the end of the story. Matching a significant competitor's bid price is not likely to be a recipe for success. What needs to happen is for intrapreneurship (i.e., internal out of the box thinking) to take over and propel our IPT leads to work to meet *and* beat their targets. To energize that process, we need to put in place some form of bonus scheme that rewards IPTs based on their performance in beating targets without diminishing overall solution desirability.

Back to PTW Framework Phase 1, Step 1

The Top Down customer/competitor budget and price estimation aspects of Phase 1, Step 1 are focused on determining the customer's addressable budget for this opportunity, which is:

- The amount of money that the customer has budgeted for the overall opportunity; *minus*
- The % of the available budget that is *not* likely to be applied directly to the contracted opportunity in question.

Next, we must determine each competitor's likely reaction to the (we have to assume) known addressable budget. For PTW purposes, this can be developed by several methods that will be explained. This approach, we will call it **Approach 1**, determines where competing bidders have priced and won similar bids as a % of customer addressable budgets, either to:

- This customer; or
- Other customers in general.

Developing a Top Down PTW for a competitor by developing discounts to a known or imputed addressable budget has to consider many issues. The take-downs reflect that competitor's past pricing behaviors, such as relationships of their past winning bid price/s to past addressable budget/s.

This approach to Top Down target pricing relies heavily on information concerning recent contract awards for the same/similar requirements, products or services. Regardless, this sort of information must always be augmented with likely bidder future behavior such as:

- Circumstances and current market conditions;
- Future prices; and
- Likely pricing strategies.

To establish a reasonable balance between documented history and the likely, yet uncertain, future, a PTW practitioner cannot merely use history as the predictor. Instead, we must understand that the opportunity at hand is not historical, or even happening in real time. The opportunity that the Home Team, the competitors, and the PTW Team are facing may not even be awarded for many months and will extend five years, or more, beyond that point in time.

Together, these two estimates comprise the first two elements of a parametrically-derived Top Down PTW, or more accurately, a Top Down "price to beat."

For PTW purposes, it is unwise to try to factor in any "best value" advantages that could, should or may accrue to certain competitors—PTW must strive to ignore everyone's hype and abstain from drinking anyone's bathwater!

Top Down Competitor PTW Analysis—Approach 2

If developing Top Down competitor PTWs by relating past pricing behavior to corresponding addressable budgets (Approach 1) is not possible, how can this important step be accomplished? **Approach 2** provides a means of deducing where competitors are likely to target their bids based on who they are in relation to the opportunity.

If PTW is modeling an incumbent, then we can assume that their Top Down PTW could be expressed as:

- Their adjusted (see below) incumbent contract value; *minus*
- 10% (reflects where an insurgent typically has to price to unseat an adequate incumbent); *minus*

- Another 5% (to reflect acknowledgement of the fact that an insurgent would expect a defensive discount to be applied by the incumbent); *and possibly minus*
- Another percentage take-down to represent what the new acquisition is looking for as its "to be" *modus operandi*, such as implementation of a productivity improving standardized approach like the Information Technology Infrastructure Library (ITIL).

Incumbent contractors rarely manage their costs very closely, choosing instead to strike a balance between minimizing costs and keeping the customer happy. What happens is that, over a contract's life cycle, bloat occurs, often because over-qualified (and compensated) people become assigned to the incumbent's contract.

As an example, if the requirement for a particular labor category is that a candidate has to have three years of relevant experience then, at the end of a five-year contract, assuming the candidate is still doing the same job, they would be increasingly over-qualified and most likely, therefore, over-paid. This means that there often needs to be an adjustment to the incumbent's contract value to remove such cumulative bloat.

The other issues related to what it takes to unseat incumbents of all performance levels have already been discussed.

If, on the other hand, PTW is modeling an insurgent, then their Top Down target price could be expressed as a 15% discount to the incumbent's adjusted contract value to reflect a:

- 10% offensive discount; *plus*
- Further 5% discount to counter the incumbent's expected defensive discount.

A general point needs to be made. PTW is part science and part art—but so is fashioning a solution and a proposal response. It is, therefore, up to each PTW practitioner to develop his or her own personality and view as it relates to the competitive world. This book provides clues that are intended to lead would-be PTW practitioners to certain conclusions, but they are just clues, not absolutes. Future PTW practitioners must fashion their own views and metrics based on their own supportable perceptions of reality.

Budget Realities

No matter what—Reality Models that quantify the "real" opportunity, or whatever—budget reality rules. If it ain't in the budget, it doesn't exist. Therefore, no matter what else changes (unit prices, volumes, technologies), customer budgets are likely to remain relatively static. They may increase slightly or decline gradually, but rarely, if ever, are government budgets going to breathe to accommodate the needs of a specific contract.

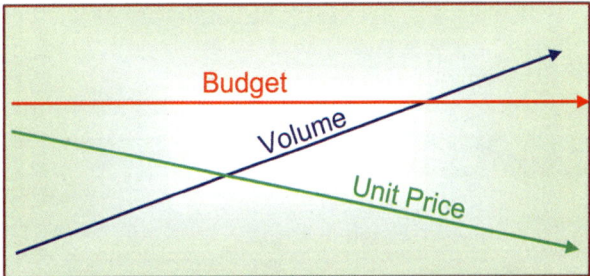

FIGURE III.9

Figure III.9 indicates that the volume usage of an item can only increase if its unit price is reduced to allow the resulting cost to fit within the prevailing budget. Great examples of this are telecommunications services that are IPv4-based, data storage, etc.

But there are other commodities that governments tend to deny the existence of as project costs—chief among them is the cost of energy. While our underlying budget may not be changing radically, energy consumption increases as its unit cost increases. This is the reason that energy is a great area to address as a Total Cost of Ownership (TCO) issue.

PTW Framework Phase 1, Step 2— Evaluation Modeling

The Basic Evaluation Model (BEM) is developed using the DRFP/RFP's opportunity evaluation scheme (e.g., the Section M, or equivalent). Until an opportunity matures to the point where the customer reveals an actual evaluation scheme, a representative scheme from the same or a different customer for the same or a similar opportunity have to be used by PTW practitioners as a baseline until the real thing appears.

For PTW to progress based on a DSOO or a DSOW, a stand-in BEM will be needed as a scoring baseline against which competitor teams and the Home Team can be graded and stack-ranked.

As shown in **Figure III.10**, a BEM consists of:

- An evaluation criteria tree as the Y axis of the evaluation matrix; and

- Allocation of award points to each evaluation criterion in a manner that ensures that all adjectival references (i.e., this is more significant than that) are met and that all criteria sum to a maximum available point score (say 1,000) or follow quantitative references.

Opportunity ID	Available Award Points
Customer Agency	
Basic Evaluation Model	
Overall Evaluation	1000
Overall Evaluation Rank	
Non-Price Evaluation (Sum of Factors 1 - 3)	600
Non-Price Evaluation Rank	
Factor 1 - Technical Issues	300
Factor 2 - Management Issues	200
Factor 3 - Past Performance Issues	100
Factor 4 - Price ($M)	400

FIGURE III.10

(As will be seen, the competitive bid teams and the Home Team will be arrayed to form the X axis of the evaluation matrix.)

The BEM shown in the preceding table will:

- Allow each non-cost evaluation criterion to be rated, documented and ranked for all bid teams;

- Use likely competitor Top Down budget-based price target estimates to develop an inverse allocation of available price points to each competitive bid team (i.e., the lowest target price gets all of the price award points); and

- Aggregate evaluation points for all bid teams to help determine the Home Team's PTW, based upon a bid price that yields a price point score that, when added the Home Team's aggregate non-cost point score, exceeds all of the other bid teams' aggregated point scores by a small margin.

The BEM shown represents an overall 1,000 award points that are allocated 60/40 to non-price evaluation factors over the price evaluation factor.

As will be seen, this BEM is used as follows:

- All competing teams (including the Home Team) are rated as to the percentages they are believed to be able to earn for each non-price evaluation criterion (Factors 1 through 3);

- Percentages are applied to the respective available points for each non-price factor to yield an aggregated non-price point score for each team; and

- Price point scores (Factor 4) are computed using the inverse relationship of the lowest likely bid price to each team's likely bid price. Using this approach, the lowest priced offeror gets all of the 400 price award points.

Note: The BEM shown is a "best value" example since, unlike many actual evaluation schemes, it values price award points and non-price award points identically.

Another important issue for PTW practitioners to remember is that the evaluation playing field is rarely level. Accordingly, price usually has a larger effect than stated in the customer's Evaluation Model because price is normalized to the lowest priced acceptable bid (which gets all of the price award points), whereas bidders are rarely, if ever, awarded all points available for a non-price evaluation criterion. The reason for this? It is extremely difficult for the customer to ascribe, and support, perfection to any bidder's proposal.

The PTW practitioner needs to regard RFP evaluation quantities potentially as works of fiction and, as such, as an opportunity for gaming exploitation. RFP evaluation quantities are developed well in advance of the opportunity contract being awarded and usually represent the customer's collective guess at what will be reasonably quantitatively required. This estimate gets pressed into service as a baseline for evaluating competitor pricing.

Would-be contractors and the incumbent, if there is one, do research to determine their views of reality quantities. The purpose is so that differences between the Evaluated Case and the Reality Case can be exploited during gaming. (See Section V of this book for more detail on Phase 3, Step 9 Gaming.)

The Phase 1, Step 2 Evaluation Modeling Process

Figure III.11 shows that a completed BEM is fed by Phase 1, Step 1 research and canvass results, which:

- Provide the basis for the SWOTs (item b. in the graphic) and the non-cost evaluation criteria scorings; and

- Determine the addressable budget for the opportunity and the take-downs, or discount, from that budget that each competitive bid team is supportably likely to target.

Note that, as always, interaction with the opportunity's information cloud is continuous. Also note that the lower case alpha characters that prepend items shown in the graphic below are used in several of the section headings that follow (e.g., the b. in the title relates to item b. in the next topic heading, and so forth.)

Competitor SWOT Summaries (b)

Competitor and Home Team SWOT Summaries are needed to provide provenance support for PTW's non-cost evaluation point scoring. PTW practitioners need to reduce this information to SWOT Summaries that sing, like the set shown in **Figure III.12**.

	Strengths	Weaknesses
Internal Factors	• Size, vast resources & bench strength • 21st century technology leadership • Willingness and capability to invest • Powerful BD & lobbying capabilities with strong customer access	• Size & vast bureaucracy • Risk averse • High cost structure • Unionized workforce • Limited knowledge of specific core requirements
	Opportunities	**Threats**
External Factors	• Customer desire for new face and fresh ideas • Inculcate the customer environment with the way (methods and tools) that this bidder does	• Poor relations with unionized workers • Traditional customer base eroding – need to backfill that erosion
	Factors Increasing pWin	Factors Decreasing pWin

FIGURE III.12

The reason for the summaries is because detailed SWOTs often run into page-upon-page of bid rationale, team detail, strengths, weaknesses, past performance citations, and other elements.

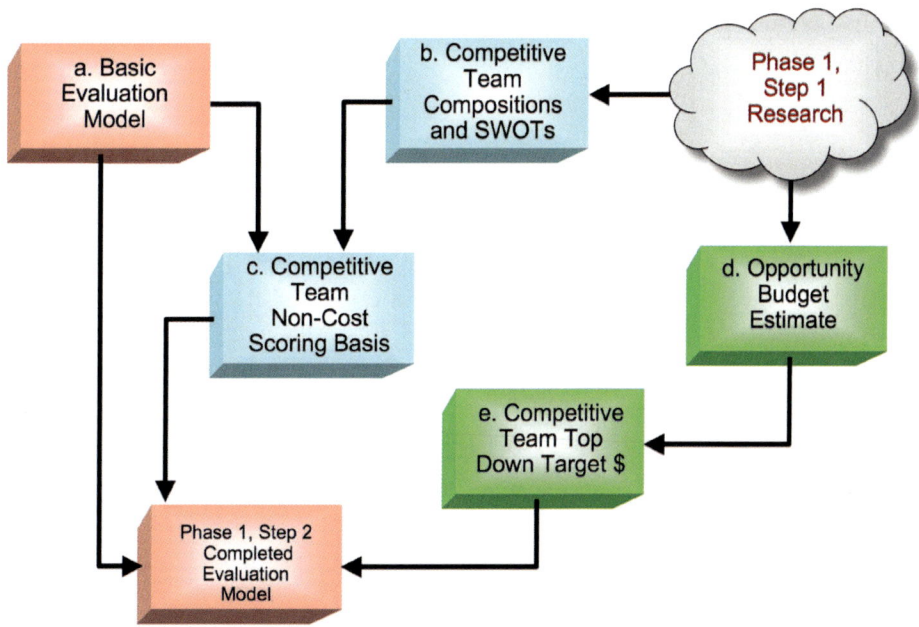

FIGURE III.11

Program XYZ Proposal Evaluation Criteria	Available Award Points	#1	#2	#3	Home Team
Sub-factor 1: Program Management	100	Why Blue?	Why Green?	Why Green?	Why Green?
Sub-factor 2: Field Overhauls	85	Why Green?	Why Green?	Why Yellow?	Why Green?
Sub-factor 3: System Modifcations	75	Why Green?	Why Blue?	Why?	Why Green?
Sub-factor 4: Engineering Support	60	Why Blue?	Why Green?	Why Blue?	Why Blue?
Sub-factor 5: Logistics	45	Why Yellow?	Why Green?	Why Red?	Why Green?
Sub-factor 6: Small Business Program	35	Why Green?	Why Green?	Why Blue?	Why Blue?
Key		> 90%	> 80% to 90%	> 70% to 80%	< 70%

FIGURE III.13

Color Coding as a Basis for Non-Cost Evaluation Scoring (b)

Another approach to coming up with non-cost evaluation scoring would be to adopt a scheme similar to the Past Performance Risk Analysis Group (PPRAG) that the U.S. Air Force was favoring for so long. (Most recently, the USAF has been drifting away from this approach and adopting a stance that says, simply: if a bidder is acceptable, open the price envelope and see if it is a winner.)

In **Figure III.13**, the evaluation sub-elements of mission capability are stratified by color for each of the competitive bid teams and the Home Team. At the bottom of the panel is a key that explains the percentage ranges covered by each color.

Using this sort of scheme, PTW practitioners can assess more broadly how the competitors and the Home Team are likely to be viewed in terms of non-cost evaluation criterion scoring. This information can be transformed into evaluation score quantifications as shown below.

Opportunity ID	Available Award Points
Customer Agency	
Basic Evaluation Model	
Overall Evaluation	1000
Overall Evaluation Rank	
Non-Price Evaluation (Sum of Factors 1 - 3)	600
Non-Price Evaluation Rank	
Factor 1 - Technical Issues	300
Factor 2 - Management Issues	200
Factor 3 - Past Performance Issues	100
Factor 4 - Price ($M)	400

FIGURE III.14

Provenance for Non-Cost Evaluation Scoring (c)

The purpose of **Figure III.14** is to rationalize and provide provenance for the BEM example's non-cost evaluation factor scores for each identified competitor and the Home Team.

In **Figure III.15**, at the intersection of each non-cost evaluation area and a competitor or the Home Team, there are spaces for positive and negative issues to be documented and sized. In either case, sizing can be positive or negative in the range of 30% down. This positive % is added to the negative % and the result is added to the nominal %, which is shown in the top left cell of the table.

By these means, the preceding table translates summary SWOT information and other research into quantifiable scoring information that is used to develop and support competitor and Home Team Evaluation Model scores.

The top left nominal value, 70% in this case, is the value that must be met for a team to remain a viable contender, i.e., within the competitive range. This nominal value is set by the PTW Team's knowledge of, and view of, the customer's scoring habits.

Budget Projection (d)

The budget that we will use to complete our Example BEM is $55M over the term of the contract. For our purpose, the budget is also the addressable budget.

70%	Represents Our Nominal Evaluation % of Available Non-Cost Evaluation Points for this Program									
PROGRAM NAME: XYZ		The Competitive Bid Teams						The Home Team		
DEPARTMENT/ AGENCY	EVALUATION APPROACH	#1		#2		#3				
Customer Agency	Standard	Rationale(s)	Attractions & Detractions (% Points from Nominal level)	Rationale(s)	Attractions & Detractions (% Points from Nominal level)	Rationale(s)	Attractions & Detractions (% Points from Nominal level)	Rationale(s)	Attractions & Detractions (% Points from Nominal level)
Major Non-Cost Evaluation Areas	Key Issues									
Factor 1: Technical Issues	Positive	Incumbent - processes, teammates and personalities well known to evaluators	22.5%	Innovative "best value" approach based on risk reduction and lessons learned	20.0%	Innovative approach to reduce risks and costs and improve control of processes	20.0%	Innovative approach based on risk reduction, lessons learned, cost control and process improvements	20.0%
	Negative	No innovation	-5.0%	Solution issues	-5.0%	Solution issues	-5.0%	None	0.0%
	Net Effect		87.5%		85.0%		85.0%		90.0%
Factor 2: Management Issues	Positive	Incumbent - processes & personalities well known to evaluators	20.0%	Approach based on best practices and lessons learned	15.0%	Approach based on best practices and lessons learned	15.0%	Innovative approach based on best practices, lessons learned, cost control and process improvements	20.0%
	Negative	No innovation	-5.0%	Solution issues	-5.0%	Solution issues	-5.0%	None	0.0%
	Net Effect		85.0%		80.0%		80.0%		90.0%
Factor 3: Past Performance	Positive	Incumbent - processes & personalities well known to evaluators	22.5%	Several similar past performances	17.5%	Several similar past performances + on incumbent team	20.0%	Many similar past performances	20.0%
	Negative	Not known for innovation	-5.0%	None	0.0%	None	0.0%	None	0.0%
	Net Effect		87.5%		87.5%		90.0%		90.0%

FIGURE III.15

Top Down Competitor PTW Analysis— Approach 3

Approach 3 provides another means of deducing where competitors are likely to target their bids, based on where they are in relation to the opportunity. For Approach 1, we needed certain knowledge of competitor pricing behaviors related to addressable budgets. For Approach 2, deduction drove our discounting of the addressable budget.

For Approach 3, as shown in **Figure III.16**, we use the reaction that each of the competitors is likely to have, in terms of a discount (or take-down) to the addressable budget, against 20, or more, key Top Down Strategic Pricing issues like those shown. Each PTW practitioner needs to develop his/her own set of issue areas of this type that best fit the nature and purview of the supported business opportunities.

Moreover, whenever a take-down is asserted, a rationale for that discount must be explained in the Take-down Rationale column in the table. For instance, if Competitor #1 is the incumbent, they would be likely to use a Defensive Discount (Item #6), whereas an insurgent would most likely use an Offensive Discount (Item #7).

The other Top Down Strategic Pricing issues shown in the table are explained by the comments to the far right in the graphic. Not all take-down issues apply to all opportunities or to all competitors. Note that it is always desirable for a PTW practitioner to define and develop his/her own set of Strategic Pricing issues and reuse them and refine and augment them over time.

The take-down percentages that the PTW practitioner assesses against each applicable Strategic Pricing issue are summed by competitor and used as Approach 3 to determine each competitor's Top Down target prices. Note that in the preceding table, because there are no take-downs shown, the sum of each competitor's take-down is zero.

Note: The Home Team's pricing is calculated in the table on page 55 (Figure III.17). It is a reaction to the resulting target price and the non-price scoring.

Issue #	Strategic Pricing Issues	Potential Competing Bid Team Price Takedowns			Takedown Rationales	Comments
		#1	#2	#3		
1	Company is in play				Why ?	May sacrifice future viability for a WIN
2	Pricing is a Reality Model				Why ?	Allows price gaming to be focused on what your team believes reality to be—probably a "baked in" given
3	Level setting existing contract's baseline				Why ?	Done by incumbents; anticipated by insurgents. Avoids the "we may know too much" syndrome
4	Converting off-site workers to on-site workers				Why ?	Done by incumbent; anticipated by insurgents
5	Vacant premises could be leveraged				Why ?	Cost avoidance potential
6	Defense discounting				Why ?	Done by incumbent; anticipated by insurgents
7	Offensive discounting				Why ?	Done by insurgents—what level of price advantage does it take to unseat this incumbent
8	New Cost Center				Why ?	Reduces labor rates and avoids the customer having to pay for things they do not need—for major opportunities only
9	Uncompensated Overtime				Why ?	May be disallowed or frowned upon—should be well supported
10	Teammates only after award				Why ?	Maximizes pricing flexibility and avoids onerous up-front commitments and markups
11	Discounting price				Why ?	Apparent loss leader—up to 50% of CY1 price or eating transition costs
12	Blending to lowest cost sub/suppliers				Why ?	Needs pricing note that stipulates actual bill will be based on teammate doing work not the blended rate
13	Residual value				Why ?	Can reduce hardware costs when technology insertion is mandated
14	Make subcontractors live within prime's unloaded labor rates				Why ?	To be effective the prime labor rates must be more aggressive than the average subcontractor's
15	Aggressive mapping of required labor categories to company labor grades				Why ?	Drives to the lowest priced, yet capable, team labor categories avaliable
16	Team employees				Why ?	Lowers cost basis—associated with #14
17	Making PM an indirect cost				Why ?	Avoids direct cost (unless incumbent is already avoiding PM direct costs)
18	Bidding to expected future ODC and labor costs				Why ?	Bidding future expected technology price points and labor rates that are not being quoted today—probably a "baked in" given—can be a "wash"
19	Projecting new hires in the out-years				Why ?	Avoids inflation for 1 or more Cys
20	Play the differences between salary/labor review cycles year-ends				Why ?	Highly bid dependent
	Potential Team Total Discount From Addressable Budget	0.00%	0.00%	0.00%		

FIGURE III.16

Opportunity ID	Available Award Points	"Top Down" Comparative Evaluation							
Customer Agency		Available Award Point Percentages & Bid Prices				Normalized Point Scores			
Basic Evaluation Model		#1	#2	#3	Home Team	#1	#2	#3	Home Team
Overall Evaluation	1000					920.00	902.50	905.00	922.61
Overall Evaluation Rank						(2)	(4)	(3)	(1)
Non-Price Evaluation (Sum of Factors 1 - 3)	600					520.00	502.50	505.00	540.00
Non-Price Evaluation Rank						(2)	(4)	(3)	(1)
Factor 1 - Technical Issues	300	87.5%	85.0%	85.0%	90.0%	262.50	255.00	255.00	270.00
Factor 2 - Management Issues	200	85.0%	80.0%	80.0%	90.0%	170.00	160.00	160.00	180.00
Factor 3 - Past Performance Issues	100	87.5%	87.5%	90.0%	90.0%	87.50	87.50	90.00	90.00
Factor 4 - Price ($M)	400	$55.0	$55.0	$55.0	$57.5	400.00	400.00	400.00	382.61

FIGURE III.17

Completing the Basic Evaluation Model (BEM) (e)

Now that we have assembled all of the ingredients, we can complete our simplistic Basic Evaluation Model (BEM).

Figure III.17 brings together all of the non-price and price evaluation modifiers and calculates the price that the Home Team needs to think about bidding in order to win the largest number of overall award points to apparently win the job by a small margin—all items being as presented.

In the hypothetical case presented above, the Home Team scores so well on non-price evaluation items (540 out of 600 possible non-cost points) that it does not have to be low price for this possibly "best value" competition. Of course, this sort of outcome rarely happens, since, as discussed earlier, price is the key award determinant in 85% of all truly competitive award decisions. Recall that price has an inverse relationship when calculating normalized point scores using the price that wins marginally for the Home Team in terms of overall award points.

The fatal flaw in this example (that an astute observer may have spotted) is that the Home Team's price that allows them to win by a small margin exceeds the addressable budget. This is an impossible or, at best, an unlikely outcome. The reason we find ourselves in this situation is because we ascribed no take-downs to any of our competitors in the panel that appeared earlier under the heading Top Down Competitor PTW Analysis—Approach 3. This would imply that we expect each of them to bid at addressable budget. That is most unlikely.

A Word About Scoring Evaluation Models

Evaluation Model scoring to develop the percentage of a given non-cost evaluation criterion's available points that are to be awarded to a given bid team is based on an impression of that bid team that a PTW practitioner develops as a result of compiling SWOTs and eliciting street talk from a canvass. When scoring bid teams against evaluation criteria, the PTW practitioner is playing the ultimate customer.

Figure III.18 is a guide for scoring each non-cost evaluation criterion for a particular bid team (including the Home Team). Without such a guide, there may be a tendency to clump bid team scores

For Use In Scoring Each Non-Cost Evaluation Issue			
Quality Bands	Grades w/in Band	% Of Points Earned	Comments
Excellent	++	95	Slam dunk - great content, well presented
	+	94	
		93	
	-	92	
Very Good	++	91	Very good content, well presented
	+	90	
		89	
	-	88	
Good	++	87	Good content, well presented
	+	86	
		85	
	-	84	
Fair	++	83	Fair content, well presented
	+	82	
		81	
	-	80	
Adequate	++	79	Marginally acceptable
	+	78	
		77	
	-	76	
Poor	++	75	Serious issues
	+	74	
	-	73	
	-	72	
	--	71	
Failed		70 & <	Inadequate

FIGURE III.18

too closely. By laying out the range shown, the PTW practitioner should first settle on a band (e.g., Very Good), and then decide where within that band a particular bid team places in terms of its ability to earn available evaluation award points.

Remember, even with a scoring scheme like the one shown, the PTW practitioner still has to provide supporting rationales for awarded scores.

Defining an Opportunity's Strategic Strike Zone (SSZ)

A bid's SSZ is a pictorial representation of the competitive standings that are defined by Evaluation Model scorings for the Home Team and the competitors. An SSZ takes an often complex Evaluation Model and translates it into a simplified XY plot graphic that provides an "at a glance" view of the competitive situation. See **Figure III.19**.

On the SSZ's X axis is *affordability*, while the Y axis represents *desirability*.

The affordability axis is bracketed by:

- Available addressable budget (as the high end); and
- The perceived cusp of unrealistic pricing (as the low end).

The desirability axis, on the other hand, is bounded by the:

- Highest theoretically available aggregate non-cost score, which rarely exceeds 95%, since 100% is really hard for anyone to ever truly justify (as the high end); and
- Nominal score (below which no bidder can go and remain in the competitive range) or the lowest competitor's aggregate non-cost score (as the low end).

The purpose of the SSZ is to focus the Capture Team on:

- Understanding the Home Team's posture, relative to that of the competitors as distilled by the PTW Team; and
- What it is going to take, in the PTW Team's opinion, for the Home Team to occupy the winning position in the SSZ.

Defining the SSZ for the opportunity starts at the end of Phase 1, when it is presented to the Capture Team and continues by plotting where in the SSZ each targeted competitive bid is likely to be at the end of:

- Phase 2—the Partially Gamed, Bottoms Up PTW for Encounter 2; and
- Phase 3—the Fully Gamed, Bottoms Up PTW for Encounter 3.

To demonstrate how the SSZ is developed, let us consider the slightly more complex Evaluation Model shown in **Figure III.20** and see how it translates into an actual SSZ.

To calculate where on the desirability axis each team is, we must calculate their awarded aggregate non-cost points as a percentage of the aggregate available non-cost award points. For example, for competitive bid team HAL (they are the Home Team) in the following Evaluation Model table, this is ~1,154 out of 1,250, or ~92.3% as plotted in the earlier SSZ graphic for Team HAL.

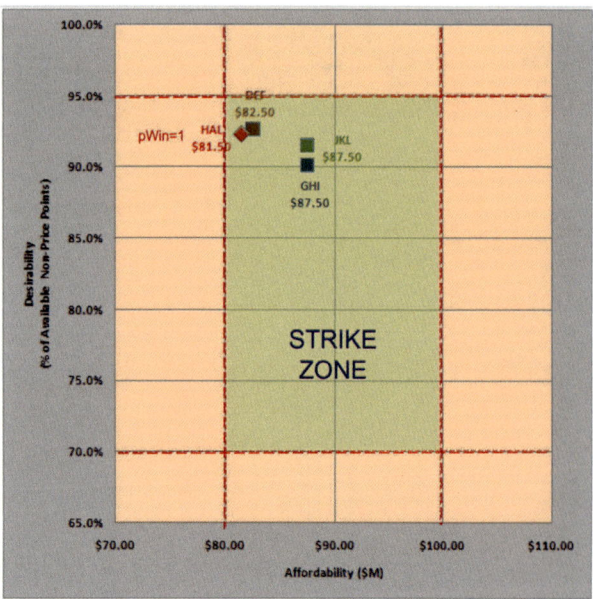

FIGURE III.19

Evaluation Criteria Set	Points Available	Percentage Scores				Normalized Point Scores			
		HAL	DEF	GHI	JKL	HAL	DEF	GHI	JKL
Overall Evaluation	1750					1653.8	1651.9	1592.5	1609.7
Overall Evaluation Rank						1	2	4	3
Non-Price Issues	1250					1153.8	1158.0	1126.8	1144.0
Rank						2	1	4	3
Mission Suitability	1000					923	923	896	919
A. Technical Approach & Understanding	500	94.5%	94.0%	90.0%	93.5%	472.5	470.0	450.0	467.5
B. Management Approach, Compensation & Staffing	300	90.0%	91.0%	88.5%	90.5%	270.0	273.0	265.5	271.5
C. Safety & Health	100	90.0%	90.0%	90.0%	90.0%	90.0	90.0	90.0	90.0
D. Small Business Utilization	100	90.0%	90.0%	90.0%	90.0%	90.0	90.0	90.0	90.0
Past Performance	250	92.5%	94.0%	92.5%	90.0%	231.3	235.0	231.3	225.0
Phase 1 "Top Down" Target Prices ($M)	500	$81.5	$82.5	$87.5	$87.5	500.0	493.9	465.7	465.7
		Addressable Budget ($M)							$100.00

FIGURE III.20

The affordability axis is either the target price that PTW has calculated and provided support for, or it is the number that the Home Team needs to think about to earn a slight advantage in terms of overall award points.

The result is the SSZ shown in the preceding graphic wherein:

- The tradespace that exists between competing bid teams and the Home Team is highlighted; and
- The Home Team's potential to improve their desirability and move closer to the top left extremity of the graphic becomes obvious.

In the preceding SSZ graphic that uses PTW's view of each team's non-cost and price award point standings at the end of Phase 1, we can see that Team DEF is our biggest competitive threat, whereas Teams GHI and JKL are relative outliers. To counter DEF's expected slightly more desirable posture we, HAL, need to bring our price down to a point where we can earn enough price award points to lead the award point stakes by a small margin.

Encounter 1—What PTW Needs to Impart to the Capture Team

With the completion of the SSZ, along with all of the other Phase 1 ingredients that we have been developing, we are now ready for Encounter 1 with our Capture Team. It is now PTW's task to present:

1. An overview of PTW's Phase 1 findings, which needs to cover:
   - The competition;
   - The evaluation scheme;
   - The addressable budget;
   - Competing teams' SWOTs;
   - Competing teams' ability to earn available non-price evaluation points;
   - Competing teams' Top Down prices and their respective abilities to earn available price evaluation points;
   - What the Home Team needs to do to win based on their position within the SSZ; and
   - Identification and rationalization of Phase 2 competitive targets.
2. Procurement details:
   - Program objectives and scope;
   - Known customer hot buttons and other issues;
   - Schedule and WBS; and
   - Labor category and ODC requirements.
3. Competitive and Home Team details including detailed team compositions and Strengths, Weaknesses, Opportunities and Threats (SWOTs).
4. Materially relevant opportunity scuttlebutt including street talk and the contacts that were made or attempted.

The PTW Team's job is to provoke a serious discussion to ensure that the Capture Team buys in to the PTW view or, if not, how their view differs, and why.

In any event, PTW practitioners must always take copious notes and be *infocentric* by documenting comments and pre-positioning all new information by ingesting it into the corporate database, or Infocenter.

The key takeaways from Encounter 1 include agreement on:

- Which competitors are to become the targets for the Phase 2 Bottoms Up portion of the PTW study; and
- A timetable for completing the remaining phases of the PTW study.

Phase 1 of the Progressive PTW Problem

As explained in the book's Foreword, Section VII of this book presents a PTW problem that progresses from Phase 1 to Phase 2 before concluding with Phase 3. Microsoft Excel spreadsheet models pertaining to the PTW Framework phases are available on demand by emailing a request to:

training@caisisco.com

For those readers who are interested in working the portion of the progressive PTW problem that relates to this, the first phase of the 3-Phase, 10-Step PTW Framework, please turn to the beginning of Section VII of this book.

Section IV

Phase 2 of CAI/SISCo's PTW Framework

Developing the Partially Gamed Bottoms Up PTW

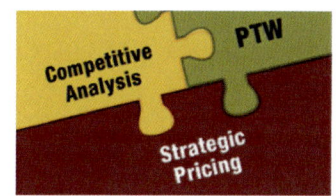

Section IV presents the details of Phase 2 of the 3-Phase, 10-Step PTW Framework which develops the Bottoms Up "Partially Gamed" PTW for the targeted competitive bid teams.

Phase 2 of the PTW Framework

As shown in **Figure IV.1**, Phase 2 of the framework involves Steps 3 though 7.

Phase 2 of the PTW Framework develops the *Partially Gamed* PTWs for the competitive bid teams selected as targets for Bottoms Up analysis at Encounter 1, which concluded Phase 1. As will be seen, the Bottoms Up PTW, or Price *To Do* the job that is produced by this phase, is developed for each targeted team by estimating their WBS leaf position activities in terms of labor and Other Direct Costs (ODCs) and rolling up the results in the Step 6 Basis Of Estimates (BOE) Model.

In addition to conventional targeted competitors, valid, yet unconventional Phase 2 PTW targets can include developing "street" views of:

- The Home Team's likely bid price; *and/or*
- The proverbial "Bidder from Hell" wherein the strongest attributes of all competitive bid teams are brought together in a fictional, super-competitor team.

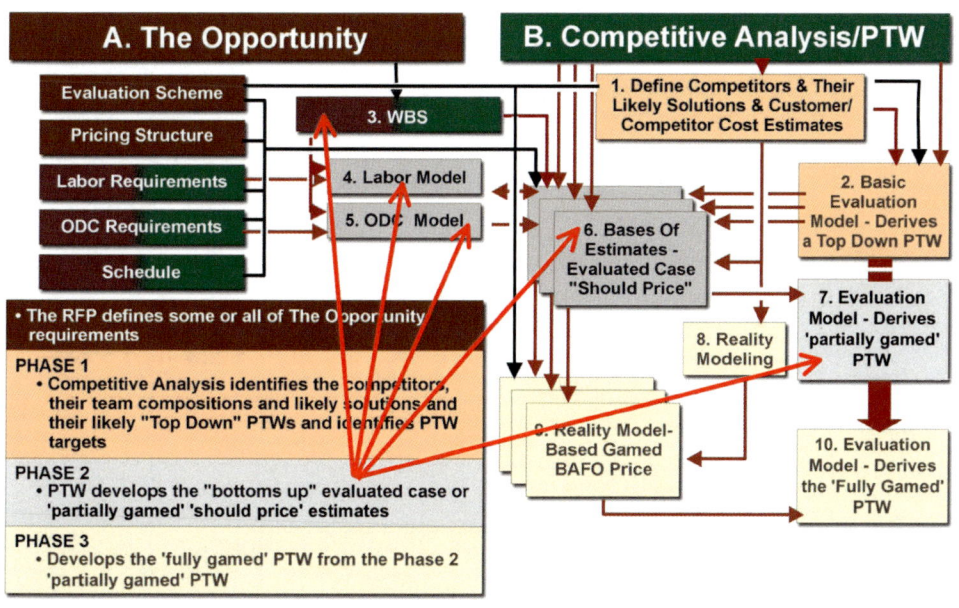

FIGURE IV.1

Before we leave the subject, some issues that relate to unconventional PTW targets need to be aired, such as:

- Are we trying to see how good the PTW practitioners are rather than trying to win the job?; *and/or*
- Are we trying to right mind the Capture Team as to the importance of price?

Years ago, my observation was that Capture Teams were not above amusing themselves by having PTW practitioners try to discover what the Capture Team already knew. Happily, these days we seem to have left that sort of unhelpful thinking behind and now both the Capture Team and PTW are pooling their knowledge and analyses and are focused on the real task—what it is going to take to win the business.

As shown in the framework graphic on the previous page, Phase 2, Steps 3 through 5 (the WBS, the Labor Model and the ODC Model) of this phase feed Step 6 (BOE Model) to yield these PTW outputs:

- A better definition of targeted competitor SWOTs and likely solution/s;
- A Contract Line Item (CLIN) by CLIN buildup of the entire opportunity for each of the targeted bid teams;
- A WBS element level price estimate for use in "apples to apples" comparisons with the Capture Team's estimates;
- Each targeted competitive bid team's *Partially Gamed*, Bottoms Up versions of the third of the three PTW parametric elements described near the beginning of Section III.

Phase 2, Step 7 updates the Evaluation Model rankings of each targeted competitive team against each evaluation criterion. As needed, non-cost points are re-aggregated and re-ranked to determine each team's revised evaluation point scoring potential. Then targeted competitor Phase 2, Step 6 PTW estimates are introduced to complete the updated Step 7 Evaluation Model.

Phase 2 culminates in PTW's Encounter 2 with the Capture Team, where PTW practitioners will present the Phase 2 results and findings, listen to Capture Team comments and concerns, and take copious notes and ingest and pre-position them as part of the corpus of information that relates to the opportunity, the competitors, and the customer.

PTW's Suite of Modeling Elements

Before we embark on a discussion of models that PTW should rely upon and adapt, let us share a view of what pre-positioned and leverageable modeling assets a PTW practitioner has to have in his or her quiver. Rapid adaptability of these models to the subject opportunity's needs (e.g., contract duration, evaluation set, WBS, labor categories, etc.) are crucial to a PTW Team's ability to be effective for the Capture Team and get its job done on time.

The taxonomy of CAI/SISCo's basic PTW model suite is shown in the **Figure IV.2**. The major division is between Target-Specific modules (i.e., modeling elements that relate to individual targeted competitive teams), and Multi-Target modules (i.e., those elements that relate to comparison of multiple teams, including the Home Team).

The *Target-Specific* **Modules** are described and discussed below:

- The **Input Module** consists of constants (e.g., statutory taxes, etc.), a depiction of a targeted competitive bid team's structure (e.g., prime or joint venture, subcontractors, suppliers, fees and other non-calculated uplifts), budget data, the opportunity's CLIN structure, and the WBS.
- The **Labor Module** consists of labor categories and salaries (defining what types of labor and their corresponding salary levels aged to the contract's most probable start date); team members' corporate personalities as they relate to developing labor fringe and overhead rates, developed team member labor rates; results of likely team blending (i.e., which teammates participate in which labor categories); resulting team wrap rates; and productivity curves that depict how various categories of work covered by the WBS are likely to behave over time.
- The **ODC Module** consists of a Bill Of Materials of Other Direct Costs (ODCs), an ODC price basis, and technology inflator/deflator curves showing how ODC prices are likely to change over time.

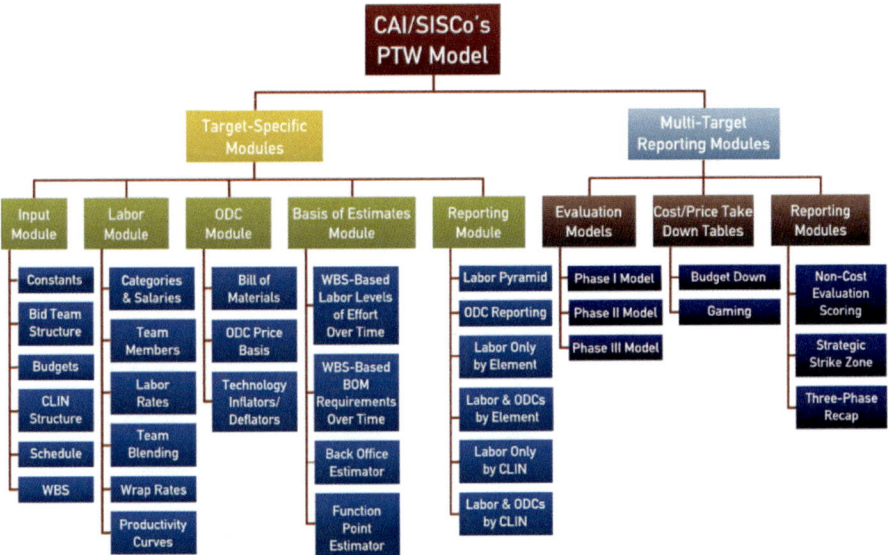

FIGURE IV.2

- The **Basis Of Estimates Module** consists of the means of estimating WBS-based Labor Levels Of Effort (LOE) and BOM requirements over time; possibly a back office estimator (to cover costs that are incremental to normal personnel and other back office functions that need to be augmented because the subject opportunity represents non-core business); and other elements such as a function point estimator, used to develop software development manpower estimates.

- The **Reporting Module** produces rate sheets, analyses of labor usage by labor category (sometimes referred to as labor pyramids), and a host of WBS- and CLIN-based reports and tables.

The *Multi-Target* Reporting Modules are described and discussed below:

- The **Evaluation Models**, as noted in Phase 1 discussions in Section III of this book, may change as a PTW study progresses from Phase 1 to Phase 2 and then Phase 3.

- The **Cost/Price Take Downs** cover tables that develop team target prices that live within the addressable budget and the results of Phase 3 gaming of the Phase 2 Partially Gamed PTW results.

- The **Reporting Modules** that develop non-cost evaluation scoring, Strategic Strike Zone (SSZ) graphics, and the three-phase recap that develops the Final, Fully Gamed PTW.

PTW Framework Phase 2, Step 3—The WBS for Bottoms Up Analysis

There is little left to say about an opportunity's Work Breakdown Structure (WBS) that wasn't said in Section III of this book. The WBS is a hierarchical representation of a Statement Of Work (SOW), the purpose of which is to:

- Decompose the required activities into major, often time-phased and discretely managed areas of work; and

- Further decompose the major work areas into tree structures comprised of discrete work packages.

The WBS is either provided, in whole or in part, in the DRFP/RFP (a very rare occurrence) or must be developed by PTW from the SOW. Realize that this is precisely what the Home Team and the other bidders have to accomplish—just do it!

Each leaf position element of the WBS is likely to:

- Have a discrete periodicity (e.g., daily, one time, monthly, etc.);

- Be associated with a single team member;

- Have its likely cost and price estimated in terms of labor categories and Levels Of Effort (LOE)—Step 4 develops labor rates;

- Employ Other Direct Cost (ODC) requirements—Step 5 develops discounted and deflated/inflated ODC prices; and
- Implement curves describing relative intensity and/or productivity improvements over time.

As shown in the framework graphic at the beginning of this section, the Step 3 WBS is used in the PTW Framework as the Y axis of the Phase 2, Step 6 Basis Of Estimate (BOE) Model. On the X axis of the BOE Model, the labor categories (and Step 4 labor rates), ODCs (and Step 5 prices), and various curves are arrayed.

PTW Framework Phase 2, Step 4— The Labor Model

For PTW purposes, a Labor Model is somewhat like a payroll program in the sense that both start off with gross pay. The Labor Model, however, produces labor category billing rates rather than the payroll program's net pay.

Labor requirements, in terms of the labor categories and grades (backed up by position descriptions) needed to accomplish the work required by the opportunity, once determined, are entered into a Labor Model.

As already noted, labor requirements may be partially or fully described in the DRFP/RFP *or* they will have to be derived from a SOW to define:

- The number of labor categories needed to staff and accomplish the opportunity—this may vary from a low of ~20 to a high of ~200 labor categories; and
- The education and experience levels that attach to each labor category.

The Labor Model requires these labor category inputs:

1. Average salary levels by work location from survey sources (see the discussion that follows) *or*, if indicated,
   - prevailing Service Contract Act (SCA) or Collective Bargaining Agreement (CBA) rates;
2. Cost Of Living Adjustments (COLAs) for each work location (e.g., New York City, it shouldn't surprise anyone to learn, has a significantly higher cost of living than does Martinsburg, WV) *and/or*, if needed,
   - overseas uplifts of many sorts; and
3. The percentage of each labor category, by work location, that each targeted competitive team member is likely to be supplying.

These allocations and assertions must strive to:

- Meet the solicitation's subcontracting or industrial participation requirements; and,
- Mirror the capabilities and corporate personalities of the members of the competitive team being modeled. For instance, if a competitive team member specializes in security, then it would be reasonable for a PTW practitioner to assume that the team member would participate in, or own, labor categories related to security.

Survey sources for the U.S. and other country salary level information include:

- The Economic Research Institute (ERI), which is more government-focused;
- Mercer, which tends to relate mainly to commercial labor realities rather than government; and
- The many other surveys that can provide important salary information.

Regardless of which salary survey source a PTW practitioner uses, it is important to:

- Know which survey is favored by the customer agency and the competitors, too; and
- Understand the limitations, if any, of the survey you choose to use.

With respect to survey limitations, the following anecdote is instructive:

> Several years ago, we asked one of the companies CAI/SISCo was considering using for salary information what questions they asked those they surveyed concerning security clearances held. The response was: "Huh?"

You have been warned!

About Corporate Personality

Just like individuals, corporations have personalities too. While an individual's personality revolves around issues such as religion, politics, and the like, a corporation's personality for PTW purposes relates mostly to employer pecuniary considerations such as how employee healthcare costs are handled, vacation policies and such. Some firms pay the entirety of family healthcare costs while others pay the employee's healthcare costs but not for the employee's family coverage. Still other companies only contribute a percentage of the employee's healthcare costs.

Labor rates, as will be explained in the next subsection, are developed by adjusting a baseline set of about 50 rate component values to approximate *each* member of a competitive bid team's corporate personality. Healthcare costs are just one of the elements.

Accordingly, whatever is deemed likely to happen to healthcare or any other employer expenses during the term of the opportunity that PTW is studying will have an effect on future labor rates. Over time, healthcare costs to the employer could be seen to be rising, staying the same, or even ceasing to be an employer issue.

Corporate organization, revenues, employee head counts by division, Internal Research & Development (IR&D) levels and myriad other items need to be factored into personality, since they all impact the way in which labor rates and Other Direct Costs (ODCs) are built up.

Labor Rate Build-Up Realities

Figure IV.3 shows how the Labor Model's rate build-up approach works for a typical competitive bid team. First, PTW has to determine for each competitive bid team how they are likely to staff the opportunity. This could be one, or a mix of more than one, of the following:

- They already have the required complement of employees;
- They are planning to acquire needed employees from the incumbent; or
- They are planning to hire other employees to accomplish the work they hope to win.

Regardless, PTW has to assume that survey-based salary levels are the great leveler of the Direct Labor (DL) shown to the left of the graphic. All bidders, as the theory goes, have to fish for help in the same labor pool, or set of survey sub-pools (e.g., quartiles from a survey).

The Labor Model needs to develop fully loaded (i.e., labor rates that include all cost elements and fees) Contract Year One (CY1) off- and on-customer-site labor rates. (An off-customer-site labor rate implies contractor site. This rate would have to include all of the overhead items, such as contractor office or factory space costs, implicit in the labor rate build-up graphic.) It also has to be able to produce rates for telecommuting labor categories that have been enabled by the Internet for some labor categories engaged in certain types of work.

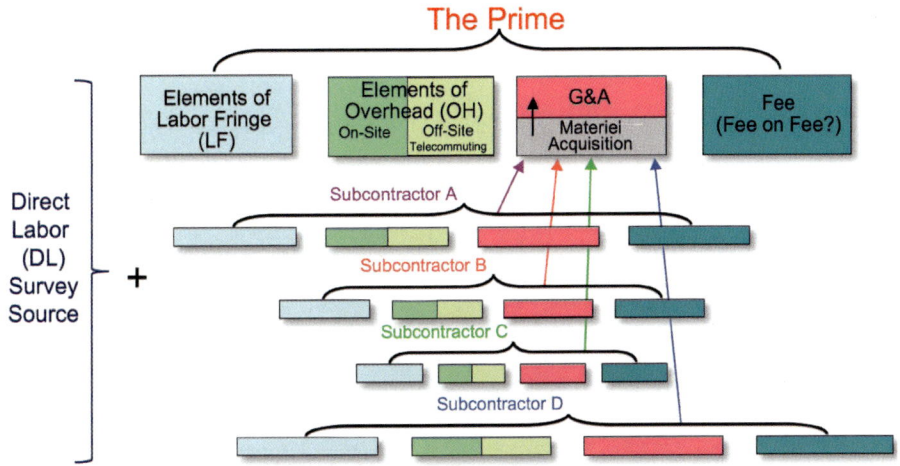

FIGURE IV.3

For the Prime, labor rates are developed by adjusting rate component values to approximate the "corporate personality" of the Prime and its need to recoup the overall *future* cost of Labor Fringe (LF), Overhead (OH) (as it applies to contractor site, customer site, or telecommuting labor), General & Administrative (G&A) expenses (e.g., corporate headquarters, the corporate jet, etc.), plus Fee. Of course, fee may be straight fee, in the case of a Time & Materials (T&M) contract type, or, in the case of a Cost Plus Award Fee (CPAF) contract, broken down into Base Fee and Award Fee. Let's say Base Fee is 3%—this portion of the overall fee will always be earned by the contractor. Award Fee, on the other hand—say a further 7%—is assessed and paid out based on the customer's view of contractor performance.

As an example of an LF rate component value, let us go back to how healthcare insurance costs are handled in the United States. As already stated, some companies cover the entire cost of employee healthcare for the employee and their family. Others only cover the cost of the employee's healthcare. Yet others only cover a portion of the employee's healthcare costs. Regardless, the costs of whatever a firm provides in this regard is part of its corporate personality and it will need to be recouped as part of the labor rates it hopes to charge to the customer.

The process of developing labor rates is identical for each of the subcontractors on a team. Of course, we would be using each subcontractor's corporate personality settings in the Labor Model instead of the Prime's. The difference relates to how subcontracted labor is brought on board a Prime's bid. As shown in the previous Figure IV.3, subcontracted labor may be:

- Unburdened by any sort of uplift;
- Burdened by a modest material acquisition uplift (e.g., 1% to cover associated administration costs);
- Burdened with the Prime's full G&A; or in extreme cases,
- Fully burdened with full Prime G&A *and* Prime Fee.

Competitive issues will drive PTW practitioners to pick the most appropriate burdening approach for subcontracted labor. In some cases, CY1 labor rates are calculated using the following formula:

*Labor Rate = (((DL * (1+LF%+OH%)) * (1+G&A%)) * (1+Fee%))*

In other cases, the formula used to calculate CY1 rates could be:

*Labor Rate = ((((DL * (1+LF%)) * (1+OH%)) * (1+G&A%)) * (1+Fee%))*

There are other variations, too.

Developing Labor Rates for CY2 and Beyond

For PTW purposes, what escalator needs to be used, and how is such an escalator to be derived and/or developed? The escalator could be a single Compound Annual Growth Rate (CAGR) from a source like a U.S. Government-Wide Acquisition Contract (GWAC) that escalates year-over-year labor rates uniformly.

The CY1 labor rates developed by the Labor Model are translated into out-year rates using multiplier/s that, in living memory, have almost always been inflationary.

The overall cost of a 3% CAGR adds up quickly, and the PTW practitioner must always ask himself if his assumptions are competitive, since:

- Over the last four years of a five-year contract it adds ~5.82%;
- Over the last six years of a seven-year contract it adds ~8.65%; and
- Over the last nine years of a ten-year contract it adds ~12.77%.

Or should PTW practitioners be developing more competitive and variable escalation rates that, for instance, are the sum of how we believe the major sub-aggregations of computed CY1 labor rates are likely to behave over time? For instance:

- The DL portion of a labor rate (let's call that 100 points) may be predicted to escalate at 1.5% per annum;
- The LF portion of the labor rate (say a further 40 points), driven by healthcare and other cost increases, may be predicted to escalate at 10% from a given year to the next; and

- The OH portion of the labor rate (say another 20 points), driven by space and energy cost increases, may be predicted to escalate at 5% from a given year to the next.

Or should we really be engaging the out-year (i.e., CY2, and beyond) problem by escalating rates at the individual labor category level?

Forward Pricing Healthcare Costs

The following discussion is provided as an example of how the PTW practitioner must view the future of major labor cost elements for targeted competitors. Presently, in the U.S., healthcare costs can add anywhere from 5% to 12.5% on top of direct labor (i.e., salary) to an employer's cost of employing an employee. This cost has to be recouped via labor rates.

Therefore, drilling down to identify the likely *now* real cost of this labor fringe element to a targeted competitor is critical to PTW analysis. Equally important is how the employer's cost of healthcare is likely to behave over time.

To establish a firm's adjusted basic healthcare costs to develop a forward pricing curve for this item across a contract's duration, the PTW practitioner has to consider the following sorts of issues (**Figure IV.4**):

- What is the prevailing cost of a single premium family healthcare policy for an average age, healthy employee? *This is shown as an assumed $15,000 per year in the graphic.*

- How does the cost of the single policy cited above apportion among the employee's and the employee's family coverage? *The graphic shows an assumed 50/50 cost split.*

- What buying power (i.e., the number of employees to be covered by the healthcare plan) does the target competitive firm have and what is the likely discount that their "bulk" purchase will bring over the single policy purchase price? This element covers target company employee demographics such as single employees, employees that do not require healthcare benefits, etc. *The graphic shows that for a company with 1,000 covered employees, a 33% discount from the single policy rate may be reasonable.*

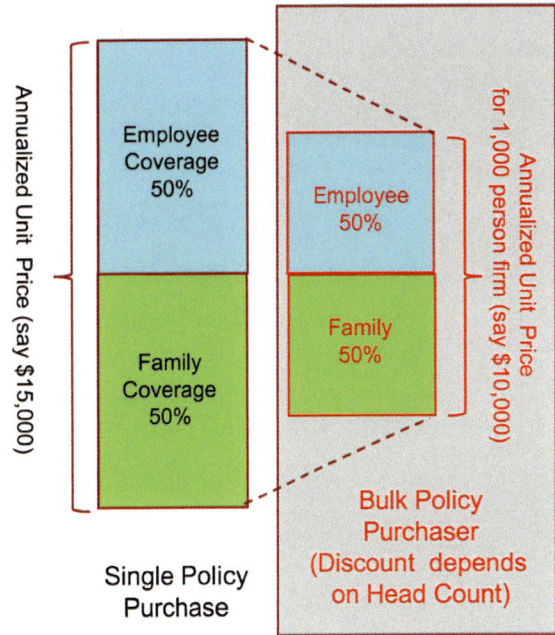

FIGURE IV.4

But this only identifies the likely now cost of a PTW target's premium family healthcare policy for an average age, healthy employee. The next set of issues gets into other aspects of what we have been calling "corporate personality." These include employee contributions to either the cost of employee coverage, family coverage, or both. Experience in the U.S. government services marketplace indicates that employee-only contributions to the cost of the employee's healthcare costs range from 0% to 60%, or more.

In addition, there are the other forward pricing considerations that are likely to converge to form a forward pricing curve for the contract's out years. These include:

- Rising healthcare costs that are likely to be offset by employee benefit decreases, such as deductible or co-pay increases;

- When (and if) Obamacare kicks in; and,

- If Obamacare is deemed to become law, whether or not healthcare insurance is likely to cease to be a feature of *this* employer's employee benefits package.

Why the Wrap Rate Build-Up Approach Should Be Favored

Because PTW is dealing with the future and a yet-to-be-won opportunity, the labor rate build-up approach described must always be favored and used. The reason is that any other approach is going to be historical, and is unlikely to be useful as a basis for developing forward priced labor rates for PTW purposes. Notwithstanding, some PTW practitioners try to take shortcuts by:

- Using purchased wrap rates derived from competitor financial filings;
- Buying wrap rates based on unsubstantiated company data benchmarked against unsubstantiated market segment average data; and
- Using labor rates garnered from awarded contracts and other awards and using these in some fashion even though they have no idea how they may have been gamed, blended or otherwise manipulated.

A possible exception could be when a PTW practitioner is developing labor rates that are discounts to a GWAC's contract ceiling rates. Even if the labor rates a PTW practitioner is developing are based on discounts from GWAC ceiling rates, the build-up approach is still preferred. The reason is this—by developing built-up rates, we can then see what, if any, discounts from the GWAC rates can be afforded and, therefore, more accurately estimate the overall price of a competitor's labor.

Data sources for wrap rate element build-up settings include:

- The PTW Team's pre-positioned and continually updated knowledge of a wide swath of "corporate personalities" from which those of the targeted team members can be drawn;
- Likely team member roles on the competitive team;
- The relative importance of the opportunity to the competing Prime; and
- Whether any members of a targeted team are in play (e.g., are they an acquisition target, etc.).

Wrap rate element sources include corporate websites, former employees, etc. Calibration sources for PTW's wrap rate and labor rate results can be found in recent awards of GWAC task orders or Blanket Purchasing Agreements (BPAs) made under GSA, or equivalent, schedules.

Other questions that affect wrap rate build-ups include:

1. Is a targeted competitive bid team likely to propose a separate cost center or even bid as a Joint Venture (JV)?
2. Is Uncompensated Overtime (UOT) a factor? (more on UOT in a moment);
3. Where will the work be done?
   - On-site or off-site?
   - In a low or high COLA area?

If Item 1 is the case, then history is of no use to us in calculating the bidding entity's labor fringes and overheads. Rate build-up is the only way to go.

Why Non-Wrap Rate Build-Up Approaches Should Be Avoided

Some time back, a U.S. customer showed me a wrap rate report on one of their competitors that they had purchased over the Web. This document purported to provide the target company's prevailing on- and off-customer-site wrap rates in two flavors, DOD-specific and non-DOD-specific. My customer had paid several thousand dollars for this product, for which they received three pages of unsubstantiated company wrap rate data benchmarked against unsubstantiated market segment average data. And this as an afterthought to a several-page litany of unwanted, and mainly irrelevant, contract information. What a crock!

Perhaps if you had just come down from Mars and wanted to find out the range of possible wrap rates, this could be helpful. (By the way, wrap rate uplifts range from a low in the 30th percentile, that barely covers statutory taxes, to 200%, or more, for the C-level trench coat and briefcase brigades.) But if you are looking for the wrap rate that a specific competitor is likely to bid for a specific opportunity, you won't find it by buying anyone's view of history. To accomplish that goal, you will have to understand opportunity specifics and the future we all face.

Here's why...

> When pricing bids (as either an incumbent or an insurgent), the Wayne Gretzky rule should be followed. A sports reporter once told the ice hockey great that his success was down to always being where the puck was. In his response, Gretzky provided great insight by stating that his success was not due to being where the puck was, but being where it was going to be. So it is with wrap rates. Anyone who bids a five-year (or longer) contract using his own or a competitor's historical, or even prevailing, wrap rates, is a loser. The secret is to bid tomorrow's wrap rates based on the assumption that the job will be won.

There is a lot more to this issue. PTW practitioners often ask what Competitor X's wrap rate is, as if knowing this would be helpful in developing a pricing strategy. Wrap rates alone, however, are relatively useless information. First, there is the issue of teaming. With the exception of a small business bidding a small job, most bid teams comprise multiple member companies that bid composite labor rates for each labor category, never a one-size-fits-all wrap rate. Also, large companies are now masking their predictability with respect to labor wrap rates by bidding out of meta-organizations that include several large major sub-divisions or internal Joint Ventures (JVs).

Moreover, a low wrap rate can be achieved by staffing a project with very high-salary individuals. Many labor fringe costs (e.g., healthcare costs that are employee benefits) and overhead uplifts are fixed dollar amounts; consequently, they form a smaller percentage of high salaries, leading to a lower wrap rate. Thus, we have a situation where a low wrap rate is associated with a (relatively) high price. The converse could be true as well: a high wrap rate might be associated with a low price.

Furthermore, since an overall wrap rate is a weighted average of a number of individual wraps, it can be skewed higher or lower as a result of the mix of individuals involved. In this connection, it must be noted that a wrap rate developed for one labor category mix cannot reasonably be used to uplift the direct labor costs of a different mix.

PTW practitioners and pricing professionals typically examine as many as 50 different micro wrap rate elements to understand how bids need to be priced. The guiding principle is this: PTW and bid pricing must be based on where reality will be, not where it has been, or even is presently.

A Word about Uncompensated Overtime

Figure IV.5 on the next page tells the following Uncompensated Overtime (UOT) story:

> If a firm's employees typically work 45-hour work weeks but are paid only 40-hour salaries, then the firm can, if need be, develop its hourly labor rates by dividing weekly costs by 45 rather than by 40, resulting in (more) aggressive bid rates.

RFPs tend to treat UOT in one of three ways:

1. Its use is forbidden.
2. It's acceptable if the bidder can demonstrate that UOT is a long-standing aspect of their corporate culture.
3. UOT is not mentioned, in which case, PTW practitioner BEWARE!

A Word about GWACs

Government-Wide Acquisition Contracts (GWAC) in the U.S. (aka Framework Contracts in the UK) limit awardees to "ceiling" labor rates and allow bidders for Task Orders under the GWAC to discount their agreed-to highest allowable or ceiling labor prices. This begs some explanation.

GWAC contracts amount to licenses to enable the holder to hunt for business on the GWAC's preserve. To win a GWAC, a firm typically has to establish labor rates that are good for the term of the contract. These are the ceiling rates that cannot be exceeded, but which can be discounted if work volumes and GWAC Task Order (TO) desirability dictate. Coming up with an appropriate discount can be done by holding up a wetted finger to the wind or by analysis.

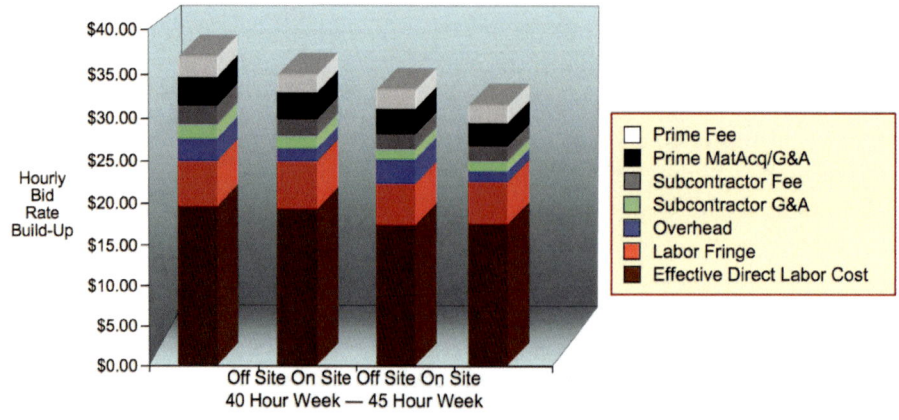

Sample Labor Rate Build-Up Element	40-Hour Week		45-Hour Week	
	Off Site	On Site	Off Site	On Site
Prime Fee	$2.35	$2.23	$2.11	$2.00
Prime M/A and/or G&A	$3.14	$2.97	$2.81	$2.67
Subcontractor Fee	$2.09	$1.98	$1.88	$1.78
Subcontractor G&A	$1.39	$1.32	$1.25	$1.19
Subcontractor DL Overhead	$2.88	$1.44	$2.59	$1.29
Subcontractor Labor Fringe	$5.77	$5.77	$5.17	$5.17
Effective Direct Labor (DL) Cost	$19.23	$19.23	$17.24	$17.24
Total Rate	$36.86	$34.95	$33.05	$31.34

FIGURE IV.5

At CAI/SISCo, we always perform build-ups on the GWAC labor categories that apply to a particular TO and use the resulting rates to establish and support discount levels from the GWAC's prevailing ceiling rates.

An astute observer will quickly see that GWAC awardees can develop similar contract duration evaluated prices by using either:

- High CY1 ceiling labor rates with a low out-year escalator; *or*
- Low CY1 ceiling labor rates with a high out-year escalator.

Off-Site Labor Opportunities

Labor that is housed in company offices or factories is burdened with space, cafeteria, and myriad other costs. This creates a ~5% to ~15% premium on top of on-government-customer-site labor rates. This premium covers contractor space (e.g., Class A office space or factory or warehouse space) costs, furniture, etc.

With today's ubiquitous Internet (which one can think of as shipping lanes for the 21st century), *for some labor categories*, telecommuting has become a viable and lower cost alternative to traditional contractor-site labor. To a government customer with space and other constraints, on-site labor is sometimes a less attractive option.

For bids that involve large quantities of contractor-site labor, telecommuting labor can reduce the overall cost of a bid. To establish a basis for introducing telecommuting into their strategies, bidders need to carefully segregate off-site labor into categories that:

- Can be reasonably supported by means of telecommuting; and
- Can be priced only marginally above on-site rates.

And the good news is that telecommuting has a basis in law since the U.S. government, at least, has policies that are aimed at, whenever possible, weaning the working population away from non-essential fossil fuel usage to effectively "bring the work to the people rather than the people to work." More recently, saving money has also become front and center, too.

Here is the basis in law:

> In accordance with section 1428 of Public Law 108-136, an agency shall generally not discourage a contractor from allowing its employees to telecommute in the performance of Government contracts. Therefore, agencies shall not:
>
> a. Include in a solicitation a requirement that prohibits an offeror from permitting its employees to telecommute unless the contracting officer first determines that the requirements of the agency, including security requirements, cannot be met if telecommuting is permitted. The contracting officer shall document the basis for the determination in writing and specify the prohibition in the solicitation; or
>
> b. When telecommuting is not prohibited, unfavorably evaluate an offer because it includes telecommuting, unless the contracting officer first determines that the requirements of the agency, including security requirements, would be adversely impacted if telecommuting is permitted. The contracting officer shall document the basis for the determination in writing and address the evaluation procedures in the solicitation.

Developing Blended Labor Rates to Lower Evaluated Prices

The tables that follow (**Figure IV.6**) relate to a hypothetical bid team developing a labor pricing strategy for a hypothetical opportunity. The top halves of each table are identical. Our bid team consists of Company X, the Prime, and two subcontractors, Company Y and Company Z. Each team member's PTW-developed wrap rates for high-end, mid-range, and low-end labor categories are shown in the top halves of the tables.

A wrap rate dictates the price that the customer pays for each dollar of direct labor. For example, in the tables, Company X has a wrap rate of 300% which implies that the customer will pay $3 for every $1 of direct labor cost, or salary. Note that Company Z's wrap rates are significantly lower than Company X's, and that Company Y's are in between.

Bid Team	Labor Category Grouping Wrap Rates		
	High	Medium	Low
Company X	300%	250%	200%
Company Y	250%	200%	160%
Company Z	200%	175%	145%

Bid Team	Job Labor Category Grouping Requirements		
	High	Medium	Low
Company X	20%	20%	10%
Company Y	5%	5%	20%
Company Z	0%	0%	20%

Bid Team	Composite Blended Wrap Rate		
	High	Medium	Low
Company X			
Company Y		214%	
Company Z			

Bid Team	Labor Category Grouping Wrap Rates		
	High	Medium	Low
Company X	300%	250%	200%
Company Y	250%	200%	160%
Company Z	200%	175%	145%

Bid Team	Job Labor Category Grouping Requirements		
	High	Medium	Low
Company X	15%	10%	0%
Company Y	5%	7.5%	25%
Company Z	5%	7.5%	25%

Bid Team	Composite Blended Wrap Rate		
	High	Medium	Low
Company X			
Company Y		197%	
Company Z			

FIGURE IV.6

In the mid section of each of the tables, the team members have allocated among themselves shares of 100% of the labor needed to do the job, which consists of:

- 25% to high-end labor categories;
- 25% to the mid-range; and
- 50% to the low-end.

If we can imagine that we are looking at dollars instead of percentages, the first table would evaluate at $214 while the second table evaluates at $197. Thus, without even breaking a sweat, we have reduced our evaluated price by $17. Can we go lower?

If one can accept that the most advantageous contract that can be awarded is one that has the customer paying the contractor for the entire contract on Day 1, then how far can we take our blending example? This is about as realistic as proposing that Company Z do all of the opportunity's work as low-end labor and, by that means, reduce our wrap rate dollars to $145.

The overarching question related to issues such as these is: Will the dogs (i.e., the customer) eat the dog food that the contractor is serving up? That is, among other things, the reason that PTW needs to spend time, as discussed in Section III, answering such questions while developing situational awareness.

The Labor Model in Perspective

Figure IV.7 brings together the major aspects of the Labor Model. As shown, these are as follows:

- At the top left are the labor categories along with their attributes, including aged salaries;

- In the middle is our infocentrically developed and maintained Knowledge Base, which holds our basic Labor Rate Model along with pre-positioned information on inflation, COLAs, and corporate personality presets, among other information. Together, these elements are used to produce the populated Target Team Labor Rate Model; and

- At the top right is the interface with the Step 6 Basis Of Estimates (BOE) Model, which is fed labor rates by the Labor Model and, in turn, feeds back labor category usages from which participation levels are determined.

The Labor Model also employs labor category usage (i.e., needed labor hours) estimates derived from Phase 2, Step 6 (the BOE) to develop individual team participant and overall team direct labor wrap rates for CY1. The model calculates the effects of likely salary and other element escalations/de-escalations for contract out-years (i.e., CY2 and beyond). As shown in the graphic, the Labor Model also interacts with the Step 6 BOE Model to generate a tally of % monetary utilization of each required (e.g., Small Business or other) participant category.

The Labor Model produces year-over-year:

- Unblended and blended uplifts and wrap rates;

- Unblended and blended on- and off-site and telecommuting labor rates;

- Labor costs; and

- Small Business (SB) participation %s.

PTW Framework Phase 2, Step 5— The ODC Model

Other Direct Costs (ODCs) for PTW purposes are all of the non-labor items that a bidder must furnish to satisfy the needs of the requirement and implement the proposed solution. These inanimate goods and services can be:

- Travel and living expenses;

- Space—office, factory, and laboratory—you name it; and

- Part of a service embedded in a CLIN. For example, equipment or packaged software that enables a managed service. Also spares and maintenance labor.

Each *materially relevant* ODC item—let's leave the paper clips out of PTW—will have its own pricing and discounting approach that PTW has to model. Each category of ODC will have its own:

- Inflation/deflation profile; and

- Life cycle.

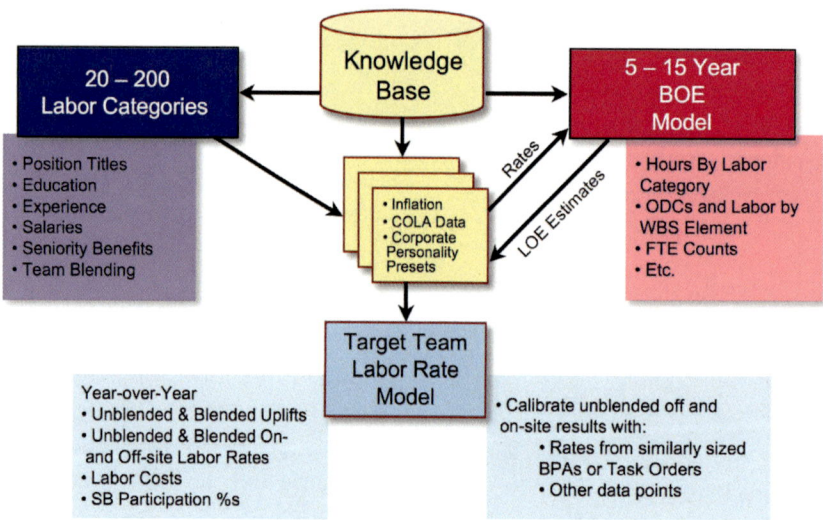

FIGURE IV.7

PTW practitioners must quantify the likely *PRICE* of materially relevant ODCs.

Rather like what was described for labor and the Labor Model in the Step 4 discussions, ODC requirements are entered into an ODC Model. Required ODCs may either be described in the DRFP/RFP or will have to be derived by implication from the SOW.

There may be *many* ODC items or components needed to satisfy a program's requirements. Non-labor (other direct) costs include:

- Boxes, circuits, supplies, etc.; and
- Items that may need to be developed and built, bought and adapted, or bought and integrated.

For each *materially relevant* ODC item, we need to:

- Identify its make, model, a price basis, and an ODC type;
- Determine the required quantity of each item; and
- Estimate the likely quantity discount from the price basis that each targeted competitor is likely to receive.

For each ODC type, curves have to be developed to represent likely future deflationary and/or inflationary effects over the duration of the program.

Several industry sources exist for major technology curve data, e.g., iSuppli.

The Step 5 ODC Model uses such technology curves to help develop fully loaded prices for ODC items for each competitive team by:

- Adjusting the baseline set of item issues enumerated above, along with the corporate personality of each targeted bid team's participants; and
- Applying individual targeted bid team uplifts to account for likely material handling, G&A and fee requirements.

Change, the Only Constant

Figure IV.8 relates to change, which PTW practitioners need to recognize is the only real constant. Everything changes over time: technology, companies, people and even the relative desirability of, and need for, labor categories.

To understand the graphic more fully, let us use the trusty iPod as our example. Apple did not invent the MP3 digital audio encoding format for music, but they did conceive the iPod appliance that made its debut at the end of 2001, yes 2001.

MP3s had long been an Enthusiast's pastime. Apple filled the Visionary role and helped their incubus vault over the chasm by making the iPod appealing as a practical and soft solution for those Pragmatists who had been amassing music on hard media such as music compact discs (CDs). Eventually, the Conservatives caught on and the Skeptics finally came on board.

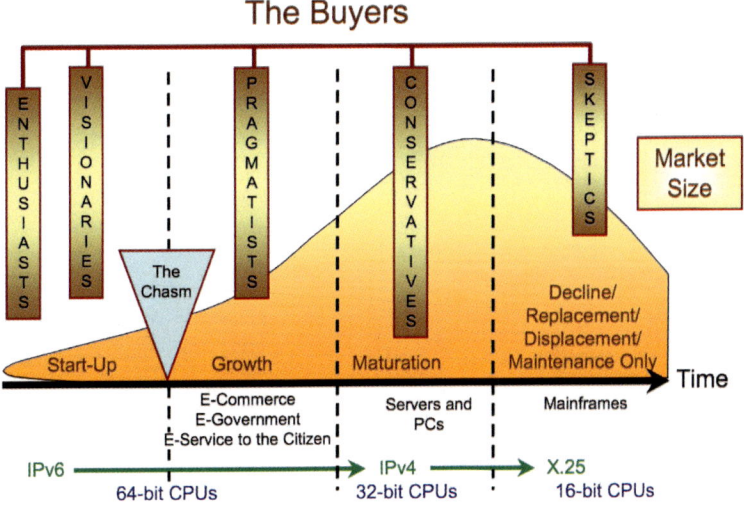

FIGURE IV.8

As one example of change over time, in 2000 a "hot" labor category was the systems administrator. These were the people who could make large servers sit up and beg. And at the time, they were as scarce as hen's teeth and, as a result, they commanded premium salaries. Today, this function is largely performed by expert system software embedded in the server's operating system.

With respect to other items, we can look at Internet Protocol version 4 (IPv4), the workhorse of the Internet in 2010, and see that IPv6, the next big thing in packet networks, is entering the market from stage left, even as X.25, the pre-Internet packet technology, is leaving the scene stage right.

The same thing is happening with PCs and servers; 32-bit CPUs dominate today while 64-bit CPUs are entering stage left and 16-bit CPUs are exiting stage right.

ODC Discounts and Deflators

ODC discounting is driven primarily by the size of the opportunity and the relative desire of each bid team to win. If the bidder is the manufacturer of the ODC or a service supplier for it, their discounting posture will be dictated by the deflator discussions that follow.

Deflators and/or inflators, as shown in **Figure IV.9**, are developed by summing the year-over-year individual effects of these constituent elements:

- Competition—how will competitive factors affect the cost basis of prices going forward?
- Technology—how will technology lower the cost of providing the item/service going forward?
- Volume—how will increases and/or decreases in usage and/or demand change the future cost of providing the item or service?

PTW practitioners must develop each constituent element's take-down or plus up for each contract year and form them into curves that are then summed to form a single curve. **Figure IV.10** shows this view of lifecycle deflation profiling that can be used to lower the projected cost basis of a bid.

At the top left, we see a set of discrete technology deflation and/or inflation curves. The pie charts beneath these curves show a series of CLINs broken down to where each slice of the pie corresponds to a discrete technology. The CLIN deflation profiles to the right meld the portions of the CLINs and the technology curves to provide the composite CLIN Deflation Profiles.

	CY1	CY2	CY3	CY4	CY5	CY6	CY7	CY8	CY9	CY10	Total
DATA DISCOUNT CURVES											
DataMovers – On-Net	25%	25%	25%	25%	25%	25%	25%	25%	25%	25%	
DataMovers – Off-Net	15%	15%	15%	15%	15%	15%	15%	15%	15%	15%	
DATA DEFLATION CURVES											
	CY1	CY2	CY3	CY4	CY5	CY6	CY7	CY8	CY9	CY10	
DataMovers – On-Net	100%	94%	86%	80%	73%	65%	51%	41%	33%	30%	
DataMovers – Off-Net	100%	94%	86%	80%	73%	65%	51%	41%	33%	30%	

DATA DEFLATION CURVE BUILD-UP

Inputs:					Cost Breakdown					
Initial Margin %	30%				Time Cost	20%				
Resulting Cost %	70%				Resulting Volume Cost	30%				
DataMovers On-Net Washout Years	7				Annual Time/Tech. & Equip Factor					
DataMovers Off-Net Washout Years	5					15%				

DataMovers	CY1	CY2	CY3	CY4	CY5	CY6	CY7	CY8	CY9	CY10
New Margin %	30%	26%	22%	18%	14%	7%	-5%	-14%	-20%	-23%
New Tech Cost %	14%	12%	10%	9%	8%	8%	7%	7%	6%	6%
New Volume Cost %	56%	56%	53%	53%	51%	51%	49%	49%	47%	47%
New Total Cost %	70%	68%	64%	63%	59%	59%	56%	56%	53%	53%

DataMovers Reduction Category	CY1->CY2	CY2->CY3	CY3->CY4	CY4->CY5	CY5->CY6	CY6->CY7	CY7->CY8	CY8->CY9	CY9->CY10
Competition Factor	3.65%	3.93%	4.87%	3.76%	6.68%	11.62%	9.55%	5.73%	2.82%
Technology Factor	2.10%	1.52%	1.13%	0.85%	0.66%	0.52%	0.41%	0.33%	0.27%
Volume Factor	0.00%	2.67%	0.00%	2.42%	0.00%	2.20%	0.00%	2.00%	0.00%
	5.75%	8.11%	6.00%	7.03%	7.34%	14.34%	9.96%	8.07%	3.09%

FIGURE IV.9

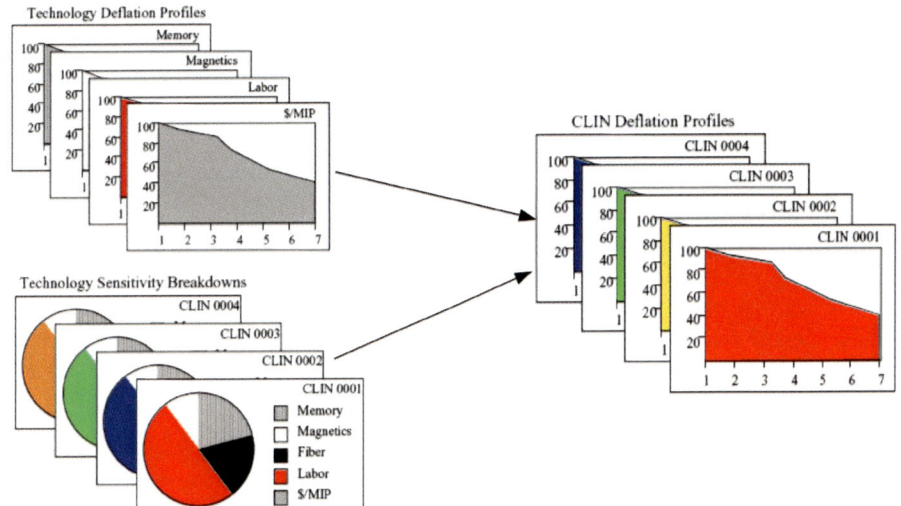

FIGURE IV.10

Be aware that technology deflation curves are not always uniform. For instance, the price of a disk drive with twice the capacity of a smaller cousin is not likely to be twice the price. When capacity is factored in, it would not be unusual for the larger device to have a price that is more like 1.5 times the price of the smaller device. The reasons for this may relate to these devices having different storage and access technologies within an identical form factor.

In developing the annual take-downs that form technology deflation curves, the question is: What weight should one give to the historical curve versus the future curve? Should it be 50/50? Should it be 0/100? What? PTW practitioners need to address this issue and revisit their results frequently.

Solution Development to Lower Costs

As society begins to fully consider the negative effects we may be having on the environment, there is intense interest in ongoing issues such as affordability and increased interest in newer issues such as, what can we do about global warming? Both issues require us to find newer approaches to existing problems when developing solutions. **Figure IV.11** presents a way in which this dual goal may be achieved.

On the right hand side of the graphic, there is a server farm consisting of 64 **single core** servers. This configuration is very capable of meeting the peak computing needs of its user community.

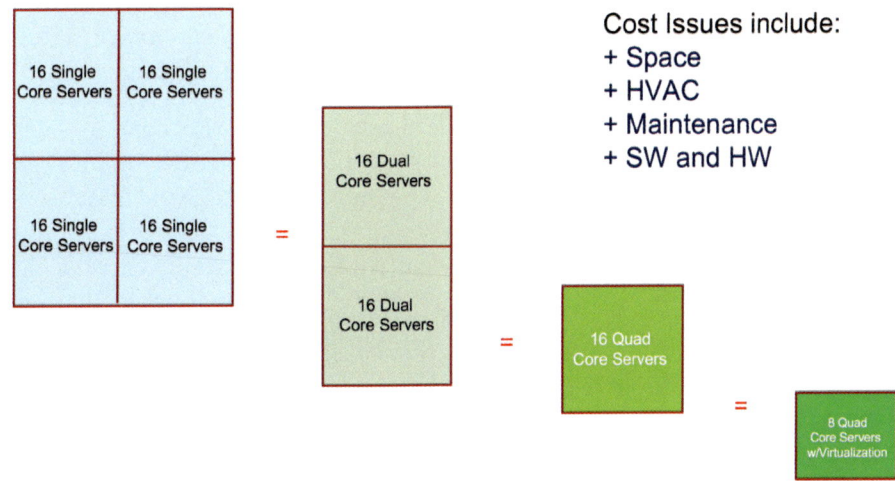

FIGURE IV.11

Going from left to right, there are other server farm configurations shown that, let's assume, can also handle the prevailing workload. They are:

- 32 **dual core** servers;
- 16 **quad core** servers; and finally
- 8 **quad core** servers with virtualization.

The point is that, as we go from left to right in the graphic, our costs go down from the cumulative savings when:

- Less space is needed;
- Less costly energy is needed to run servers and HVAC systems;
- Less maintenance is needed, since we have fewer boxes, software instances, wires, etc.; and, most likely,
- Significantly less hardware and software will have to be acquired to support the requirements.

This is win, win, win, win.

Commoditization—The Signs

Other Direct Cost (ODC) price erosion in the out years of a contract is somewhat inevitable due to the cumulative effect of one, or more, of the following on prices:

- Increased competition;
- Application of newer technologies; and
- Greater production volumes.

This, of course, is of vital interest to PTW practitioners, and generally leads to commoditization.

Commoditization is the process that, over time, emasculates the discriminators, allure, cachet and price premiums of products and services. The signs of commoditization include:

- Standardization;
- Increasing competition;
- Prevalence of look-alike products and services;
- Perception that all suppliers are fundamentally the same;
- Decreasing desire on the customers' part to look at new options or features;
- Increasing preference among customers to base purchasing decisions on price;
- Reluctance among customers to pay for anything perceived to be unnecessary; and
- Decreasing profit margins.

The stages that product categories go through leading to commoditization are:

- Start-up;
- Proof of concept;
- Shake-out phase;
- Stabilization;
- Maturity and saturation; producing…
- Commoditization.

Monitoring and Adjusting Pricing Curves

PTW practitioners are required to project their views of where the future is taking us. Sometimes curves that shape future ODC price points can be over- or under-estimated and may need to be adjusted as the future unfolds.

Figure IV.12 describes a contract that supplies minutes of long distance telephone service to a government customer. At the beginning of Contract Year One (CY1) of this 10-year contract (let's say it consisted of a five-year base period followed by five one-year option periods), based on the evaluated call minute volumes, this bidder was charging $.075 per minute. By the end of CY10, the unit price was reduced to $.03 per minute.

Halfway through the contract, when unit prices had been reduced to $.045, the customer called the contractor to demand prices that were at least competitive with low cost long distance offers that routinely interrupted family dinner time. The customer's position is that they are recompeting the contract and the additional option years on the incumbent's contract will not be exercised.

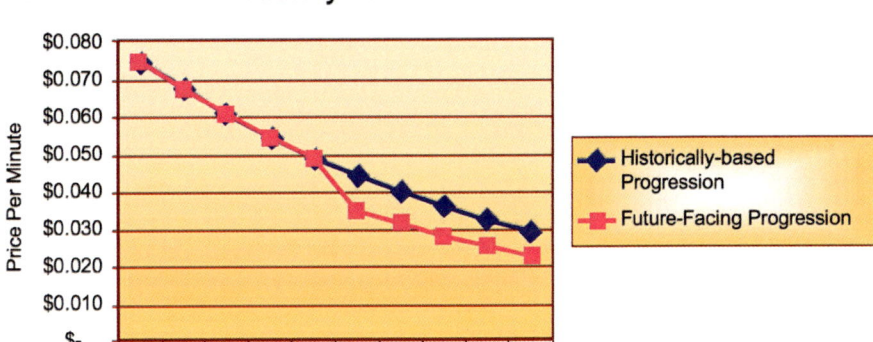

FIGURE IV.12

Perhaps the incumbent contractor should have been monitoring contract prices against commercial reality. When significant disparity was detected, they should have unilaterally offered more competitive prices.

The contractor's response to the recompete would be to abandon the blue price points and curve and chart a new trajectory (the pink line) for CYs 6–10. The question that this could raise is this: If service can be sold now at the new price point, why wasn't it possible to predict the new price as part of the original winning bid?

The blue line for CYs 6–10 follows the old contract's (i.e., the incumbent's) price erosion curve to arrive at possible bid price points. The pink line for CYs 6–10 is the PTW Team's view of the pricing needed to fend off insurgent bidders and use incumbency advantages using technology insertion, competition, and volume increases to plot a new price erosion curve.

Remember, while a conservative view of the future can be used to develop forward pricing, not being aggressive enough when predicting the future is often a formula for defeat in price-sensitive situations.

PTW Framework Phase 2, Step 6— The BOE Model

The BOE Model develops the *Partially Gamed Bottoms Up Basis Of Estimates* (BOE) for each of the targeted bid teams. The WBS (produced by Phase 2, Step 3) is used as the Y axis of the BOE Model.

The X axis of the BOE Model is designed to meet all opportunity requirements throughout the opportunity's contractual period:

- Labor categories and labor hour prices from Phase 2, Step 4 Labor Model; and
- Quantities of labor category hours and ODCs needed to meet requirements.

Developmental items will have to be estimated as a combination of labor and ODC components.

Often, the PTW practitioners have to determine which labor categories will be required to do the work and to estimate the Level Of Effort (LOE) that will be required of each needed labor category. ODCs, such as boxes, supplies, travel, etc., in required or estimated quantities, over time, will be included in the BOE. ODC prices will be drawn from the Phase 2, Step 5 BOE Model.

Producing WBS-Based BOEs

The BOE Model that the PTW Team generates to produce the *Partially Gamed* Bottoms Up "should price" for targeted competitive teams must cover the entire evaluated duration of the opportunity.

At the leaf position, or extremity, of the WBS, a BOE may consist of:

- A set of hours by the Phase 2, Step 4 labor categories that collectively are estimated to be required to accomplish each WBS leaf position task. If the task relates to software development, this may be backed up by:
  - A function point analysis—in the case of software development,
  - An application point analysis—in the case of application enhancement or maintenance requirements, or
  - An engineering estimate—in the case of hard (physical) or soft (logical) engineering of a developmental item, or both;
- A collection of Phase 2, Step 5 ODCs (we could call them configuration items) required to host or support the WBS element task; and
- Other Phase 2, Step 5 ODCs such as hardware and software maintenance, space costs, and travel and living expenses.

Each WBS leaf position's estimate will have a discrete periodicity (e.g., daily, monthly, one time, etc.). Labor and ODC BOE quantity estimates are multiplied by labor rate and ODC unit prices for each Contract Year (CY).

The aggregate prices, once rolled up, may be factored to account for year-over-year reductions or other fluctuations to produce a targeted team's BOE. This BOE-based aggregation represents PTW's view of a competitor's Price To Do the job, or its *Partially Gamed* PTW that the Home Team now has to figure out how to beat.

Key to a successful encounter with a Capture Team is having sufficient provenance to support all assertions. This is especially true when it comes to ODCs.

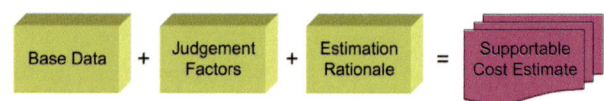

FIGURE IV.13

As shown in **Figure IV.13**, four key questions concerning consequential ODCs have to be answered. They are:

1. What is the base data that was used?
2. Why is the base data relevant?
3. What adjustments were made to the base data?
4. Why are the adjustments appropriate?

Being armed with answers to these sorts of questions will help ensure that PTW encounters with the Capture Team will generate much more light than heat.

WBS-Level BOE Development

Developing a BOE for a WBS element is much less of an "engineering" task than one may think. PTW practitioners must master this skill, and so should all those who purport to do solution development or pricing as part of Capture Teams.

As an example, let us use a 7 x 24 service desk requirement that supports some 1,000 users for hardware, software, and telecommunications issues. We are told that historical trouble call volumes are based on 30% of the users calling the service desk on average three times a month. This results in 900 calls per month, or ~30 calls per day.

The requirement is that we answer calls within one minute and provide detailed updates every two hours until a given trouble ticket has been cleared.

We also need to agree to a Service Level Agreement (SLA) that goes on to state that 50% of the troubles have to be cleared within two hours, 75% within four hours and 100% within eight hours.

First, to staff this requirement, we need to anticipate the need for the following labor categories:

- A service desk manager;
- Service desk shift leaders;
- Service desk staffers;
- Hardware technicians;
- Software technicians; and
- Telecommunications technicians.

We will also need labor rates for each of our identified labor categories.

Second, a concept of operations has to be developed, and that might go something like this:

- The service desk manager has four full-time shift leaders who rotate to cover 7 x 24 (168 hours per week), including holidays;
- The service desk manager doubles as the weekday shift leader; and
- Shift leaders double as "technicians at large."

In addition to the shift leader, each shift has to be staffed with at least two service desk staffers (response time issue) and at least one of each technician type.

Third, we need to populate the BOE with our monthly estimates of required billable hours by labor category. **Figure IV.14** presents our completed BOE for this WBS item.

Labor Category	Hourly Rates	#FTEs	Monthly Hours	Monthly $ Estimate
Service Desk Manager	$75.00	1	160	$12,000
Service Desk Shift Lead	$60.00	4	640	$38,400
Service Desk Staffer	$35.00	10	1,600	$56,000
Hardware Technician	$50.00	4	640	$32,000
Software Technician	$52.50	4	640	$33,600
Telecommunications Technician	$55.00	4	640	$35,200
Total Monthly Cost Estimate		27	4,320	$207,200

FIGURE IV.14

Having created a BOE like this, PTW practitioners need to be thinking of future leverage. Our service desk BOE, and the thought processes behind it, need to be added to our template library, ready to be leveraged and improved (and replaced in the template library) by the next PTW practitioner who needs to grapple with a service desk requirement.

The BOE Model in Perspective

Figure IV.15 shows how the BOE Model brings together work elements, bid elements and prices to produce the Partially Gamed, Bottoms Up PTW for a given targeted competitor. The WBS, when coupled with periodicity at its leaf position, is the "what" of the BOE. The schedule determines "when" in time the various work elements defined in the WBS are to happen. The Labor Model and the ODC Model provide the year-over-year unit prices.

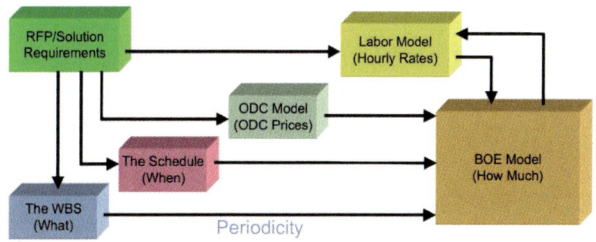

FIGURE IV.15

The BOE Model must cover both fixed and variable costs. Fixed costs may relate to continuing costs such as covering the cost of a contractor's Project Management Office (PMO). Variable costs relate to Indefinite Delivery, Indefinite Quantity (IDIQ) contract issues, such as:

- How many sites are likely to be involved?
- How many items and/or hours will be bought?

The BOE Model has also to produce many useful reports for each targeted competitor, including:

- Hours by labor category by CY;
- ODCs and labor by WBS element, by CY;
- Full Time Equivalent (FTE) head counts by CY;
- Scaling by CY and within CY; and
- Dollars by CY, by WBS element and by targeted competitive team member.

The Bottoms Up, Partially Gamed PTW produced by the BOE Model is a granular, WBS-driven PTW. Initial results may reveal numbers that are lower or higher than the Top Down Phase 1 PTW bogey that was shared with the Capture Team at Encounter 1.

PTW practitioners should never rush to judgment by presuming that their first cut BOE Model is producing realistic partially gamed competitor prices. Results have to be carefully audited since the Bottoms Up PTW errors are not unusual, given that the BOE Model represents the confluence of complex elements.

PTW has to be prepared to spend quality time:

- Revising technical and management approaches ascribed to targeted competitors;
- Reassessing allocation of Levels Of Effort (LOEs) across the WBS; and
- Calibrating the audited PTW results for each major WBS element in preparation for Encounter 2 with the Capture Team.

Additional Thoughts on BOEs & BOMs

Estimation is an art and a science. For instance, neither engineers nor PTW practitioners can accurately predict everything that will be needed when developing a BOM for an item such as a washing machine. To address the potential for under-estimation, a cost component entitled "Things We May Have Forgotten" is added to the list of sub-assemblies and labor requirements that comprise the BOM. The value of this catch-all item can easily range from 2.5% up to 25% depending on the estimator's perception of how well the rest of their BOM represents a complete and workable solution.

PTW Framework Phase 2, Step 7— Evaluation Model

At this point, the PTW Team can use the Evaluation Model to reassess their initial scoring of each evaluation criterion and, if deemed necessary, re-rate, re-document and re-rank the Home Team and each targeted competitive bid team.

Remember that the Evaluation Model that is now available may be different from the one used to evaluate competitors at the end of Phase 1, Step 2. PTW must always use the latest one. The Phase 2, Step 7 Evaluation Model now uses the Bottoms Up *Partially Gamed* PTW estimates for targeted competitors from the Phase 2, Step 6 BOE Model to re-develop the inverse allocation of evaluation points available to the Price evaluation factor.

Aggregated evaluation points for competing bid teams are used, along with the PTW practitioner's view of the Home Team's non-price evaluation scores, to derive the "Partially Gamed" PTW needed for the Home Team to prevail by a small margin in the evaluation points earned stakes.

Encounter 2—What PTW Needs to Impart

With the completion of the SSZ, along with all of the other Phase 2 ingredients that we have been developing (and the Phase 1 artifacts that we have been improving during Phase 2), we are now ready for Encounter 2 with our Capture Team. PTW's Encounter 2 task is to present an overview of Phase 2 analysis, covering:

Summary findings:

- Competition (updated, if needed);
- Evaluation scheme (updated or refreshed, if necessary);
- Competitive team standings;
- Detailed non-price evaluation item scores (updated, if necessary);
- Partially gamed bottoms up prices and point scores; and
- What the Home Team now needs to do to win, based on its Phase 2 position within the SSZ.

Procurement details such as:

- Program objectives and scope (updated, if necessary);
- Known customer hot (and cold) buttons and other issues (updated, if necessary);
- Schedule, WBS, labor category and ODC requirements (updated, if necessary); and
- Additional information such as Non-Recurring Engineering (NRE) needed to, for instance, develop a prototype, and/or software development estimates.

Targeted competitive team Bottoms Up PTW details, to include:

- Capture strategy;
- Productivity improvement and escalation curves;
- Rate cards;
- Labor pyramids;
- BOM lists;
- Details of targeted competitor Partially Gamed PTW results; and
- Completed price tables.

Materially relevant opportunity scuttlebutt, including:

- Detailed SWOTs (updated, as needed); and
- Street talk and contacts made (updated, as needed).

The PTW Team's job, as always, is to provoke a serious discussion to ensure that the Capture Team "buys in" to the PTW view or, if not, to explain how their view differs and why. In any event, PTW practitioners must always take copious notes and be *infocentric* by documenting comments and pre-positioning all new information by ingesting it into the corporate Infocenter.

It may become clear at Encounter 2 that the Capture Team's solution and BOE cannot be modified to support the Bottoms Up bogeys and meet the price levels of the calibrated Phase 2 PTW results. PTW is not in the business of killing deals—PTW's role is to present the facts and let the Capture Team and senior management decide how best to interpret them.

What Is/Is Not in the Partially Gamed PTW

At the end of Phase 2, we are only at the Partially Gamed, Price To Do the job PTW level—there are several material issues that *are* in the targeted competitor Phase 2 evaluation results, and some that *are not yet* included. Items that *are* included are:

- Solution;
- Labor requirements;
- ODC needs;
- Team composition; and
- Team SWOTs and likely past performance citations.

Chief among the issues that *are not yet* included in Phase 2 PTW results are:

- Degrees of "Must Win";
- Incremental cost avoidance approaches, sunk costs, and otherwise stranded capacity (telecom, space, etc.);
- Post-award opportunities to re-compete subcontractor participation;
- One or more of the targeted competitors being in play;
- Risk-averseness, aggressive assumptions, underpricing CY1;
- Service Level Agreements (SLAs) that are aggressive, passive, or creative;
- Possible share-in-savings approaches (e.g., proposing a "to be" way of doing the work using commercial best practices such that the contractor gets reimbursed for actual "to be" operating costs plus gets a share of the delta between "as is" costs and "to be" costs) that are aggressive, analysis-based, etc.; and
- Best value issues, including what this might encompass, how it would be supported, and why the customer should or would care.

Phase 2 of the Progressive PTW Problem

As explained in the book's Foreword, Section VII of this book presents a PTW problem that progresses from Phase 1 to Phase 2 before concluding with Phase 3. Microsoft Excel spreadsheet models pertaining to the PTW Framework phases are available on demand by emailing a request to:

training@caisisco.com

For those who are interested in the Progressive PTW Problem that relates to this, the second phase of the 3-Phase, 10-Step PTW Framework, please turn to Phase 2 of the Progressive PTW Problem in Section VII of this book.

Section V

Phase 3 of CAI/SISCo's PTW Framework

Fully Gaming the Partially Gamed Bottoms Up PTW

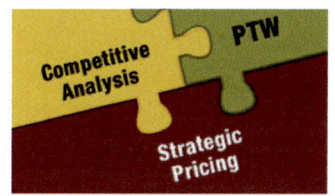

Section V presents Phase 3 of the 3-Phase, 10-Step PTW Framework which develops the Bottoms Up "Fully Gamed" PTW for the targeted competitive bid teams.

Phase 3 of the PTW Framework

As shown in **Figure V.1**, Phase 3 of the PTW Framework involves Steps 8 through 10.

This phase of the PTW Framework develops Fully Gamed PTWs from Phase 2's Partially Gamed, Bottoms Up results for those competitive bid teams that were selected as targets for Bottoms Up analysis at Encounter 1.

Phase 3, Steps 8 and 9 yield the following PTW outputs:

- A CLIN by CLIN Reality Model (Phase 3, Step 8) that depicts what we expect the customer to buy, in what quantity, and when we expect them to buy it;

- A Delta Margin Gaming (DMG) Model (Phase 3, Step 9) showing how margins and/or costs need to be adjusted by CLIN to exploit the differences between the government's Evaluated Case and our Phase 3, Step 8 Reality Case; and

- A "Fully Gamed" version of the third of the three PTW parametric elements first mentioned in Section II of this book, for each targeted bid team.

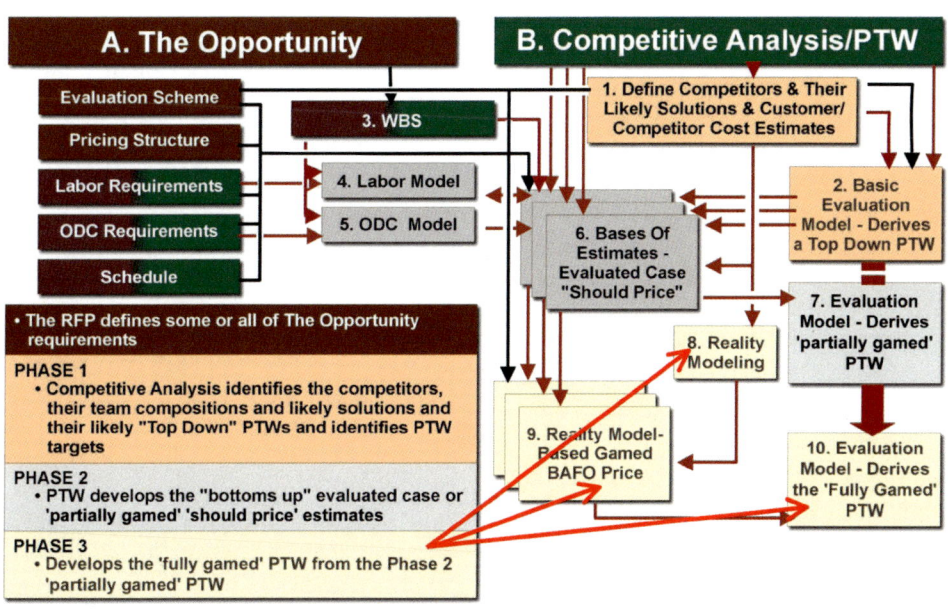

FIGURE V.1

Phase 3, Step 10, the Final Evaluation Model, adjusts the SWOTs and non-cost evaluation item rankings of each competitive bid team against each evaluation criterion, re-aggregates and re-ranks them to determine each team's revised evaluation point scoring potential.

PTW estimates for this Final Evaluation Model iteration are developed by Phase 3, Step 9. These results, in turn, are used to develop the Home Team's PTW which, as always, is the price that, when turned into cost award points and added to the Home Team's total non-cost award points, puts the Home Team marginally ahead.

Phase 3 culminates in the PTW Team's Encounter 3 with management, pricing, and some elements of the Capture Team. The PTW Team presents its findings, listens to comments and concerns, take copious notes, and ingests and pre-positions them as part of the corpus of information that relates to the opportunity, the competitors, and the customer.

PTW Framework Phase 3, Step 8— The Reality Model

Evaluation quantities (labor hours, quantities of ODCs, etc.) that are used as the basis for evaluating bid prices are usually significantly at odds with eventual reality. This is the case because all the customer is usually trying to develop is a basis for conducting the competition, not a definitive numerical statement of need.

Reality Modeling's role is to size the magnitude of the likely CLIN level divergence (plus or minus) of either the Home Team (for Strategic Pricing purposes) or a targeted competitor (for PTW purposes) from the customer's Evaluated Case.

Of course, not all opportunities have evaluation quantities that can be used in conjunction with a Reality Model to create the basis for gaming. If the DRFP/RFP simply evaluates "One Lot," there is nothing that a Reality Model can do to provide a basis for gaming.

In this case, PTW will need to use another of its gaming approaches. This is explained later in this section under *An Alternative Phase 3, Step 9 Price Gaming Approach*.

Reality modeling is accomplished by means of a process that PTW practitioners sometimes refer to as *informed quantification*, the process of studying the customer need and environment to more accurately determine what they are likely to actually buy and when they are likely to buy it. In addition to having to be quantitatively realistic, PTW views of a targeted competitor's Reality Case cannot exceed addressable budgets.

Figure V.2 presents a simple Reality Model example.

	Contract Year 1		
Cases	Desktop PCs	Laptop PCs	Explanation
Evaluated	500	500	What The Customer Evaluates & Expects To Buy
Reality	300	700	What The Contractor Expects To Sell
Unreality	-200	+200	The Exploitable Delta – Used By Gaming

FIGURE V.2

In the table, we have depicted a one-year opportunity that is evaluating the purchase of 1,000 PCs—500 laptops and 500 desktops. The question that the Reality Model row seeks to answer is: How many of each PC type do we expect to sell?

If, as shown, our research of the customer environment indicates that they are only likely to buy 300 desktops, but buy additional laptops, then we will have created negative and positive *unreality*. Unreality is that precious commodity that strategic pricers use to game bid prices. The approach is this: if an item is over-evaluated (e.g., desktops in our table) relative to our view of reality, then we move money out of that unit price and add it to the price of an under-evaluated item or items.

So that the reader does not get the impression that Reality Models only apply to inanimate objects such as desktop and laptop PCs, we could just as easily have labor categories such as systems analyst and senior systems analyst. The concept is identical.

How Is a Reality Model Developed?

A Reality Model is developed using the following information:

- The CLIN pricing structure and evaluation quantities from the RFP;
- Information gleaned from the customer, the competition, and the environment;
- Technological forecasts that dwell on where key elements of the opportunity solution are likely to go and when;
- The budgetary "winds of change" i.e., how budgetary predictions are likely to affect future spending;
- How competitive vehicles may eat into the opportunity as it unfolds; and
- Assessments of likely aftermarket potential.

The Reality Model presents the PTW practitioner's version of how they expect each targeted competitor to view the opportunity's potential that:

- Could happen; and
- Targeted competitors are judged to reasonably be able to help make happen.

The results of this step, if executed, feed the Phase 3, Step 9, Delta Margin Gaming process.

Forecasting and Estimating Contract Potential

To PTW, whenever the opportunity involves evaluation quantities, forecasting and estimating contract potential in a Reality Model is crucial; that is, crucial to being able to develop winning pricing and arrive at the best evaluated price within profit constraints.

Reality modeling in support of PTW looks at the customer environment (e.g., budget issues, mandated imperatives, etc.) and DRFP/RFP evaluated quantities to determine if the evaluated case is reasonable and, if not, determine **what is** reasonable.

PTW needs to look into overall conditions, which include:

- Pent-up demand;
- Realistic FY buying patterns; and
- Budget constraint forecasts.

PTW also needs to look into specific conditions, which cover:

- CLIN-by-CLIN realities (e.g., item desirability, etc.).
- Whether CY1 evaluated case quantities are going to be met, given: government contract startup issues, contractor mobilization realities, and order processing creakiness.
- Technology insertion—how will this affect out-year reality?

Other considerations that PTW practitioners need to address in coming up with a targeted competitor-specific Reality Models include:

- Is there opportunity expansion/contraction (e.g., base closings, etc.)?
- Are other contract vehicles competing for this business?
- Could overall dollar potential be met by other means, such as aftermarket potential?

For those of you who think that there is something immoral about gaming bids using a Reality Model, or by any other means, remember this old saw:

> **Never confuse bidding with doing.**

What it means is that, regardless of the situation, the bid documented in your proposal is directed at winning the job. Doing the job once the opportunity has been won is another matter entirely. Don't get ahead of yourself by trying to do the job in your proposal.

Ways of Estimating the "Real" Opportunity

The "Real" opportunity, as it relates to PTW, is the opportunity's potential, by evaluated CLIN, that the PTW practitioner ascribes to each targeted competitor. "Real" opportunity knowledge is crucial to all bidders for developing the best price within profit constraints, and winning.

Market understanding uncovers the basis for gaming opportunities. The following example, though aged, is instructive:

> A circa 1975 U.S. Navy Rework Facilities RFP evaluated a family of compute servers and five (5) very high end printer systems. The RFP evaluated five Xerox 9700 printer systems which, at that time, were selling for about $500K each. The Xerox 9700 could take a digital image of a new or modified "fix it" manual, copy it, collate it, develop a cover for it, and bind the resulting manual for use by technicians repairing or upgrading systems on board naval vessels.
>
> The Xerox 9700 appeared to be a solution made in heaven, and, except for its size, was considered to be a "must have" item when the RFP was being developed months earlier. The company that eventually won the bid asked its local-to-the-facilities salespeople to nose around at the five facilities. Their findings indicated that three facilities had no space to accommodate a Xerox 9700, which was the size of a large pickup truck.
>
> Using the "reality" that only two Xerox 9700 printer systems were likely to be sold, the eventual winning bidder priced printers at 60% of cost, and spread the difference between printer prices and printer costs across the server prices (which the customer badly needed to buy).
>
> This bidder's price evaluated low, and won the award. What happened over the course of time was that zero printers were sold, the Present Value (PV) of the bid looked good, and the profit was exceptional.

The moral, once again, is that things are liable to change from RFP development to contract execution time. While each of the Navy Rework Facilities had planned to get a Xerox 9700 printer system when the RFP was being developed, after award, it turned out that all of them had since found other ways to meet their "fix it" manual printing needs.

Contrasting the Evaluated and Reality Cases

As with the previous example, what is really interesting about Reality Models is that it often turns out to be much less important for the PTW practitioner or a Home Team pricer to call reality precisely. What *is* critical is that PTW practitioners and pricers *must* make some sort of attempt at shedding light on eventual reality and use it to game their results.

As another case in point, consider **Figure V.3**. This represents an opportunity out of the old DOD DISA organization's contracting arm. As the use of cell phones became widespread, there had been a proliferation of U.S. military personnel entering into individual contracts with carriers in Europe and elsewhere. These contracts were, for the most part, priced at retail, and expensed.

DISA sought to award a single contract to consolidate cell phone service agreement purchases at rates that were commensurate with the large body of users that U.S. personnel represented. The opportunity covered cellular voice and cellular data. At the time, cellular voice was the heavy hitter, whereas cellular data was just getting off the ground.

In the graphic, the dark blue and red lines represent the *evaluated* quantities for cellular voice and cellular data, respectively. So the PTW Team went to town to determine the Reality Model for these items.

It was evident that the Evaluation Model swept several items under the rug, including:

- Existing contracts could only be gradually accessioned over the first Contract Year (CY1) to the new contract, not all at once; and
- The compound escalation rates that were used to develop year-over-year evaluation quantities looked to be anything but real.

Digging deeper, the PTW Team began to see that cellular voice demand would be severely diminished over time at the hands of cellular data that was supporting a steady stream of new applications such as texting and game playing, and today (with 20/20

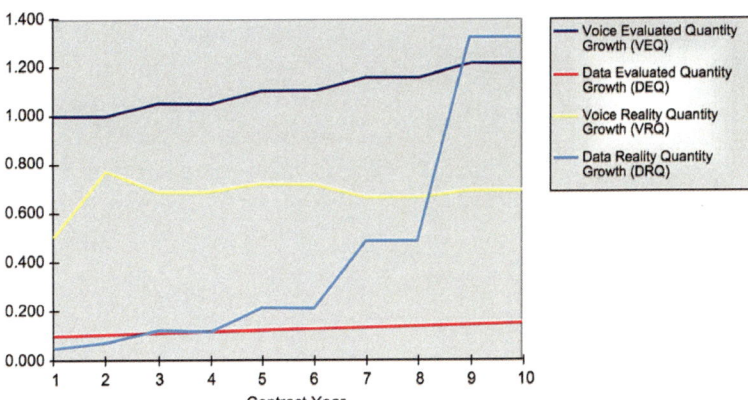

FIGURE V.3

hindsight), tweeting, internet access, and so forth. When the PTW Team coupled this future view with the fact that the military tends to be comprised of young, tech savvy people with time on their hands, the imperative for them to communicate asynchronously became evident and was seen to be a key demand driver.

The resulting Reality Model is represented on the graphic by yellow and light blue lines. These lines represent the *reality* quantities that PTW developed for cellular voice and cellular data, respectively. Basing pricing on the delta between the Evaluated Case and the Reality Case allowed a small reseller of cellular service to win a major contract from under the noses of several major European cell companies.

Once again, PTW did not call it spot on. For instance, the cellular data "hockey stick" happened a couple of years earlier than predicted but, once again, the fact that the whole Reality Model situation was considered gave the Home Team a significant advantage over the competition.

A Word about Engineering Change Proposals (ECPs)

For jobs that are won by bidding to a barebones interpretation of a Statement Of Objectives (SOO) or a Statement Of Work (SOW), Engineering Change Proposals (ECPs) should be seen as the means that the winning bidder has of giving the customer what they really wanted or what they really need. How can, or does, this happen?

Suppose there is an acquisition that seeks to acquire a satellite constellation that communicates with its earth stations by means of lasers. Let us also assume that there are numerous significant technical issues that will need to be solved in order for any solution to actually work.

So, as a prudent bidder, a firm may opt to submit what one might describe as a barebones or "Swiss cheese" bid. The concept is that the bid is made against the cheese and the holes in the cheese (those issues that are present day imponderables) become future ECP fodder.

Accordingly, ECPs, if they reasonably apply, should be viewed as an integral part of the aftermarket potential of a job. Thus, the value of ECPs need to be quantified and accounted for in the PTW practitioner's Reality Model.

This strategy, however, is not without calculated risk. The risks to the contractor may include:

- Having to deliver what was bid; and
- Being assessed as a poor performer or a bait and switcher.

Note: Not actively seeking ECPs can result in the delivery of an unworkable solution and an unhappy customer. This applies equally to the contractor and the customer.

If the customer, with its PMO support contractors, can't define precisely what the hypothetical satellite constellation that communicates with its earth stations by means of lasers needs to do then, they should expect ECPs to cover any or all of the unknowns. There are numerous instances where large amounts of money have been expended to produce inadequate results, either because expectations were unrealistic or progress was not well managed.

Reality Modeling Information Sources and Examples

PTW does not need to stoop to questionable activities such as dumpster diving and so forth to generate needed information. Open Source information is everywhere—it just needs to be mined.

For PTW purposes, the major categories of need are:

- Competitor-related;
- Customer-related; and
- Opportunity-related.

For Reality Modeling, the key category is customer-related information. To plumb this category, at least in the U.S., one can read the Office of Management and Budget's (OMB) tea leaves. From its vantage point, OMB looks at scorecards that compare individual government activity costs with comparable agency and commercial activity cost levels. These comparisons can be revealing. Here is one example:

> In 2004, the U.S. Defense Logistics Agency's (DLA) departmental computing costs were seen by OMB to be a significant high side outlier. With the advent of affordable minicomputers in the 1970s and 1980s, DLA activities had increasingly shunned using centralized mainframes and embraced departmental computing. By 2004, according to solicitation documents, DLA had some 1,600 departmental computer systems, each housed in raised-floor computer rooms, tended by flocks of acolytes (operators, systems administrators, systems programmers, etc.), which had an aggregate cost that raised a significant red flag at OMB. The result was the initiation of a consolidation requirement that became a major recentralization opportunity aimed at reducing preconsolidation costs by more than 30%.

Another non-OMB example is this.

> A few years ago, when the U.S. Department of Education was looking to outsource its Student Loan processing requirements, a comparison with commercial "best practices" revealed this: Education had been paying $1.19 to service an average transaction, whereas the commercial banking world was doing this for less than $0.20.

Other information sources include all of the sources described in Section VI under *General Research Sources: Finding Opportunity, Agency, and Competitor Information*, plus:

- Marketing and sales calls;
- Talking to people (and remembering the details);
- Budget documents and exhibits;
- Government workforce statistics;
- Agency five-year plans and other forward-looking documents;
- OMB publications;
- Your firm's internal knowledgebase; and
- Knowledge gathered at facilitation sessions.

One can also engage in behavioral modeling exercises to determine reality demand. These include:

- Right sizing—reassessing the *overall requirement* to reflect budget, project and manpower realities;
- Scheduling—reassessing the *demand variation over the contract life* to reflect budget, project and manpower realities; and
- Rebalancing—adjusting the *product mix* (at system and subsystem level) to reflect buying habit realities (the devil is in the details).

There is also bidder-created unreality. This is where the winning bidder has control of, say, the makeup of a "standard server configuration" that, for evaluation purposes, is attractively priced but which turns out to need add-ons to enable it to perform adequately. Of course, the winning bid includes add-ons that are, most likely, expensive but which buyers have to order from the contract unless they want to void their warranty. By means such as these, bidders can *create* exploitable unreality.

PTW Framework Phase 3, Step 9— Gaming the Partially Gamed PTW

The PTW practitioner has several approaches that can be used to approximate a targeted competitor's Price *To Win* the job using that competitor's Price *To Do* the job. Because PTW is usually operating within short turnaround times (typically 30 days, but rarely 60 days), PTW practitioners tend to use an approach that CAI/SISCo has called Delta Margin Gaming (DMG) since the mid-1980s. DMG exploits the unreality (i.e., negative and positive differences) between:

- What the customer is going to evaluate and when (the Evaluated Case)—as seen, this rarely comes close to eventual reality; and

- What PTW expects the targeted bidder to want to sell, tempered by what the customer is likely to buy and when (the Reality Case).

DMG's focus is on moving margin out of over-evaluated CLINs and into under-evaluated ones. DMG is more effective at reducing evaluated prices as unreality increases. To be worthwhile, DMG requires that over-evaluated CLINs be priced near, at or below cost, thus lowering the price floor.

The DMG Model estimates the effects of gaming and produces the likely "gamed" BAFO prices for the targeted competitive bid teams. DMG's impact increases as the price floor is lowered.

Caution: PTW practitioners and pricers have to always beware of unrealistic pricing. The case law for unrealistic pricing uses the unlikely relationship between the price of chef's hats and tablecloths. If the price of the lower valued item exceeds that of the higher valued, then unrealistic pricing can be alleged.

Note: Gaming can be accomplished using a targeted competitor's likely granular pricing strategies instead of DMG. (See *Additional Pricing Strategies for PTW Practitioners* in Section VI for more detail.)

Delta Margin Gaming— The PTW Practitioner's Edge

Figure V.4 is a cartoon that tells a story. On the left is the Partially Gamed PTW (call it the Initial Submission, if you will) or Price *To Do* the job.

To its right is the Price *To Win* the job (one may call this the Best And Final Offer (BAFO) price), which is considerably lower. This version uses gamed unit prices **and** *evaluation* quantities.

Because the rightmost "As Executed" case uses gamed unit prices **and** *reality* quantities, there is a reasonable expectation that a bidder will be able to yield more profitable business out of a contract won using DMG than is implied by the Partially Gamed PTW or Price *To Do* the job.

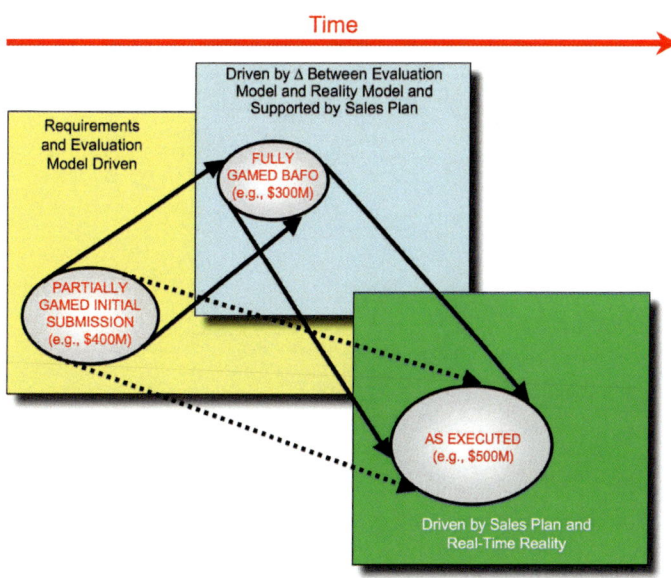

FIGURE V.4

What we are looking to maximize is what the hedge fund people refer to as *alpha*, i.e., the ability to do better with respect to overall margin than the *beta*, or basic, case may suggest. The next topic explains how this can work.

Delta Margin Gaming: Solve for Lower Price or Higher Profit?

Figure V.5 presents a Delta Margin Gaming (DMG) example. While this example covers the maintenance of several items of hardware and their respective failure rates, it could equally apply to a set of labor categories and set of evaluated hours.

On the left side of the table are eleven (11) **Mail-Back/Carry-In** items (shaded in grey) that constitute a hypothetical opportunity for which bidders are required to provide unit prices. The Evaluation Model is typically unrealistic inasmuch as each item is uniformly evaluated to fail 15 times in a contract year.

What an astute bidder can be expected to do is to get its smart people to look at these 11 items and assess what the most likely number of annual failures will be, based upon their knowledge of the actual products. These orange shaded cells provide the actual or Reality Case failure quantities, the unit price to fix each failure for that item, and an annual cost to repair the item. Once we have established that the bidder whose pricing we are about to game would be happy with an overall margin of 12.5% (see top right, in grey) we can let the games begin.

The result cases shown in the matrix are as follows, and they are explained below:

- Ungamed;
- Gamed for Profit; and
- Gamed for Price.

The **Ungamed** price (yellow cells) is developed by multiplying "evaluated failures/year" by "unit cost to repair" prices prior to tacking on the desired 12.5% profit margin. The result is the $71,803 evaluated price shown, and lo and behold, the margin comes in at 12.5%.

The **Gamed for Profit** price (green cells) uses the deltas between Evaluated and Reality Case failures to develop unit prices that are then multiplied by the evaluated quantities, and that result is uplifted by the 12.5% margin to form a bid that is aimed at maximizing profit. The result is the $71,803 evaluated price shown which, instead of yielding the desired 12.5% profit margin, yields a whopping 68.9% margin. Note that under-evaluated item bid prices

					Profit Markup Target Set At:					12.50%
Mail-Back/Carry-In Maintenance					Ungamed		Gamed for Profit		Gamed for Price	
Item	Estimated Actual # Failures/Year	Unit Cost To Repair	Annual Cost To Repair	Evaluated Failures/ Year	Fixed Markup Unit Price	Evaluated Price	Delta Margin Unit Price	Evaluated Price	Delta Margin Unit Price	Evaluated Price
1	20	$150	$3,000	15	$168.75	$2,531.25	$199.24	$2,988.60	$132.68	$1,990.22
2	35	$1,200	$42,000	15	$1,350.00	$20,250.00	$2,789.36	$41,840.41	$1,857.54	$27,863.04
3	19	$55	$1,045	15	$61.88	$928.13	$69.40	$1,041.03	$46.22	$693.26
4	0.2	$60	$12	15	$67.50	$1,012.50	$0.80	$11.95	$0.53	$7.96
5	6	$150	$900	15	$168.75	$2,531.25	$59.77	$896.58	$39.80	$597.07
6	9	$1,500	$13,500	15	$1,687.50	$25,312.50	$896.58	$13,448.70	$597.07	$8,955.98
7	8	$750	$6,000	15	$843.75	$12,656.25	$398.48	$5,977.20	$265.36	$3,980.43
8	18	$60	$1,080	15	$67.50	$1,012.50	$71.73	$1,075.90	$47.77	$716.48
9	19	$50	$950	15	$56.25	$843.75	$63.09	$946.39	$42.02	$630.24
10	23	$130	$2,990	15	$146.25	$2,193.75	$198.58	$2,978.64	$132.24	$1,983.58
11	4	$150	$600	15	$168.75	$2,531.25	$39.85	$597.72	$26.54	$398.04
			Evaluated Total Price			$71,803.13		$71,803.13		$47,816.29
			Estimated Reality Sales Value			$81,086.63		$121,763.39		$81,086.63
			Total Annual Cost to Repair			$72,077.00		$72,077.00		$72,077.00
			Profit Potential			12.5%		68.9%		12.5%

FIGURE V.5

(e.g., Item 2) are increased, and costs for over-evaluated items (e.g., Item 7) are minimized.

The **Gamed for Price** price (light blue cells) also uses the deltas between Evaluated and Reality Case failures to develop unit prices that are then multiplied by the evaluated quantities, and that result is uplifted by the 12.5% margin to form a bid that is aimed at minimizing the overall evaluated price.

The result is the $47,816 evaluated price shown, which yields the desired 12.5% margin. Note that under-evaluated item costs (e.g., Item 2) and over-evaluated item costs (e.g., Item 4) are only uplifted by the desired 12.5% profit margin.

Also note the rows underneath the **Evaluated Total Price** row in the last table. **Estimated Reality Sales Value** presents what our reality quantities would yield in terms of aggregate sales assuming our view of reality is accurate. (This equates to the "As Executed" portion of Figure V.4 on page 87.) The **Total Cost** row simply sums the **Yearly Cost to Repair** column.

Here is the bottom line:

- The Ungamed bid probably ends in a loss because it doesn't do anything;
- The Gamed for Profit bid probably also fails to win because the bidder has been too greedy; and
- The Gamed for Price bid is just right because it meets objectives while hitting an (apparently) aggressive price point.

But be warned, this DMG example presented is too simplistic. The major problem is that there are clearly no built-in "collars" that prevent unit prices from going way high or way low. Accordingly, the results shown produce unit prices that are likely to be considered either *unrealistic* or *unbalanced*. The bottom line is that to make DMG work well, you will need a fairly sophisticated model that allows both costs and desired margins to be defined in addition to setting how far beneath or above cost a gamed unit price can be.

An Alternative Phase 3, Step 9 Price Gaming Approach

As was discussed earlier in this section, it is not always possible to turn a Partially Gamed PTW into a Fully Gamed one using Reality Models and a Delta Margin Gaming (DMG) Model.

In these cases, we may use a table to approximate the effect of gaming on each competitor's likely, Partially Gamed Bottoms Up PTW.

Figure V.6 on the next page uses a set of Strategic Pricing take-down issues. These issues would not have been baked into the Phase 2, Step 7 Partially Gamed Bottoms Up PTW, but for fully gamed purposes, now need to have their relative applicability and intensity developed.

The take-down items shown in the table relate to each targeted competitor's ability, based on their perceived relationship to the opportunity, and/or the customer, and/or their teammates, to:

1. Avoid costs. Cost avoidance represents a take-down from the Price *To Do* the job that relates to a targeted competitor being judged by the PTW practitioner as having the ability to avoid certain costs. Let us assume that the subject opportunity is to develop and integrate three black boxes into a system of some sort. PTW may have information that suggests that Bidder #1 has already developed one of the boxes, while Bidder #2 has developed two of them. Hence the take-downs that would have to be supported in the table by row entries in the Bid Team Specific Comments column.

2. Successfully raise Engineering Change Proposals (ECPs) aimed at giving the customer what they really need above and beyond what was asked for and bid (recall the double pill versus single pill solution example from Section I).

3. Trade on customer environment knowledge such as might alert a bidder to ways the contractual landscape may be changed after award.

4. Renegotiate subcontractor prices post-award.

5. Avoid cost by offshoring or onshoring labor from nations with lower labor costs. For instance, if Competitor #1 is an insurgent with a history of bidding aggressive offshoring, they would be likely to have a steep offshoring discount whereas other bid teams may not.

6. Take-down prices because the opportunity has some extraordinary strategic value to a particular bid team. It could be that one or other of the competitors may see the opportunity as a small fish to catch a bigger fish later on.

Item 7 is not a take-down at all. Indeed, it is a plus-up. This item, and others like it, relate to bids that involve potential risks to the competitive bid team, such as that which strikes fear into the hearts of most government contractors—Firm, Fixed Price (FFP).

The Item 7 shown is the management risk pool that provides funds to cover overruns, and the like, when FFP bids are being priced. (In the UK, for instance, FFP bids are much more common than in the U.S.)

Once populated, the targeted competitor columns are aggregated to provide a net take-down to each competitor's Partially Gamed PTW. This assumes that the Delta Margin Gaming (DMG) approach could not be employed for the opportunity at hand.

Note: This aggregate discount must only be applied to the estimated portion of the partially gamed team results; plug numbers cannot be "gamed."

Clearly the number and types of take-down categories that are possible are limited only by a PTW practitioner's imagination, experience and ingenuity.

Issue #	Typical Strategic Cost-Based Pricing Take-Down Issue	Relative Importance (10 is high)	Potential Competing Bid Team Price Influence			Bid Team Specific Comments	General Comments
			#1	#2	#3		
1	Cost Avoidance		5.00%	10.00%	2.50%	Bidder #1 rationale	A bidder's ability to avoid costs by leveraging existing assets and capabilities (e.g., facilities, developed software, IR&D, etc.)
						Bidder #2 rationale	
						Bidder #3 rationale	
2	Engineering Change Proposals (ECPs)		0.00%	5.00%	5.00%	Bidder #1 rationale	Propensity to raise ECPs to meet the delta between what the customer needs and what was asked for in the RFP and priced in the vendor's proposal
						Bidder #2 rationale	
						Bidder #3 rationale	
3	Customer Environment Knowledge		2.50%	0.00%	5.00%	Bidder #1 rationale	When a bidder has a close relationship with a customer what advantages may be wrung from such relationship
						Bidder #2 rationale	
						Bidder #3 rationale	
4	Bearing Down On Subcontractors & Suppliers		2.50%	2.50%	0.00%	Bidder #1 rationale	The tactic is to "bid to win" and upon award informing the subs and suppliers of the price points that were needed to secure the award
						Bidder #2 rationale	
						Bidder #3 rationale	
5	Offshoring		25.00%	10.00%	0.00%	Bidder #1 rationale	The extent to which bidders may utilize offshore labor in lieu of indigenous labor to reduce costs
						Bidder #2 rationale	
						Bidder #3 rationale	
6	Strategic Loss Leader		0.00%	0.00%	0.00%	Bidder #1 rationale	The advantage that a bidder is likely to realize by proposing to bid the opportunity out of a new, zero-based Cost Center or through a JV
						Bidder #2 rationale	
						Bidder #3 rationale	
7	Management Risk Pool		15.00%	5.00%	12.50%	Bidder #1 rationale	The premium that gets added back to an estimate to provide a risk cushion
						Bidder #2 rationale	
						Bidder #3 rationale	
	Net Effect		20.00%	22.50%	0.00%		

FIGURE V.6

PTW Framework Phase 3, Step 10— Final Evaluation Model

The Final Evaluation Model allows each evaluation criterion to be re-rated, documented, and re-ranked for each targeted competitive bid team.

The Phase 3, Step 9 Fully Gamed PTW results for targeted competitors are substituted in the Phase 3, Step 10 Evaluation Model for the Partially Gamed PTW estimates. The fully gamed results are used to reallocate the evaluation award points available to the price evaluation factor.

Aggregated evaluation points for competing bid teams are used, along with the PTW practitioner's view of the Home Team's non-price evaluation scores, to derive the Fully Gamed PTW that allows the Home Team to prevail by a small margin in terms of overall evaluation points earned.

Encounter 3—What PTW Needs to Impart

Having accomplished all Phase 3 steps, the PTW Team is now ready for Encounter 3, the third and final encounter with our Capture Team, or at least parts of the Capture Team augmented for sure by pricing, finance, and management people. The PTW Team's task is to present an overview of Phase 3 findings covering:

- Competition (updated, if needed);
- Evaluation scheme (updated or refreshed, if necessary);
- Competitive team standings;
- Detailed non-price evaluation item scores (updated, if necessary);
- *Fully Gamed* Bottoms Up prices and point scores and *how these items were gamed or otherwise derived*; and
- What the Home Team now needs to do to win based on their Phase 2 position within the SSZ.

All other information that was presented at Encounter 2, but which may have sustained updates, becomes part of the readout package, but it is typically relegated to the status of backup material for Encounter 3. This would include:

1. Procurement details such as:
   - Program objectives and scope (updated, if necessary);
   - Known customer hot (and cold) buttons and other issues (updated, if necessary);
   - Schedule, WBS, labor category and ODC requirements (updated, if necessary); and
   - Additional information such as Non-Recurring Engineering (NRE) and/or software development estimates.

2. Targeted competitive team Bottoms Up PTW details, to include:
   - Capture strategy;
   - Productivity improvement and escalation curves;
   - Rate cards;
   - BOM lists;
   - Details of targeted competitor Partially Gamed PTW results; and
   - Completed price tables.

3. Materially relevant opportunity scuttlebutt, including:
   - Detailed SWOTs (updated, as needed); and
   - Street talk and contacts made (updated, as needed).

The PTW Team's job, as always, is to provoke a serious discussion to ensure that the audience buys in to the PTW view or, if not, how their views differ, and why.

In any event, PTW practitioners must always take copious notes and be *infocentric* by documenting comments and pre-positioning all new information by ingesting it into the corporate Infocenter.

Conclusion

From Top Down PTW to the Partially and Fully Gamed Bottoms Up PTWs

In **Figure V.7**, which we have already seen in Section II, we are told that the 3-Phase, 10-Step PTW Framework progresses for a particular competitor from an Addressable Budget, to a Phase 1 Top Down Target Price, to a Bottoms Up, "Partially Gamed" PTW, to this, the Fully Gamed PTW.

Figure V.8 reiterates how the three phases within the PTW Framework waterfall to produce the Fully Gamed PTW. The phases are driven by the latest available acquisition documents and, all the time, interact with pre-positioned and freshly acquired information that is accessioned to the Home Team's Infocenter as it is acquired.

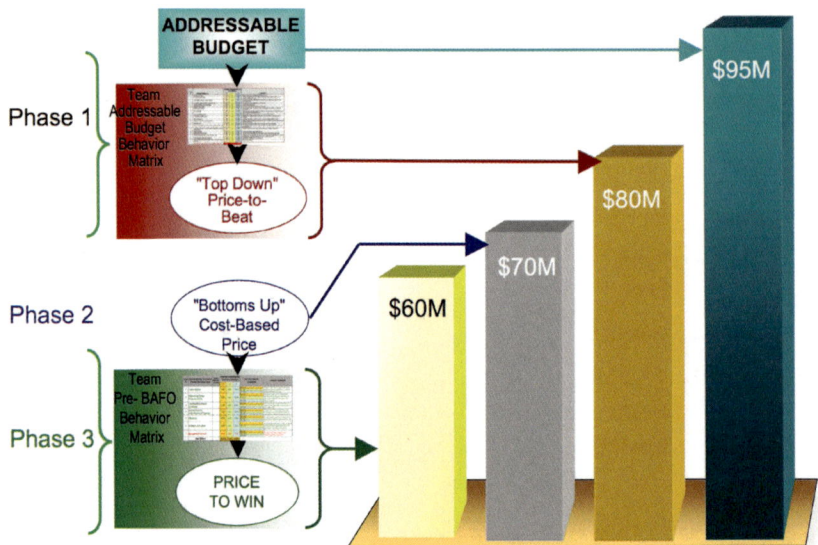

FIGURE V.7

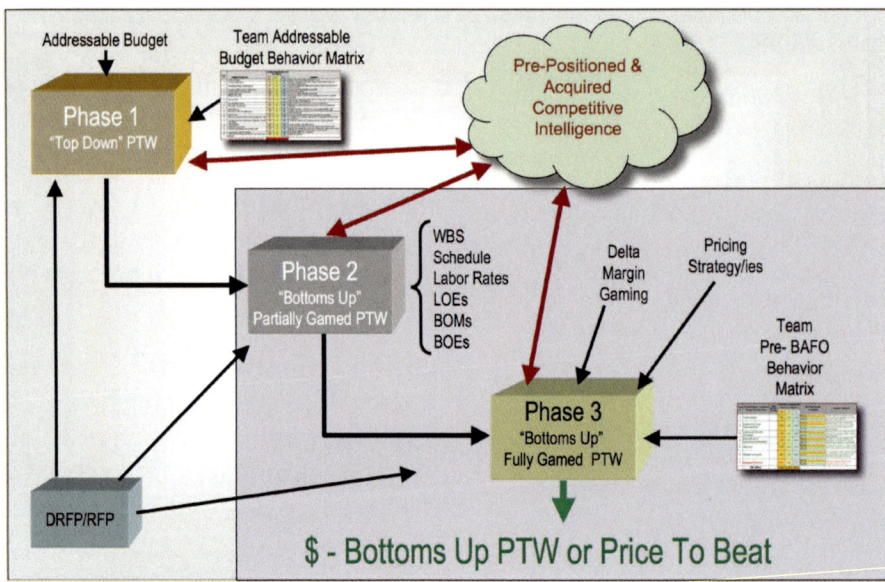

FIGURE V.8

How the Fully Gamed PTW Is Related to pWin

Our Bottoms Up PTW process (Phases 2 and 3 of the PTW Framework) has now developed a:

- Partially Gamed PTW; and
- Fully Gamed PTW—the Partially Gamed PTW adjusted for the aggregate affect of competitor/s anticipated price gaming (i.e., Delta Margin Gaming (DMG), other strategies, take-down tables, etc.).

We now need to develop a Final, Fully Gamed PTW which is the Fully Gamed PTW plus *or* minus a "comfort factor." We will get to that in a moment, but right now is a good time to ask why.

As we have gone through each of the three phases, our goal has always been to have the Home Team be the marginally highest award point scoring team. This equates to winning by a very small monetary margin, and it is not often the case that major bids are won by small amounts, especially if an incumbent is involved.

We know that pWin = f(P, NP, SP, μ), where:

- P = Price factors;
- NP = Non-Price factors;
- SP = Strategic Pricing factors; and
- μ = Error term, which is analogous to what we are calling our "comfort factor."

Thus, we can assert that the relationship between PTW and pWin is:

- Partially Gamed PTW = f(P, NP);
- Fully Gamed PTW = f(P, NP, SP); and
- Final, Fully Gamed PTW = f(P, NP, SP, μ).

This last item, the Final, Fully Gamed PTW delivers a pWin of 1 (i.e., 100%). Not .87, not .93, but 1.

All PTW deals with are pWins of 1.

Setting the Home Team's Final, Fully Gamed PTW

So as our PTW study draws to a close, we will have, for each of the targeted competitors, a:

- Phase 1 budget-based Top Down PTW result;
- Phase 2 Bottoms Up Partially Gamed PTW result; and a
- Phase 3 Bottoms Up Fully Gamed PTW result.

Figure V.9 presents a phase-by-phase recapitulation of where each targeted competitive bid team and the Home Team ended up. The prices shown in the table contributed to overall phase point scores that enabled the Home Team to win in terms of overall points by often small price margins.

To accomplish this and stay in the game, the Home Team was given the following price targets:

- Phase 1—$127.5M;
- Phase 2—$121M; and
- Phase 3—$101M.

Since well-performing incumbents and otherwise strong competitors are unlikely to be beaten by a small dollar amount, the Home Team, in this instance, is judged by the PTW Team to need a comfort factor of ~-5% to bring them under Competitor #2's likely Fully Gamed Bid Price, which points to the Home Team's need for a Final, Fully Gamed PTW of $95.95M.

PTW Phase Recapitulation	All $ In $M				Home Team Comfort Factor	
	#1	#2	#3	Home Team	-5%	
Addressable Budget	$141.02					
Phase 1 "Top Down" Results	$123.40	$130.45	$135.00	$127.50		
Phase 2 "Bottoms Up" Partially Gamed Results	$132.00	$125.00	$127.50	$121.00		
Phase 3 "Bottoms Up" Fully Gamed Results	$105.60	$96.88	$127.50	$101.00	$95.95	Is the recommended PTW

FIGURE V.9

> **Remember:**
> **You can only do the job**
> **if you can win the job.**

Phase 3 of the Progressive PTW Problem

As explained in the book's Foreword, Section VII of this book presents a PTW problem that progresses from Phase 1 to Phase 2 before concluding with Phase 3. Microsoft Excel spreadsheet models pertaining to the PTW Framework phases are available on demand by emailing a request to:

training@caisisco.com

For those who are interested in pursuing the progressive PTW problem that relates to this, the third and final phase of the 3-Phase, 10-Step PTW Framework, please locate Phase 3 of the Progressive PTW Problem in Section VII of this book.

Section VI

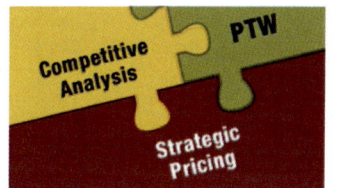

Food for PTW Thought

PTW practitioners must, in a general sense, become students of the entire environment in which their employers and/or customers operate. The reasoning is this: the broader your environmental understanding, the easier it will be to appreciate opportunity specifics. Following are several general "food for thought" issues that PTW practitioners should consider—there are many, many more.

Routes to the Government Labor Market

Granted, every government market for labor is somewhat unique, and there are some global issues that transcend specific situations. **Figure VI.1** that follows does several things.

First, the column entitled **Labor Rate Categories** shows high end (e.g., those that deal with C-level executives such as CIOs, CTO, CFOs and the like), mid range (e.g., solution architects down to designers and developers), and low end labor (e.g., computer operators, service desk staffers, down to the those who pick up dead animals from military base runways, etc.) categories.

In itself, this is probably no great revelation. When, however, this is linked with the brackets shown to the left of the labor rate categories column, the concept of "corporate personality" comes into focus a little more.

The purple bracket, at least in the U.S. federal government marketplace, should, in my opinion, bring to mind firms such as Accenture, Booz-Allen, and Deloitte. The red bracket may bring to mind companies like Computer Sciences Corporation (CSC), Lockheed Martin, and SAIC. The green bracket, in my view, applies to no firm I can cite.

The other aspect to the Labor Market graphic that should appeal to PTW practitioners is what company attributes entitle which companies to supply labor, at least, to the U.S. government. As shown under **Contracting Avenues for Acquiring Labor**, most U.S. government contracts can only be awarded to companies that are certified as being Cost Accounting Standards (CAS) compliant.

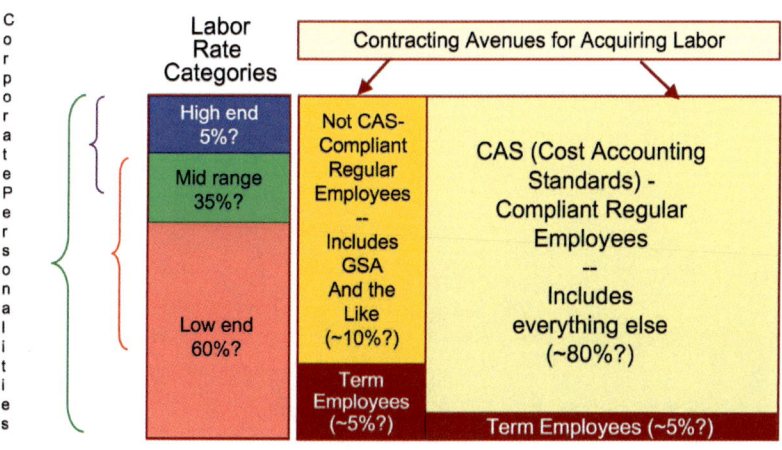

FIGURE VI.1

The graphic suggests that this may be ~80% of all labor that the U.S. government buys from contractors; it could easily be higher than that. The remainder of labor that contractors supply comes from non-CAS compliant sources (these include GSA Schedule holders) and from staff augmentation firms who have been showing up on bid teams supplying term employees on a "We've got a job, you've got a job" basis.

PTW practitioners must become students of the competitive environment, be curious about why things are the way they are, and be interested in learning everything they can about the competition.

The Landscape Is Always Changing

Nothing stays the same forever, even in the marketplace for goods and services provided to government. The economic downturns that are experienced nationally or globally from time to time can have profound implications.

To most investment houses, the rates of return that are typically enjoyed by government contractors usually generate little or no interest. Economic downturns, however, have the effect of making government contractors quite desirable when contrasted with commercially-oriented counterparts.

Accordingly, in an otherwise volatile commercial market, a number of prominent government contractors have been acquired precisely because of their long-term business basis, accompanied by their modest, yet predictable, margins.

Here are a couple of questions (and answers) for those who are, and those who aspire to become, PTW practitioners.

Question 1—What do the following U.S. companies have in common?

- ARINC
- Booz-Allen
- Dyncorp International
- Schafer Corporation
- SRA International
- TASC
- Vangent

Answer 1—At the time of publication, each of these firms was owned by U.S. investment groups such as Carlyle, Cerebus, KKR, and Veritas. There are more examples and there are likely to be even more in the future.

Question 2—What do you suppose these new owners have in mind as their long-term strategy?

Answer 2—Multiple choice—some or all of these? Will they...

- Squeeze costs to improve profits?
- Bid aggressively to put business on their books? and/or
- Ready these firms for resale?

When engaged in predicting a future that includes firms in this phase of their existence, PTW practitioners must engage in a measure of crystal ball gazing.

Additional Thoughts on Developing a Top-Down PTW

Of course, a budget or estimated cost for a specific opportunity may or may not be realistic. For instance, according to a *Washington Post* article on a post-award over-billing scandal, in the heady days following 9/11:

> The Transportation Security Administration (TSA) hired a contractor "to create a state-of-the-art computer network linking thousands of federal employees at hundreds of airports to the TSA's high-tech security centers." When the opportunity was competed and awarded, it had a $1 billion ceiling value. The then TSA CIO who managed the acquisition was reported as saying, "The $1 billion was simply a guess to get the project started," and that "we knew at the time that the project would cost closer to $3 billion, but the $1 billion figure was used because it would be more palatable to Congress."

Surely this is an indictable admission. This is the way the world sometimes works—not just in government, either. "We'll pretend to estimate the cost and you (Congress) pretend to exercise oversight," to paraphrase the old Russian aphorism about the worker pretending to work while the employer pretends to pay the worker. Perhaps "government oversight" and "Congressional oversight" should both be 21st century oxymorons?

The U.S. Federal Government Staff Augmentation Marketplace

The U.S. government indirectly employs contractors to consult to, or support, government activities. Many contractors work on-site at government installations, while others work at contractor sites or in the field. This contractor workforce includes "solution" vendors, developers of all sorts, and outsourcers. These contractor employees are the *arm's length* government workforce.

This contractor workforce can be viewed as a huge sports arena where the major blocks of seats equate to government departments (e.g., Education, Treasury, Army, etc.) and these major blocks are further subdivided into major agencies and other activities. Seats are temporarily owned by their incumbent contractors and industry players compete to put their corporate imprimaturs on as many contract personnel seats as possible to:

- Maintain/increase revenues;
- Lower overheads and other costs; and
- Earn fee.

The size of the federal civilian government workforce is a deceptive measure of the size of government. As U.S. citizens continue to demand more government services, while the politicians claim to be reducing the government's size, government activities have turned increasingly to a workforce employed through contracts (not counting grants and mandates to state and local governments).

So, how big is this "arm's length" federal workforce? A *Wall Street Journal* (WSJ) article pegged the size of the U.S.'s "arm's length government workforce" in the government fiscal year (FY) 2000 as being comprised of ~12.7M souls who were costing $208B per year. This number is far greater than the ~4.25M direct employee head count at the time, which combined:

- The federal civilian workforce;
- U.S. postal workers; and
- All uniformed military personnel.

In FY 2006, the WSJ reported that federal contractor expenditures had risen to $423B—this rise was largely explained by the aftermath of 9/11.

More recently, the WSJ reported that in FY 2009, Federal contract spending reached $525B.

Altogether, the true FY 2010 federal workforce approaches ~17M, a figure that is almost nine times the size of the *actual federal civilian workforce of ~2M*—this being the reference group upon which reduced government head count claims made by politicians are typically based.

The Public-Private Partnership

Pay attention, PTW practitioners—government and industry maintain a mutual revolving door. This reality will diminish your effectiveness if you don't embrace it and wrestle it to the ground.

Career government people, with residual "access" to their former government employers, retire to join contractors or start their own consulting shops.

Employees of major contractors temporarily join the government for tours of duty to:

- Enhance their personal access and otherwise further their careers; or
- Fulfill their destinies as political appointees.

PTW practitioners must track and remember these relationship realities and make sure that they are brought out when SWOTs are being compiled and evaluation award point scores are being assessed.

The Other Big Bangs

The universe, and the Big Bang theory that appears to have supported its creation, have parallels to other environments—even the government contracting world. Medicine and technology are both involved in their own big bangs.

Every year in medicine, there are new procedures, new drugs, and even new diseases. Scientists in each of these areas are seeking financial support and remuneration and, at present, most appear to be succeeding. But how long can this really go on until a funding wall is reached?

The same is true with technology. At CAI/SISCo, we see technology concurrently expanding in all directions. One area that resonates is related to fire suppression in tanks and other military vehicles after taking a major ammunition round.

In a WW II era military vehicle, one might have counted oneself lucky if there were even an old fashioned fire extinguisher. Today, with advances in technology, it is possible to deploy an inert gas within a split second of receiving a hit. This can stop the vehicle's fuel source from exploding and, as a consequence, stop the vehicle's occupants from being incinerated.

Of course, these systems are far from free and, in any event, it is unlikely that we are going to scrimp on such items if they can be proven to improve survival odds for our best and bravest. However, technology too, is headed toward the funding wall.

Most areas of government generate more requests for project funding than there is available budget. This situation, too, must resolve itself. In the current fiscal climate, we are likely to end up spreading around the pain in such a way that all contractors are going to need to find less expensive ways of accomplishing more. This, surely, is an open door for Price To Win and everything it represents.

A Cautionary Incumbency Tale

Because PTW is focused on what competitive prime contractors and bid teams have done and could do, PTW practitioners are sometimes accused of being low-ballers. This would be valid criticism, except that, even for PTW, bid prices must always be supported with a roadmap showing how targeted competitors are likely to improve their overall profitability over time—not a "get well" strategy, but rather a "get better" strategy.

As a case in point, in the mid-1980s, three bid teams, each headed by one of the Inter-Exchange Carrier (IXC) behemoths of the day, squared off to compete for two FTS2000 contract berths worth billions under the U.S. General Services Administration's (GSA) Federal Telephone Service (FTS) vehicle. The contract supplied long distance telecommunications services to federal agencies on a "mandatory use" basis. Price competition for an FTS2000 berth, even for its day, was brutal. For instance, over the contract's 10-year life, the price for a minute of long distance telephone time plummeted from an initial price of $.27 to about $.05. A large portion of these prices charged by the IXCs was paid to local exchange carriers (LEC) to connect users, by means of local access, to the IXC networks *and* to connect from the IXC network to the user at the other end of the end-to-end circuit.

A primitive form of PTW was practiced to derive competitive price points but, as evidenced by the following, precious little effort was devoted to the "get better" side of PTW. As a result, at least one of the two FTS2000 awardees had been leaving tens of millions of dollars of pure profit on the table. Here's the story:

> As the FTS2000 contract got underway, orders rolled in. At that time, the mainstay of data communications was the T1 circuit. As you may know, a T1 circuit can carry up to about 1.5 million bits per second (Mbps), which can be split into 24 64 Kbps voice grade circuits. Of greater significance, however, is the fact that 24 voice grade lines could be carried over a T1 circuit and 28 T1 circuits could be carried by a single T3 circuit, but at about one third of the monthly recurring charge (MRC) of an equivalent number of voice grade lines or T1 circuits. For the same run, the MRC of a T3 from a LEC was roughly equivalent to the LEC's MRC for 10 T1s and, the MRC ratio was about the same for sub-T1 service.

Many of the orders that rolled in were for multiple T1 and sub-T1 circuits. Pretty soon, many government locations had ordered enough sub-T1s to justify consolidating over a single T1 and a lot of locations could have economically consolidated required T1s into T3s. And the orders kept on rolling in. By the end of the 10-year contract, it was estimated that at least 250,000 T1 circuit months had been bought from LECs that could have been aggregated into far fewer T3 circuits, and reduced the cost basis for each T1 circuit by at least 50%. The same was true for voice grade lines. Astoundingly, even though there was no requirement to pass cost savings on to the government customer, no optimization occurred.

But that was then, when the telecommunications companies were fat, dumb, and happy. The point is that they could have easily been fatter, less dumb, and much happier.

Additional Pricing Strategies for PTW Practitioners

As alluded to in Section V, there are scores of pricing strategies that strategic pricers and PTW practitioners can employ to create the competitor and Home Team bid prices. PTW practitioners need to be aware of these and ensure that their own gaming meets and beats the competitive realities of the competitors. Some of these strategies can only be used in isolation against a particular CLIN whereas, in other cases, multiple strategies can be successfully applied to a single CLIN.

Generally speaking, PTW uses many of these strategies as it converges on its Final, Fully Gamed PTWs for targeted competitors. Below is a list of some of the more common pricing strategies, along with a short explanation of each one.

The **Joint Venture** strategy seeks to leave behind both risk and/or JV partner prevailing overhead realities by creating a new or different bidding entity. Some customers do not look favorably on JV proposers. This is because they are often seen as "flags of convenience," i.e., convenient to the involved contractors, not advantageous to the customer. Be advised that a JV can be either a "populated" JV (i.e., one with an existing base of business and staff), or an "unpopulated" JV (i.e., one with no existing book of business or staff).

The **Milestone Payment** strategy seeks to define and lock in invoiceable events that a bidder can use to avoid otherwise onerous payment lead times and financing costs.

The **Cash in Hand** strategy is aimed at moving as many payments as possible to the left in time to, once again, avoid otherwise onerous payment lead times and financing costs.

The **Pricing Notes** strategy adds elaborations to a cost volume that interpret or define the limits of a pricing issue. For instance, if our cost volume includes an explanation of how we have developed blended labor rates for our bid team's labor categories, we might also want to add a pricing note that says, "We reserve the right to charge *unblended* labor rates for the team member who actually does the work."

The **Fixed Cost Allocation** strategy is aimed at recouping fixed costs independently of how and when variable cost items are ordered. For instance, this could cover recouping the cost of standing up a Project Management Office (PMO) as part of some Non-Recurring Engineering (NRE) activity.

The **Strange Attractor** strategy is used whenever an opportunity calls for a preponderance of ODC items but also includes a small amount of finitely evaluated labor. What may be possible with this strategy is to remove labor from an ODC's cost build-up by requesting that a labor Task Order (TO) be issued to cover the ODC-specific labor out of the pool of evaluated labor.

The **Labor Rate** strategies include team blending, Uncompensated Overtime (UOT), and even shaving small uplift portions from things like labor rate escalators by only applying them to the labor complement that is expected to remain at the end of a given contract year based on historical, expected attrition.

The **Lego** or **Prerequisite Pricing** strategy seeks to manage customer buying behavior by linking certain actions such as upgrading a server to having to buy upgrades and additional maintenance coverage from the contractor.

The **Capacity Pricing** strategy seeks to debrand or commoditize items with respect to forward pricing. For example, an RFP may suggest that brand name items such as printers or storage devices are favored. Compliance issues aside, by opting for capacity pricing, regardless of the actual item brand the bidder bids, future refreshes will be tied to the capability costs of generic devices (i.e., pages per minute printed, or GBs or TBs of storage) rather than brand named devices.

The **Technology Deflation** strategy allows a bidder to develop forward prices for ODCs by creating curves that deflate (or inflate) prices over time to approximate where axioms like Moore's Law are taking future technology prices. Moore's Law has it that the density of transistors on a chip doubles every two years.

The **Unequal Product Averaging** strategy takes a basket of equivalent products (e.g., printers) and produces an average price for evaluation purposes while the individual product prices will be charged for at pre-average prices when ordered.

The **Brown Bag** or **OOH** (that is Out Of Hide) strategy avoids having to price and being price evaluated for certain deliverables by making them the subject of, for instance, a lunchtime group deliverable development activity.

The **Demand Elasticity** strategy seeks to use small changes in price to stimulate large increases in demand that, presumably, generate more profit for the contractor.

The **Exploitation of Unrealistic Evaluation Quantities** strategy is covered in great depth in Section V of this book under *PTW Framework Phase 3, Step 8—The Reality Model*.

The **Bid All Options** strategy develops bids that include as many options as possible to push demand toward higher priced, more profitable, and presumably not evaluated options.

The **System Warranty and Maintenance** strategy seeks to bundle warranties and maintenance into the purchase price of each item, rather than risk the aftermarket revenues being cannibalized by others.

The **Lease** strategy provides customers with an often more immediately affordable and less risky (in terms of obsolescence) option to item use than by acquiring the item directly. By using this strategy, contractors may be able to charge more profitable price points and/or they can sell product to the maximum number and types of customer users.

For each gaming strategy earmarked for attribution to a targeted competitive team, the PTW practitioner has to:

- Establish its relevance;
- Develop a rationale for its use; and
- Possibly, provide sketches of how the strategies might be employed by the PTW targets for:
  - Initial submission; and
  - Best And Final Offer (BAFO).

Figure VI.2 presents a synopsis of the differences between the Initial Submission and the BAFO.

Characteristics	Initial Submission	BAFO
Overall Goals	Gain pricing strategy and notes approval and be in competitive range	Win with lowest evaluated price at an acceptable profit level
Risk	Assess for strategies	Mitigate and accept
Quantity Basis	Evaluated only	Estimated reality
Strategy Employment	Strategic framework included, tacit approval sought	Underlying strategies exploited within the tacitly approved framework
Pricing Basis	Discounted only	Discounted, forward priced, and gamed

FIGURE VI.2

A Word about Unintended Consequences

The law of unintended consequences is alive and well. Back in the 1970s, there was a U.S. Air Force opportunity that evaluated a large number of minicomputers and a small number of routers that the Air Force wanted to acquire. The winning bidder evidently had no appreciation of the router's pivotal role in what has become the Internet—in those days it was the Advanced Research Projects Agency Network (ARPANET)—a DOD initiative. So, ignorance led these guys to promulgate a pricing strategy that underpriced routers (which they saw no reason for anyone to want to buy) and overpriced the minicomputers. Once Air Force activities became aware that bargain basement priced routers were now available, a line formed at the contractor's door.

Faced with having to meet such demand, the contractor could have been forced into bankruptcy. The day was apparently saved by a little known U.S. Federal Acquisition Regulation (FAR) clause that states that: "A contractor does not have to supply more of an item than the government evaluated."

General Research Sources

Finding Opportunity, Agency and Competitor Information

Open Source information is generally available online from:

Blogs

Business, Trade and Professional Associations*

AFCEA, AFA, AFIO, AOC, ASIS, AUSA, GEIA, ISOA, Navy League, NDIA, Army Aviation Association, Surface Navy Association, Naval Submarine League, etc.:

- National organization and local chapter information
- Publications (e.g., AFCEA Signal & Sourcebook, JED, National Defense, and many, many others)

Chambers of Commerce, Regional Marketing, Development, Advancement Organizations, Alliances, Partnerships, Councils

Company Websites:

- Annual Reports/Quarterly Reports
- Descriptions of products, services, contract vehicles, etc.
- Investor briefings
- Company newsletters
- Job postings
- Organization charts and executive bios
- Press releases and speeches
- White papers, product and service literature

Daily Newspapers (National & Local)*:

- *Wall Street Journal, Washington Post*, etc.—too numerous to list

Industry Events*:

- Corporate sponsorship and corporate profile blurbs, exhibitor information, etc.
- Programs, speaker bios, and presentations
- Small business outreach event presentations
- Trade show marketing collateral and business cards

Trade Press* (examples only—this is by no means an exhaustive list!):

- *Air Force/Army/Navy Times*
- *Armada*
- *Armed Forces Journal*
- *Aviation Week & Space Technology*
- *Bloomberg*
- *C4ISR Journal*
- *Defense Daily*
- *Defense News*
- *Federal Computer News (FCW)*
- *Government Computer News (GCN)*
- *Government Executive*

- *Inside Defense*
- *Janes* (includes *Documental Solutions*)
- KMI Media Group (e.g., *Military Information Technology*, etc.)
- Spaceref.com
- *Washington Business Journal*
- *Washington Technology*

Government-Wide Acquisition and Other Government Websites:

- FedBizopps.gov—Opportunity synopses, interested parties lists, Industry Day attendance lists
- Defenselink.mil—Contract award announcements

Individual Government Agency Websites:

- Acquisition websites and forecasts
- Departmental budget requests
- Contract award announcements
- RFIs/RFPs and bidder lists
- Price lists—GSA schedule, state and local government multi-award contracts of various stripes
- Org charts, key executive bios, etc.

Social Media*:

- LinkedIn, Facebook, etc. and public profile data
- Glassdoor.com

Other Open Source Information (Government and Non-Government):

- Legal pleadings and judicial opinions
- Bid protest decisions
- Congressional hearing testimony
- GAO reports
- Redacted FOIA request results
- Federation of American Scientists
- Global Security.org
- Inspector General reports
- POGO

Commercially-available Subscription Databases*:

- Airframer
- Carroll Publishing
- Centurion
- Deltek (FedSources and INPUT)
- EagleEye
- Forecast International
- Frost & Sullivan
- Gale Directory
- …and many others

Note: Subscription and/or membership fees may be required for access.

**Remember:
PTW practitioners and all others must respect copyrights and terms of use.**

Section VII

The Progressive Price To Win (PTW) Problem

The Progressive PTW Problem presented in this section tracks a hypothetical opportunity (explained on the next page) through the phases of the 3-Phase, 10-Step Price To Win (PTW) Framework. While the opportunity that underpins this progressive problem presents its fair share of the twists and turns that a PTW practitioner experiences with real opportunity pursuits, it, of course, represents only a small subset of the work that would actually be required to research and analyze an actual opportunity through the framework phases.

Please read the appropriate book sections before engaging with the corresponding phase of the problem. You will notice that, as we progress from PTW phase to PTW phase, more information becomes available to the PTW practitioner. Enjoy the experience!

Note: The models that underlie the opportunity are available upon request by sending an email entitled **PTW Models Please** to: training@caisisco.com

Phase 1 of the Progressive PTW Problem

As shown in **Figure VII.1** below, Phase 1 of the PTW Framework involves Steps 1 and 2.

Phase 1 of the problem will allow you to determine:

- The customer's addressable budget;
- Competitor *top down* target prices to be developed based on past pricing behaviors; and
- The Home Team's *top down* PTW.

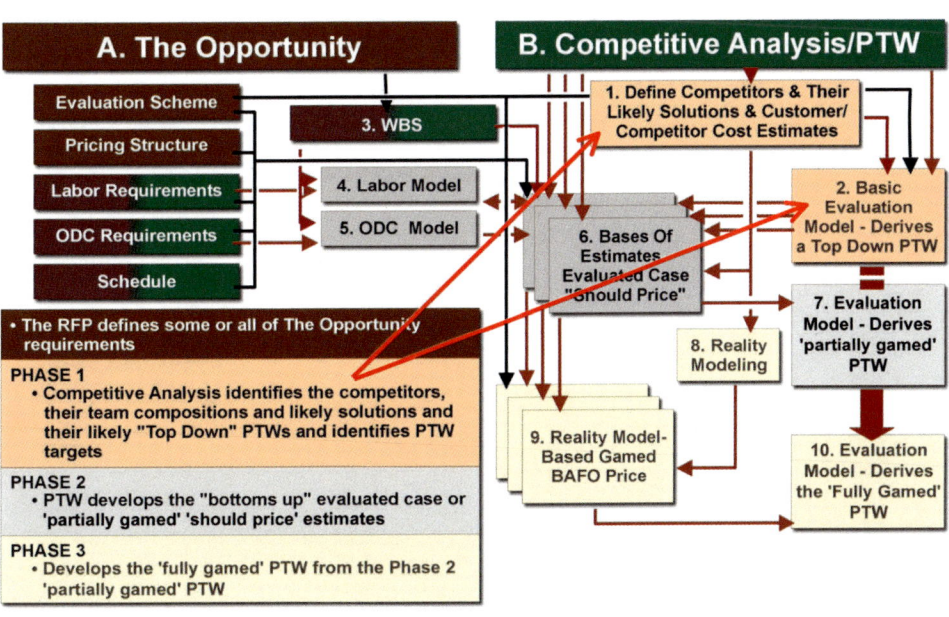

FIGURE VII.1

103

Understanding the ITCON Opportunity

ITCON, short for IT Consolidation, is a hypothetical five-year Firm, Fixed Price (FFP) opportunity at a minor government agency to consolidate three existing, geographically distributed, yet identical customer IT Operating Environments (OEs) into a single OE.

PTW research has distilled and/or developed the following competitive information: two of the existing OEs are small, with 50 users each, while the third is large, with 500 users.

According to the rather sketchy Draft RFP (DRFP), the successful bidder must:

- Take over the three "as is" OEs;
- Design and develop the "to be" environment;
- Plan the transition from the "as is" to the "to be";
- Implement and test the "to be" OE;
- Migrate the users; and
- Provide O&M (service desk, maintenance, etc.).

All elements of the consolidated solution can either be on or off the customer site. Other issues:

- The consolidated OE must be in operation with all users migrated within 18 months After Contract Award (ACA);
- "Best value" applies (see Section I for a refresher on this); and
- Small Business (SB) content has to be 25%, or more, of all labor dollars.

According to the DRFP, the contract excludes all site infrastructure and user equipment. In addition, the existing equipment originally cost $1M and has a remaining economic life of three years. This equipment can be acquired by bidders as part of their "to be" solution according to the following discount schedule:

- By the end of CY1 at 60% of acquisition cost; and
- By the end of CY2 at 30% of acquisition cost.

The customer's addressable budget over the five-year contractual period can be approximated as follows:

- Presently, the customer spends $600 per month, per user; but
- The customer's goal is to reduce its OE operating costs by 30% within two years ACA with no user head count change.

The ITCON Competitors

The competitors consist of us (the Home Team) and them.

The **Home Team** is HAL, a forward-looking Large Business (LB) systems integrator that has lots of relevant experience but no history with the ITCON customer. Our team is rounded out with Small Business (SB) PQR, who is the incumbent O&M contractor for one of the small "as is" OEs.

Our (i.e., HAL's) solution is to buy OE capacity on a utility basis at a Telco's data center. This type of solution provides our team with the advantage of built-in diverse communications.

The Competitive Bid Teams

PTW research to date has identified the following two teams as our competitors:

1. **Team ABC**, headed by ABC who is a Large Business (LB). This team is bidding a solution that consolidates the two smaller OEs into the largest existing on-site OE facility. It turns out that ABC is the incumbent O&M contractor for the largest OE.

2. **Team XYZ**, headed by XYZ, a Small Business (SB) outsourcer. This team is likely to be bidding a consolidated off-site "to be" solution hosted at their corporate data center. DEF is on this team—they are the O&M incumbent for the other small "as is" OE.

Past Bid Behavior

PTW's research has developed the following information about competitor past bid behaviors with respect to target pricing within a known addressable budget. This information supports Approach #1 (see Section III for a refresher) for setting target prices.

ABC has bid and won three similar jobs in the recent past:

- A 5-year consolidation/O&M job for which the budget was $50M and which was won for $35M;
- A 10-year consolidation/O&M job for which the budget was $100M and which was won for $77.5M; and
- A 3-year consolidation/O&M job for which the budget was $50M and which was won for $45M.

XYZ has also bid and won three similar jobs in the recent past:

- A 7-year consolidation/O&M job for which the budget was $250M and which was won for $188.5M;
- A 15-year consolidation/O&M job for which the budget was $100M and which was won for $99.5M; and
- A 5-year consolidation/O&M job for which the budget was $50M and which was won for $47.5M.

What Needs to Be Done

Use the information provided by PTW research and the ***Phase 1 Models.xls*** Excel spreadsheet book to complete the referenced tables.

First is the year-by-year **Addressable Budget Table** (**Figure VII.2**). This panel is located directly under the Evaluation Model panel shown on Excel page *Eval Model—Not Done*.

$0	Total Budget ($M)
$0	CY1 ($)
$0	CY2 ($)
$0	CY3 ($)
$0	CY4 ($)
$0	CY5 ($)

FIGURE VII.2

Enter your view of ITCON's Addressable Budget by Contract Year (CY) in the green font cells. The red font cell will calculate automatically. Note that entries are in integer dollars.

Next, we need to populate the **Top Down PTW History Table**, as shown in **Figure VII.3**, which is Excel page *Top Down—Not Done*, to calculate Team ABC's and Team XYZ's likely Addressable Budget "take-down" percentages.

This is accomplished by entering each competitor's historical citation data provided earlier under this heading into the correct table's relevant green cells. Each team's historical weighted average "Bid to Addressable Budget" % is calculated by the model.

ABC Relevant Program Citations	Addressable Budget ($M)	Bid Price ($M)	Bid $ as % of Budget
Cite 1	$0.0	$0.0	0.00%
Cite 2	$0.0	$0.0	0.00%
Cite 3	$0.0	$0.0	0.00%
ALL	$0	$0	0.00%

XYZ Relevant Program Citations	Addressable Budget ($M)	Bid Price ($M)	Bid $ as % of Budget
Cite 1	$0.0	$0.0	0.00%
Cite 2	$0.0	$0.0	0.00%
Cite 3	$0.0	$0.0	0.00%
ALL	$0	$0	0.00%

FIGURE VII.3

By completing the aforementioned Phase 1 tables, the Team ABC and Team XYZ target prices will appear in the **Evaluation Model** panel shown below in **Figure VII.4** (Excel page *Eval Model—Not Done*) overwriting the red font cells. The non-price evaluation issue areas have been pre-scored for HAL and the competitive teams.

Now use the live Evaluation Model to overwrite the green font cell to determine what price HAL will need to be targeting to marginally achieve an overall point score win—all other evaluation items being equal.

It should take you no more than 30 minutes to complete this task to establish HAL's *Top Down* PTW target. Please save your spreadsheets.

How close to the solution provided did you come?

This concludes the Phase 1 part of the Sample Problem. As you move on to Phase 2 of the problem, remember that the information provided later may supersede the available Phase 1 information. This is often the case in real life since, as time progresses and more relevant information is learned, opinions on all sorts of issues can change. For instance, a DRFP evaluation set may include an evaluation criterion that is dropped from the RFP.

ITCON Proposal Evaluation Criteria (PEC)	Available Points	Team Adjectival Score (Out of 10)			Normalized Scores		
		ABC	XYZ	HAL	ABC	XYZ	HAL
Overall Evaluation	1000				521.3	523.1	515.6
Overall Evaluation Rank					(2)	(1)	(3)
Non-Cost	600				521.3	523.1	515.6
Non-Cost Evaluation Rank					(2)	(1)	(3)
Factor 1 - Technical Approach	275				238.8	238.8	236.3
Rank					(1)	(1)	(3)
Subfactor 1: Enterprise Services	100	8.50	9.00	8.75	85.0	90.0	87.5
Subfactor 2: Transition	100	9.00	8.50	8.50	90.0	85.0	85.0
Subfactor 3: Contractor's Performance Work Statement & WBS	75	8.50	8.50	8.50	63.8	63.8	63.8
Factor 2 - Management	225				195.0	194.4	194.4
Rank					(1)	(2)	(2)
Subfactor 1: Program Leadership	100	9.00	8.75	8.75	90.0	87.5	87.5
Subfactor 2: Subcontractor Management	75	8.50	8.25	8.25	63.8	61.9	61.9
Subfactor 3: Metrics & SLA Reporting & Management	50	8.25	9.00	9.00	41.3	45.0	45.0
Factor 3 - Past Performance	100	8.75	9.00	8.50	87.5	90.0	85.0
Rank					(2)	(1)	(3)
Factor 4 - Price ($M)	400	$ -	$ -	$ -	0.0	0.0	0.0
Rank					(1)	(1)	(1)

FIGURE VII.4

Phase 2 of the Progressive PTW Problem

As shown in **Figure VII.5** below, Phase 2 of the PTW Framework involves Steps 3 through 7.

Phase 2 of the ITCON problem will allow you to determine:

- The competitors' Bill Of Materials (BOM) and their labor requirements;
- Competitor *Bottoms Up* partially gamed prices to be developed;
- Needed changes to non-cost evaluation scores; and
- The Home Team's *partially gamed* PTW.

Needed ITCON Capture Team Support

Based on the recently released ITCON RFP, the HAL Capture Team needs to develop a five-year Bottoms Up PTW for each of the ITCON competitors, Team ABC and Team XYZ, by developing their likely:

- Labor categories, team member shares and category usage estimates;
- Bills Of Materials (BOM) for expected competitive solutions; and
- Overall partially gamed PTW supported by Basis Of Estimates (BOE).

Once this has been accomplished, HAL must apply the BOE results to the Evaluation Model (which did not change from the DRFP to the RFP), as it stood at the end of Phase 1. Then we develop a modified *partially gamed* PTW target for HAL's Capture Team based on this analysis, considering the following newer competitive information.

More Intelligence

Since PTW research never sleeps, we have accumulated a number of new competitive snowflakes, as follows:

- ABC has received an innovation award from the ITCON customer;
- XYZ has just been thrown out of an unrelated customer account and is being sued for its inability to transition that customer's existing user base both on schedule and within budget. This has made it to the national press; and
- We, HAL, have arranged a corporate agreement with global telco, WorldTel, to provide value-added services, such as Continuity Of Operations (COOP), which are believed to be significant issues related to the enterprise services evaluation sub-factor.

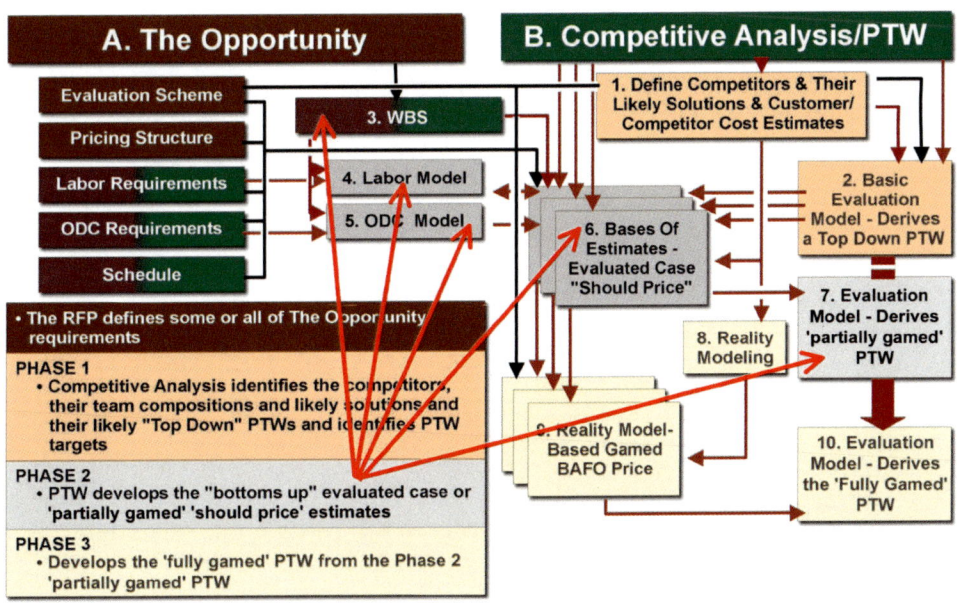

FIGURE VII.5

In addition, PTW research has discovered that the ITCON customer has 50 server-based applications. Unfortunately, it turns out that ABC presently maintains 10 of this customer's applications while the customer maintains the other 40 in-house.

What Needs to Be Done

Use the information provided by PTW research and/or the RFP and the ***Phase 2 Models.xls*** Excel spreadsheet book to complete the referenced tables.

The **Bill Of Materials (BOM)** estimation is accomplished using the *BOM—Not Done* page in the Phase 2 book.

The first BOM related issue for each of the targeted competitive bid teams is whether their solutions are to be implemented on or off of the customer's site. **Figure VII.6** for Teams ABC and XYZ covers both on-site—the blue cells—and off of the customer's site—the yellow cells.

	Team ABC ITCON BOM Elements	Periodicity	Period Cost	Team ABC's 5-Year BOM by BOM Item				
				CY1	CY2	CY3	CY4	CY5
1	On-Site Site Preparation	One Time	$100,000	0	0	0	0	0
2	On-Site Hardware	One Time	$1,000,000	0	0	0	0	0
3	On-Site COTS Software	One Time	$1,000,000	0	0	0	0	0
4	On-Site Installation & Test	One Time	$50,000	0	0	0	0	0
5	On-Site Telecom Non-Recurring Charge (NRC)	One Time	$0	0	0	0	0	0
6	On-Site Telecom Monthly Recurring Charge (MRC)	Monthly	$7,500	0	0	0	0	0
7	On-Site Hardware & Software Maintenance	Monthly	$16,667	0	0	0	0	0
8	Off-Site Space (includes HVAC)	Monthly	$16,667	0	0	0	0	0
9	Off-Site Site Preparation	One Time	$0	0	0	0	0	0
10	Off-Site Hardware	One Time	$600,000	0	0	0	0	0
11	Off-Site COTS Software	One Time	$1,000,000	0	0	0	0	0
12	Off-Site Installation & Test	One Time	$50,000	0	0	0	0	0
13	Off-Site Telecom Non-Recurring Charge (NRC)	One Time	$5,000	0	0	0	0	0
14	Off-Site Telecom Monthly Recurring Charge (MRC)	Monthly	$12,500	0	0	0	0	0
15	Off-Site Hardware & Software Maintenance	Monthly	$13,333	0	0	0	0	0

	Team XYZ ITCON BOM Elements	Periodicity	Period Cost	Team XYZ's 5-Year BOM by BOM Item				
				CY1	CY2	CY3	CY4	CY5
1	On-Site Site Preparation	One Time	$100,000	0	0	0	0	0
2	On-Site Hardware	One Time	$1,000,000	0	0	0	0	0
3	On-Site COTS Software	One Time	$1,000,000	0	0	0	0	0
4	On-Site Installation & Test	One Time	$50,000	0	0	0	0	0
5	On-Site Telecom Non-Recurring Charge (NRC)	One Time	$0	0	0	0	0	0
6	On-Site Telecom Monthly Recurring Charge (MRC)	Monthly	$7,500	0	0	0	0	0
7	On-Site Hardware & Software Maintenance	Monthly	$16,667	0	0	0	0	0
8	Off-Site Space (includes HVAC)	Monthly	$16,667	0	0	0	0	0
9	Off-Site Site Preparation	One Time	$0	0	0	0	0	0
10	Off-Site Hardware	One Time	$600,000	0	0	0	0	0
11	Off-Site COTS Software	One Time	$1,000,000	0	0	0	0	0
12	Off-Site Installation & Test	One Time	$50,000	0	0	0	0	0
13	Off-Site Telecom Non-Recurring Charge (NRC)	One Time	$5,000	0	0	0	0	0
14	Off-Site Telecom Monthly Recurring Charge (MRC)	Monthly	$12,500	0	0	0	0	0
15	Off-Site Hardware & Software Maintenance	Monthly	$13,333	0	0	0	0	0

FIGURE VII.6

The actual RFP contains rules related to the way in which the BOMs need to be developed, including:

- All one-time charges occur in CY1;
- All monthly charges begin in month 10 of CY1 and continue for the remainder of the contractual period; and
- BOM items 6 and 7 and 14 and 15 deflate by 5% compounded per CY, beginning in CY3.

The BOM estimation task is to populate the BOM for each competitive team with estimates of needed BOM costs, by CY.

Overwrite the green **or** yellow cells (but not both) with the appropriate BOM item costs for each team's solution that has been described by PTW intelligence.

The **Labor** estimation for each of the competitive bid teams is accomplished using the table from the *Labor—Not Done* Excel page in the Phase 2 book (see **Figure VII.7**).

Team ABC – ITCON Labor Categories		ABC Team Membership's % of Labor Categories		Contractor Site Hourly Rates		Customer Site Hourly Rates		Place of Performance %		Blended CY1 Fully Burdened Hourly Labor Rates			5-Year Hours by Labor Category				
		ABC - Prime	SBs	ABC - Prime	SBs	ABC - Prime	SBs	Off Customer Site	On Customer Site	Off Customer Site	On Customer Site	Location Blended CY1 Labor Rates	CY1	CY2	CY3	CY4	CY5
1	Program Manager	100%	0%	$150.00	$135.00	$142.50	$128.25	100%	0%	$150.00	$142.50	$150.00	0	0	0	0	0
2	Project Planner	100%	0%	$75.00	$67.50	$71.25	$64.13	100%	0%	$75.00	$71.25	$75.00	0	0	0	0	0
3	System Architect/Engineer	100%	0%	$125.00	$112.50	$118.75	$106.88	100%	0%	$125.00	$118.75	$125.00	0	0	0	0	0
4	Transition Specialist	100%	0%	$75.00	$67.50	$71.25	$64.13	100%	0%	$75.00	$71.25	$75.00	0	0	0	0	0
5	Operations Specialist	100%	0%	$60.00	$54.00	$57.00	$51.30	100%	0%	$60.00	$57.00	$60.00	0	0	0	0	0
6	QA Specialist	100%	0%	$75.00	$67.50	$71.25	$64.13	100%	0%	$75.00	$71.25	$75.00	0	0	0	0	0
7	Telecommunications Analyst	100%	0%	$85.00	$76.50	$80.75	$72.68	100%	0%	$85.00	$80.75	$85.00	0	0	0	0	0
8	Documentation Specialist	100%	0%	$50.00	$45.00	$47.50	$42.75	100%	0%	$50.00	$47.50	$50.00	0	0	0	0	0
9	System Maintenance Specialist	100%	0%	$50.00	$45.00	$47.50	$42.75	100%	0%	$50.00	$47.50	$50.00	0	0	0	0	0
10	Help Desk Specialist	100%	0%	$50.00	$45.00	$47.50	$42.75	100%	0%	$50.00	$47.50	$50.00	0	0	0	0	0

Team XYZ – ITCON Labor Categories		XYZ Team Membership's % Participation		Contractor Site Hourly Rates		Customer Site Hourly Rates		Place of Performance %		Blended CY1 Fully Burdened Hourly Labor Rates			5-Year Hours by Labor Category				
		XYZ - Prime	DEF	XYZ - Prime	DEF	XYZ - Prime	DEF	Off Customer Site	On Customer Site	Off Customer Site	On Customer Site	Location Blended CY1 Labor Rates	CY1	CY2	CY3	CY4	CY5
1	Program Manager	100%	0%	$150.00	$135.00	$142.50	$128.25	100%	0%	$150.00	$142.50	$150.00	0	0	0	0	0
2	Project Planner	100%	0%	$75.00	$67.50	$71.25	$64.13	100%	0%	$75.00	$71.25	$75.00	0	0	0	0	0
3	System Architect/Engineer	100%	0%	$125.00	$112.50	$118.75	$106.88	100%	0%	$125.00	$118.75	$125.00	0	0	0	0	0
4	Transition Specialist	100%	0%	$75.00	$67.50	$71.25	$64.13	100%	0%	$75.00	$71.25	$75.00	0	0	0	0	0
5	Operations Specialist	100%	0%	$60.00	$54.00	$57.00	$51.30	100%	0%	$60.00	$57.00	$60.00	0	0	0	0	0
6	QA Specialist	100%	0%	$75.00	$67.50	$71.25	$64.13	100%	0%	$75.00	$71.25	$75.00	0	0	0	0	0
7	Telecommunications Analyst	100%	0%	$85.00	$76.50	$80.75	$72.68	100%	0%	$85.00	$80.75	$85.00	0	0	0	0	0
8	Documentation Specialist	100%	0%	$50.00	$45.00	$47.50	$42.75	100%	0%	$50.00	$47.50	$50.00	0	0	0	0	0
9	System Maintenance Specialist	100%	0%	$50.00	$45.00	$47.50	$42.75	100%	0%	$50.00	$47.50	$50.00	0	0	0	0	0
10	Help Desk Specialist	100%	0%	$50.00	$45.00	$47.50	$42.75	100%	0%	$50.00	$47.50	$50.00	0	0	0	0	0

SB Labor Content	
ABC	XYZ
0%	0%

FIGURE VII.7

From left to right, there are three sets of cells that you will need to consider filling out:

1. The SBs column, which regulates how much of each labor category's hours will be applied to the various team members—remember, we have a Small Business (SB) requirement to meet;

2. The Place of Performance, On Customer Site column, which needs to either be left as is for a solution that is being implemented off of the customer's site or changed to 100% if an on-customer-site solution is being represented; and

3. The Hours by Labor Category columns, which are described in detail below, by CY.

For labor estimation, the following RFP rules apply to the labor categories shown in the previous table by competitive bid team labor categories:

- Category 1 is full time (160 hours per month) for all five years;
- Categories 2, 3 and 8 are only needed for the first six months of CY1;
- Category 4 is full-time for two FTEs for CY1 only; and
- Categories 5, 6 and 7 are half-time for one FTE during CY1 and are full-time thereafter for the remainder of the contract and the full-time FTEs are subject to the 20% rule (see below) if an off-site solution is being proposed.

The following additional RFP rules also apply to solution siting:

- If Categories 9 and 10 are on the customer site... then each of these categories must have six full-timers starting in the fourth quarter of CY1 and continuing until contract's end; and

- If Categories 9 and 10 are off of the customer site... then each of these labor categories can leverage existing resources to cover up to 20% of the six full-timer customer site requirement.

The white on red table underneath the Labor table is a SB participation counter on this Excel page that allows you to keep track of each team's SB participation.

Note: There is a labor escalator of 5% Compound Annual Growth Rate (CAGR) after CY1 that is built in to the model.

The composite cost tables in **Figure VII.8** are populated automatically as the BOM and Labor tables are completed for each competitive bid team.

Once you have completed the BOM and labor tasks, use the resulting Bottoms Up PTW estimate and new research information *to revise as needed* the Phase 1 Evaluation Matrix shown in **Figure VII.9**.

Team ABC – **Ungamed** Price						
Item	CY1	CY2	CY3	CY4	CY5	Total
BOM						$0
Labor	$0	$0	$0	$0	$0	$0
Totals	$0	$0	$0	$0	$0	**$0**

Team XYZ – **Ungamed** Price						
Item	CY1	CY2	CY3	CY4	CY5	Total
BOM	$0	$0	$0	$0	$0	$0
Labor	$0	$0	$0	$0	$0	$0
Totals	$0	$0	$0	$0	$0	**$0**

FIGURE VII.8

ITCON Proposal Evaluation Criteria (PEC)	Available Points	Team Adjectival Score as a % of Available Points			Normalized Scores		
		ABC	XYZ	HAL	ABC	XYZ	HAL
Overall Evaluation	1000				915.57	893.35	915.63
Overall Evaluation Rank					(2)	(3)	(1)
Non-Cost	600				521.3	523.1	515.6
Non-Cost Evaluation Rank					(2)	(1)	(3)
Factor 1 - Technical Approach	275				238.8	238.8	236.3
Rank					(1)	(1)	(3)
Subfactor 1: Enterprise Services	100	85.0%	90.0%	87.5%	85.0	90.0	87.5
Subfactor 2: Transition	100	90.0%	85.0%	85.0%	90.0	85.0	85.0
Subfactor 3: Contractor's Performance Work Statement & WBS	75	85.0%	85.0%	85.0%	63.8	63.8	63.8
Factor 2 - Management	225				195.0	194.4	194.4
Rank					(1)	(2)	(2)
Subfactor 1: Program Leadership	100	90.0%	87.5%	87.5%	90.0	87.5	87.5
Subfactor 2: Subcontractor Management	75	85.0%	82.5%	82.5%	63.8	61.9	61.9
Subfactor 3: Metrics & SLA Reporting & Management	50	82.5%	90.0%	90.0%	41.3	45.0	45.0
Factor 3 - Past Performance	100	87.5%	90.0%	85.0%	87.5	90.0	85.0
Rank					(2)	(1)	(3)
Factor 4 - Price ($M)	400	$13.95	$14.86	$13.75	394.3	370.2	400.0
Rank					(2)	(3)	(1)

FIGURE VII.9

The Team ABC and Team XYZ Phase 2 prices that appear in the table shown above will be entered automatically.

Determine what price HAL now needs to consider bidding to assure a win—all other evaluation items being equal.

It should take you 60 minutes or less to complete these tasks. Please save your spreadsheets.

Phase 3 of the Progressive PTW Problem

As shown in **Figure VII.10** below, Phase 3 of the PTW Framework involves Steps 8 and 10.

Phase 3 of the ITCON problem will allow you to determine:

- Competitor *Bottoms Up* fully gamed prices to be developed;
- Needed changes to non-cost evaluation scores, if any; and
- The Home Team's *fully gamed* PTW.

Since PTW research is only over when the PTW study is completed, we have accumulated a number of new competitive snowflakes, and the question is: What do we (HAL) believe the competitive bid teams can really make happen, and what will their gamed Prices *To Win* the job look like?

More Intelligence

For **Team ABC**, our PTW researchers have concluded, ITCON is a "Must Win" for them. ABC has a history of using used equipment on jobs like ITCON—equipment that has a 20% lower cost than the estimated on-site hardware costs in the RFP's BOM rules. And whenever they have the customer's trust, they have been able to pull this off.

As an application maintenance incumbent, ABC needs to maintain the ITCON incumbency and use it to help increase its share of the customer's application maintenance and modernization work.

For **Team XYZ**, ITCON is deemed to be a "Nice To Have" win. XYZ's history includes cross training and consolidation of help desk and maintenance staffs to provide acceptable customer SLAs for operating environments (OEs) with 70% of staffing normally associated with stand-alone operations.

XYZ sees economies of scale but no "aftermarket potential."

How to Game ITCON Prices

For PTW, gaming is often less a matter of the over- and/or under-evaluation of CLIN items and more a matter of how cost avoidance potential can be exploited. For ITCON, the latter is true.

Think about how the additional intelligence information supplied can, or cannot, be used to favorably adjust each competitive team's ungamed bid pricing.

While you are expected to use your creativity in formulating your solution approach, always beware of contravening the rules of the RFP!

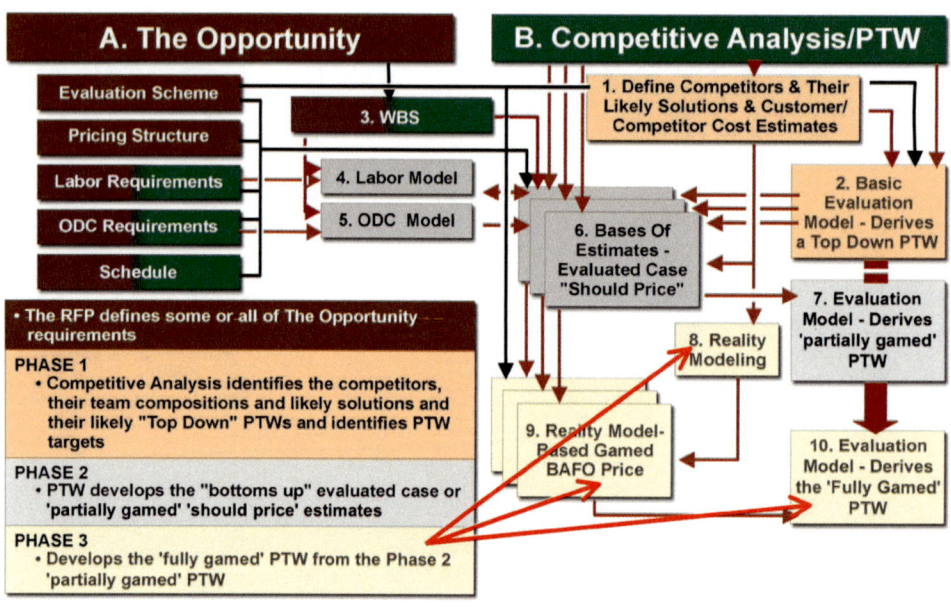

FIGURE VII.10

Once you have developed your competitive bid team strategies, implement them!

Your task is to:

- Redo your ITCON Phase 2 BOM tables and Labor tables, as needed, using the *Gaming Values* Excel page in the ***Phase 3 Models.xls*** book (see **Figure VII.11** below);
- Develop your Phase 3 fully gamed bid prices; and
- Redo the Phase 2 Evaluation table using the resulting Phase 3 fully gamed Bottoms Up PTW estimates.

Then determine what gamed price HAL now needs to be thinking about bidding to assure a win—all other evaluation items being equal.

You should need about 30 minutes to figure out an appropriate and legal gaming strategy for each competitive bid team. Be prepared to explain and defend your conclusions to your peers.

Team	Additional Labor Discount		Additional Hardware (NRC) Discount	
	Off Site	On Site	Off Site	On Site
ABC	0.00%	0.00%	0.00%	0.00%
XYZ	0.00%	0.00%	0.00%	0.00%

FIGURE VII.11

Completed Phase 1 Tables

Below, we have presented our solution to the Phase 1 problem in terms of completed tables. These can also be found in the *Phase 1 Models Done.xls* Excel spreadsheet book. The password needed to open this spreadsheet is: **PTW1**

Phase 1 Budget Table—Done

The issue here is when the 30% take-down from the "as is" budget should occur. In the sample $17.71M budget shown in **Figure VII.12**, we have taken the step down starting in CY3—we could have taken it halfway through CY2. PTW practitioners must decide these issues for themselves.

$17.71	Total Budget ($M)
$4,320,000	CY1 ($)
$4,320,000	CY2 ($)
$3,024,000	CY3 ($)
$3,024,000	CY4 ($)
$3,024,000	CY5 ($)

FIGURE VII.12

Phase 1 PTW History Table—Done

The results shown in **Figure VII.13** were developed by entering the information provided by PTW researchers into the green font cells in the table.

ABC Relevant Program Citations	Addressable Budget ($M)	Bid Price ($M)	Bid $ as % of Budget
Cite 1	$50.0	$35.0	70.00%
Cite 2	$100.0	$77.5	77.50%
Cite 3	$50.0	$45.0	90.00%
ALL	$200	$158	78.75%

XYZ Relevant Program Citations	Addressable Budget ($M)	Bid Price ($M)	Bid $ as % of Budget
Cite 1	$250.0	$188.5	75.40%
Cite 2	$100.0	$99.5	99.50%
Cite 3	$50.0	$47.5	95.00%
ALL	$400	$336	83.88%

FIGURE VII.13

Phase 1 Evaluation Model—Done

The Evaluation Model was pre-populated with non-cost evaluation criterion scores for all three bid teams. As shown, in terms of non-cost award points, Team XYZ is #1, followed by Team ABC and Team HAL, the Home Team.

The Evaluation Model then uses the results from the two panels shown in Figure VII.13 to compute Team ABC's and Team XYZ's overall award point scores. When we enter $13.75M into HAL's green font Price cell, HAL's aggregated award point score puts us, as shown in **Figure VII.14**, in the #1 overall position.

ITCON Proposal Evaluation Criteria (PEC)	Available Points	Team Adjectival Score as a % of Available Points			Normalized Scores		
		ABC	XYZ	HAL	ABC	XYZ	HAL
Overall Evaluation	**1000**				915.57	893.35	915.63
Overall Evaluation Rank					(2)	(3)	(1)
Non-Cost	**600**				521.3	523.1	515.6
Non-Cost Evaluation Rank					(2)	(1)	(3)
Factor 1 - Technical Approach	**275**				238.8	238.8	236.3
Rank					(1)	(1)	(3)
Subfactor 1: Enterprise Services	100	85.0%	90.0%	87.5%	85.0	90.0	87.5
Subfactor 2: Transition	100	90.0%	85.0%	85.0%	90.0	85.0	85.0
Subfactor 3: Contractor's Performance Work Statement & WBS	75	85.0%	85.0%	85.0%	63.8	63.8	63.8
Factor 2 - Management	**225**				195.0	194.4	194.4
Rank					(1)	(2)	(2)
Subfactor 1: Program Leadership	100	90.0%	87.5%	87.5%	90.0	87.5	87.5
Subfactor 2: Subcontractor Management	75	85.0%	82.5%	82.5%	63.8	61.9	61.9
Subfactor 3: Metrics & SLA Reporting & Management	50	82.5%	90.0%	90.0%	41.3	45.0	45.0
Factor 3 - Past Performance	**100**	87.5%	90.0%	85.0%	87.5	90.0	85.0
Rank					(2)	(1)	(3)
Factor 4 - Price ($M)	**400**	$13.95	$14.86	$13.75	394.3	370.2	400.0
Rank					(2)	(3)	(1)

FIGURE VII.14

Completed Phase 2 Tables

Below, we have presented our solution to the Phase 2 problem in terms of completed tables. These can also be found in the *Phase 2 Models Done.xls* Excel spreadsheet book. The password needed to open this spreadsheet book is: **PTW2**

Phase 2 BOM Tables—Done

Your completed BOM tables should look something like those in **Figure VII.15**. The only liberty that was taken was to avoid site preparation costs for Team ABC's on-customer-site solution. The rationale was that adding capacity to accommodate another 100 users probably would take little more than an in-place upgrade.

	Team ABC ITCON BOM Elements	Periodicity	Period Cost	Team ABC's 5-Year BOM by BOM Item				
				CY1	CY2	CY3	CY4	CY5
1	On-Site Site Preparation	One Time	$100,000	$0	$0	$0	$0	$0
2	On-Site Hardware	One Time	$1,000,000	$1,000,000	$0	$0	$0	$0
3	On-Site COTS Software	One Time	$1,000,000	$1,000,000	$0	$0	$0	$0
4	On-Site Installation & Test	One Time	$50,000	$50,000	$0	$0	$0	$0
5	On-Site Telecom Non-Recurring Charge (NRC)	One Time	$0	$0	$0	$0	$0	$0
6	On-Site Telecom Monthly Recurring Charge (MRC)	Monthly	$7,500	$22,500	$90,000	$85,500	$81,225	$77,164
7	On-Site Hardware & Software Maintenance	Monthly	$16,667	$50,000	$200,000	$190,000	$180,500	$171,475
8	Off-Site Space (includes HVAC)	Monthly	$16,667	$0	$0	$0	$0	$0
9	Off-Site Site Preparation	One Time	$0	$0	$0	$0	$0	$0
10	Off-Site Hardware	One Time	$600,000	$0	$0	$0	$0	$0
11	Off-Site COTS Software	One Time	$1,000,000	$0	$0	$0	$0	$0
12	Off-Site Installation & Test	One Time	$50,000	$0	$0	$0	$0	$0
13	On-Site Telecom Non-Recurring Charge (NRC)	One Time	$5,000	$0	$0	$0	$0	$0
14	On-Site Telecom Monthly Recurring Charge (MRC)	Monthly	$12,500	$0	$0	$0	$0	$0
15	Off-Site Hardware & Software Maintenance	Monthly	$13,333	$0	$0	$0	$0	$0

	Team XYZ ITCON BOM Elements	Periodicity	Period Cost	Team XYZ's 5-Year BOM by BOM Item				
				CY1	CY2	CY3	CY4	CY5
1	On-Site Site Preparation	One Time	$100,000	$0	$0	$0	$0	$0
2	On-Site Hardware	One Time	$1,000,000	$0	$0	$0	$0	$0
3	On-Site COTS Software	One Time	$1,000,000	$0	$0	$0	$0	$0
4	On-Site Installation & Test	One Time	$50,000	$0	$0	$0	$0	$0
5	On-Site Telecom Non-Recurring Charge (NRC)	One Time	$0	$0	$0	$0	$0	$0
6	On-Site Telecom Monthly Recurring Charge (MRC)	Monthly	$7,500	$0	$0	$0	$0	$0
7	On-Site Hardware & Software Maintenance	Monthly	$16,667	$0	$0	$0	$0	$0
8	Off-Site Space (includes HVAC)	Monthly	$16,667	$50,000	$200,000	$200,000	$200,000	$200,000
9	Off-Site Site Preparation	One Time	$0	$0	$0	$0	$0	$0
10	Off-Site Hardware	One Time	$600,000	$600,000	$0	$0	$0	$0
11	Off-Site COTS Software	One Time	$1,000,000	$1,000,000	$0	$0	$0	$0
12	Off-Site Installation & Test	One Time	$50,000	$50,000	$0	$0	$0	$0
13	On-Site Telecom Non-Recurring Charge (NRC)	One Time	$5,000	$5,000	$0	$0	$0	$0
14	On-Site Telecom Monthly Recurring Charge (MRC)	Monthly	$12,500	$37,500	$150,000	$142,500	$135,375	$128,606
15	Off-Site Hardware & Software Maintenance	Monthly	$13,333	$40,000	$160,000	$152,000	$144,400	$137,180

FIGURE VII.15

SECTION VII — The Progressive Price To Win (PTW) Problem

Phase 2 Labor Tables—Done

Your completed Labor tables should look something like those in **Figure VII.16**. The Small Business (SB) labor participation counter should hit 25% (remember we need to hit a quota for SB participation) for Team ABC and, because XYZ *is* an SB, the percentage for their subcontractor's participation relates only to keeping that sub on board, since they are an incumbent.

Team ABC - ITCON Labor Categories		ABC Team Membership's % of Labor Categories		Contractor Site Hourly Rates		Customer Site Hourly Rates		Place of Performance %		ABC Blended CY1 Fully Burdened Hourly Labor Rates			5-Year Hours by Labor Category				
		ABC - Prime	SBs	ABC - Prime	SBs	ABC - Prime	SBs	Off Customer Site	On Customer Site	Off Customer Site	On Customer Site	Location Blended CY1 Labor Rates	CY1	CY2	CY3	CY4	CY5
1	Program Manager	100%	0%	$150.00	$135.00	$142.50	$128.25	0%	100%	$150.00	$142.50	$142.50	1,920	1,920	1,920	1,920	1,920
2	Project Planner	100%	0%	$75.00	$67.50	$71.25	$64.13	0%	100%	$75.00	$71.25	$71.25	960				
3	System Architect/Engineer	100%	0%	$125.00	$112.50	$118.75	$106.88	0%	100%	$125.00	$118.75	$118.75	960				
4	Transition Specialist	100%	0%	$75.00	$67.50	$71.25	$64.13	0%	100%	$75.00	$71.25	$71.25	3,840				
5	Operations Specialist	50%	50%	$60.00	$54.00	$57.00	$51.30	0%	100%	$57.00	$54.15	$54.15	960	1,920	1,920	1,920	1,920
6	QA Specialist	100%	0%	$75.00	$67.50	$71.25	$64.13	0%	100%	$75.00	$71.25	$71.25	960	1,920	1,920	1,920	1,920
7	Telecommunications Analyst	100%	0%	$85.00	$76.50	$80.75	$72.68	0%	100%	$85.00	$80.75	$80.75	960	1,920	1,920	1,920	1,920
8	Documentation Specialist	100%	0%	$50.00	$45.00	$47.50	$42.75	0%	100%	$50.00	$47.50	$47.50	960				
9	System Maintenance Specialist	60%	40%	$50.00	$45.00	$47.50	$42.75	0%	100%	$48.00	$45.60	$45.60	2,880	11,520	11,520	11,520	11,520
10	Help Desk Specialist	60%	40%	$50.00	$45.00	$47.50	$42.75	0%	100%	$48.00	$45.60	$45.60	2,880	11,520	11,520	11,520	11,520

Team XYZ - ITCON Labor Categories		XYZ Team Membership's % of Labor Categories		Contractor Site Hourly Rates		Customer Site Hourly Rates		Place of Performance %		XYZ Blended CY1 Fully Burdened Hourly Labor Rates			5-Year Hours by Labor Category				
		XYZ - Prime	DEF	XYZ - Prime	DEF	XYZ - Prime	DEF	Off Customer Site	On Customer Site	Off Customer Site	On Customer Site	Location Blended CY1 Labor Rates	CY1	CY2	CY3	CY4	CY5
1	Program Manager	100%	0%	$150.00	$135.00	$142.50	$128.25	100%	0%	$150.00	$142.50	$150.00	1,920	1,920	1,920	1,920	1,920
2	Project Planner	100%	0%	$75.00	$67.50	$71.25	$64.13	100%	0%	$75.00	$71.25	$75.00	960				
3	System Architect/Engineer	100%	0%	$125.00	$112.50	$118.75	$106.88	100%	0%	$125.00	$118.75	$125.00	960				
4	Transition Specialist	100%	0%	$75.00	$67.50	$71.25	$64.13	100%	0%	$75.00	$71.25	$75.00	3,840				
5	Operations Specialist	50%	50%	$60.00	$54.00	$57.00	$51.30	100%	0%	$57.00	$54.15	$57.00	768	1,536	1,536	1,536	1,536
6	QA Specialist	100%	0%	$75.00	$67.50	$71.25	$64.13	100%	0%	$75.00	$71.25	$75.00	768	1,536	1,536	1,536	1,536
7	Telecommunications Analyst	100%	0%	$85.00	$76.50	$80.75	$72.68	100%	0%	$85.00	$80.75	$85.00	768	1,536	1,536	1,536	1,536
8	Documentation Specialist	100%	0%	$50.00	$45.00	$47.50	$42.75	100%	0%	$50.00	$47.50	$50.00	960				
9	System Maintenance Specialist	100%	0%	$50.00	$45.00	$47.50	$42.75	100%	0%	$50.00	$47.50	$50.00	2,304	9,216	9,216	9,216	9,216
10	Help Desk Specialist	25%	75%	$50.00	$45.00	$47.50	$42.75	100%	0%	$46.25	$43.94	$46.25	2,304	9,216	9,216	9,216	9,216

SB Labor Content	
ABC	XYZ
25.1%	78.2%

FIGURE VII.16

Phase 2 Price Tables—Done

Your completed BOM and Labor tables should create Ungamed, Bottoms Up prices that look something like the following tables in **Figure VII.17**.

Team ABC - **Ungamed** Bottoms Up Price						
Item	CY1	CY2	CY3	CY4	CY5	Total
BOM	$2,122,500	$290,000	$275,500	$261,725	$248,639	$3,198,364
Labor	$1,235,760	$1,806,034	$1,896,335	$1,991,152	$2,090,710	$9,019,991
Totals	$3,358,260	$2,096,034	$2,171,835	$2,252,877	$2,339,348	**$12,218,354**

Team XYZ - **Ungamed** Bottoms Up Price						
Item	CY1	CY2	CY3	CY4	CY5	Total
BOM	$1,782,500	$510,000	$494,500	$479,775	$465,786	$3,732,561
Labor	$1,204,416	$1,583,770	$1,662,958	$1,746,106	$1,833,411	$8,030,661
Totals	$2,986,916	$2,093,770	$2,157,458	$2,225,881	$2,299,198	**$11,763,222**

FIGURE VII.17

SECTION VII   The Progressive Price To Win (PTW) Problem

Phase 2 Evaluation Model—Done

The Evaluation Model from Phase 1 that was pre-populated with non-cost evaluation criterion scores for all three bid teams now needs to be changed to reflect the new information that was introduced at the beginning of the Phase 2 part of the problem. As can be seen, in terms of non-cost award points, Team XYZ is now #2, displaced (by virtue of the fact that they now are reckoned to be able to earn a lower number of non-cost evaluation award points) as #1 by Team ABC. Team HAL, the Home Team, still trails.

The Evaluation Model then uses the results from the two panels shown in Figure VII.17 to compute Team ABC's and Team XYZ's overall award point scores. When we enter $11.68M into HAL's green font Price cell, then HAL's aggregated award point score puts us, as shown in **Figure VII.18**, back in the #1 position overall.

ITCON Proposal Evaluation Criteria (PEC)	Available Points	Team Adjectival Score as a %			Normalized Scores		
		ABC	XYZ	HAL	ABC	XYZ	HAL
Overall Evaluation	*1000*				906.13	917.80	918.13
Overall Evaluation Rank					(3)	(2)	(1)
Non-Cost	**600**				523.8	520.6	518.1
Non-Cost Evaluation Rank					(1)	(2)	(3)
Factor 1 - Technical Approach	*275*				238.8	238.8	238.8
Rank					(1)	(1)	(1)
Subfactor 1: Enterprise Services	100	85.0%	90.0%	90.0%	85.0	90.0	90.0
Subfactor 2: Transition	100	90.0%	85.0%	85.0%	90.0	85.0	85.0
Subfactor 3: Contractor's Performance Work Statement & WBS	75	85.0%	85.0%	85.0%	63.8	63.8	63.8
Factor 2 - Management	*225*				195.0	194.4	194.4
Rank					(1)	(2)	(2)
Subfactor 1: Program Leadership	100	90.0%	87.5%	87.5%	90.0	87.5	87.5
Subfactor 2: Subcontractor Management	75	85.0%	82.5%	82.5%	63.8	61.9	61.9
Subfactor 3: Metrics & SLA Reporting & Management	50	82.5%	90.0%	90.0%	41.3	45.0	45.0
Factor 3 - Past Performance	*100*	90.0%	87.5%	85.0%	90.0	87.5	85.0
Rank					(1)	(2)	(3)
Factor 4 - Price ($M)	*400*	$12.22	$11.76	$11.68	382.4	397.2	400.0
Rank					(3)	(2)	(1)

FIGURE VII.18

Completed Phase 3 Tables

Below, we have presented our solution to the Phase 3 problem in terms of completed tables. These tables can also be found in the ***Phase 3 Models Done.xls*** Excel spreadsheet book. The password needed to open this spreadsheet book is: **PTW3**

The ITCON Phase 3 problem is significantly different from the previous phases. PTW has been confronted with two very different rationales concerning how the competitive bid teams are likely to justify to themselves (if not support to the customer) a reduction in their Phase 2 Price *To Do* the job that will effectively raise their overall evaluation point scores.

In the case of **Team ABC**, their ace in the hole revolves around Bill Of Materials (BOM) price reductions. Since changing BOM prices would contravene the stated rules of the RFP, what could they do to lower their price?

Another RFP requirement is the Labor Level Of Effort (LOE). This cannot be changed either.

What remains are the Labor rates themselves. Since these are obviously furnished by the bid teams rather than the customer, they can be changed to accommodate the savings that Team ABC is likely to project, related to using "used" equipment to implement their "to be" solution.

For **Team XYZ**, we have a similar situation, but this time price reduction possibilities are related to labor LOEs, not BOM issues. The remedy, however, is identical—we can reduce labor rates to accommodate the expected post-award reduction in LOE.

Phase 3 BOM Tables—Done

These do not change from where we left them in Phase 2.

Phase 3 Discount Tables—Done

The table in **Figure VII.19** relates to discounts from Labor Price (not LOE) estimates that relate to BOM take-downs.

Team	Additional Labor Discount		Additional Hardware (NRC) Discount	
	Off Site	On Site	Off Site	On Site
ABC	0.00%	2.25%	0.00%	0.00%
XYZ	0.00%	0.00%	0.00%	0.00%

FIGURE VII.19

SECTION VII — The Progressive Price To Win (PTW) Problem

Phase 3 Labor Tables—Done

In the case of **Team ABC**, the Phase 3 completed Labor table now uses the "Gamed" blended labor rates shown in **Figure VII.20** to implement lowered labor rates. **Team XYZ**, by contrast, has simply reduced their LOE, which, while illegal if we were submitting a proposal to this customer, is quite legitimate for PTW purposes.

Note that both approaches end up with a similar result. Make sure that the SB counter still hits 25% for **Team ABC**.

Team ABC - ITCON Labor Categories

#	Labor Category	ABC-Prime %	SBs %	Contractor Site ABC-Prime	Contractor Site SBs	Customer Site ABC-Prime	Customer Site SBs	CY1	CY2	CY3	CY4	CY5	Blended CY1	Blended CY2	Blended CY3	Blended CY4	Blended CY5
1	Program Manager	100%	0%	$150.00	$135.00	$142.50	$128.25	$273,600	$287,280	$301,644	$316,726	$332,563	$142.50	$149.63	$157.11	$164.96	$173.21
2	Project Planner	100%	0%	$75.00	$67.50	$71.25	$64.13	$68,400	$0	$0	$0	$0	$71.25				
3	System Architect/Engineer	100%	0%	$125.00	$112.50	$118.75	$106.88	$114,000	$0	$0	$0	$0	$118.75				
4	Transition Specialist	100%	0%	$75.00	$67.50	$71.25	$64.13	$273,600	$0	$0	$0	$0	$71.25				
5	Operations Specialist	0%	100%	$60.00	$54.00	$57.00	$51.30	$49,248	$103,421	$108,592	$114,021	$119,723	$51.30	$53.87	$56.56	$59.39	$62.36
6	QA Specialist	100%	0%	$75.00	$67.50	$71.25	$64.13	$68,400	$143,640	$150,822	$158,363	$166,281	$71.25	$74.81	$78.55	$82.48	$86.60
7	Telecommunications Analyst	100%	0%	$85.00	$76.50	$80.75	$72.68	$77,520	$162,792	$170,932	$179,478	$188,452	$80.75	$84.79	$89.03	$93.48	$98.15
8	Documentation Specialist	100%	0%	$50.00	$45.00	$47.50	$42.75	$45,600	$0	$0	$0	$0	$47.50				
9	System Maintenance Specialist	0%	100%	$50.00	$45.00	$47.50	$42.75	$123,120	$517,104	$542,959	$570,107	$598,613	$42.75	$44.89	$47.13	$49.49	$51.96
10	Help Desk Specialist	50%	50%	$50.00	$45.00	$47.50	$42.75	$129,960	$545,832	$573,124	$601,780	$631,869	$45.13	$47.38	$49.75	$52.24	$54.85

Team XYZ - ITCON Labor Categories

#	Labor Category	XYZ-Prime %	DEF %	Contractor Site XYZ-Prime	Contractor Site DEF	Customer Site XYZ-Prime	Customer Site DEF	CY1	CY2	CY3	CY4	CY5	Blended CY1	Blended CY2	Blended CY3	Blended CY4	Blended CY5
1	Program Manager	100%	0%	$150.00	$135.00	$142.50	$128.25	$288,000	$302,400	$317,520	$333,396	$350,066	$150.00	$157.50	$165.38	$173.64	$182.33
2	Project Planner	100%	0%	$75.00	$67.50	$71.25	$64.13	$72,000	$0	$0	$0	$0	$75.00				
3	System Architect/Engineer	100%	0%	$125.00	$112.50	$118.75	$106.88	$120,000	$0	$0	$0	$0	$125.00				
4	Transition Specialist	100%	0%	$75.00	$67.50	$71.25	$64.13	$288,000	$0	$0	$0	$0	$75.00				
5	Operations Specialist	50%	50%	$60.00	$54.00	$57.00	$51.30	$38,304	$80,438	$84,460	$88,683	$93,118	$57.00	$59.85	$62.84	$65.98	$69.28
6	QA Specialist	100%	0%	$75.00	$67.50	$71.25	$64.13	$50,400	$105,840	$111,132	$116,689	$122,523	$75.00	$78.75	$82.69	$86.82	$91.16
7	Telecommunications Analyst	100%	0%	$85.00	$76.50	$80.75	$72.68	$57,120	$119,952	$125,950	$132,247	$138,859	$85.00	$89.25	$93.71	$98.40	$103.32
8	Documentation Specialist	100%	0%	$50.00	$45.00	$47.50	$42.75	$48,000	$0	$0	$0	$0	$50.00				
9	System Maintenance Specialist	100%	0%	$50.00	$45.00	$47.50	$42.75	$100,800	$423,360	$444,528	$466,754	$490,092	$50.00	$52.50	$55.13	$57.88	$60.78
10	Help Desk Specialist	25%	75%	$50.00	$45.00	$47.50	$42.75	$93,240	$391,608	$411,188	$431,748	$453,335	$46.25	$48.56	$50.99	$53.54	$56.22

FIGURE VII.20

Phase 3 Gamed, Bottoms Up Price Tables—Done

The BOM totals in **Figure VII.21** do not change from where we left them in Phase 2. The Labor totals, however, now reflect the changes in Labor rates.

Team ABC - Gamed							+/- Difference
Item	CY1	CY2	CY3	CY4	CY5	Total	
BOM	$2,122,500	$290,000	$275,500	$261,725	$248,639	$3,198,364	$0
Labor	$1,223,448	$1,760,069	$1,848,072	$1,940,476	$2,037,500	$8,809,565	$0
Totals	$3,345,948	$2,050,069	$2,123,572	$2,202,201	$2,286,138	**$12,007,928**	$0

Team XYZ - Gamed							+/- Difference
Item	CY1	CY2	CY3	CY4	CY5	Total	
BOM	$1,782,500	$510,000	$494,500	$479,775	$465,786	$3,732,561	$0
Labor	$1,155,864	$1,423,598	$1,494,778	$1,569,517	$1,647,993	$7,291,751	($738,910)
Totals	$2,938,364	$1,933,598	$1,989,278	$2,049,292	$2,113,779	**$11,024,312**	($738,910)

FIGURE VII.21

Phase 3 Evaluation Model—Done

The only thing that changes with the Evaluation Model from Phase 2 is the Team ABC and Team XYZ PTWs. The "gamed" prices drive Team HAL, the Home Team, to a PTW of $10.95M in order to prevail in terms of overall evaluation points awarded (**see Figure VII.22**).

ITCON Proposal Evaluation Criteria (PEC)	Available Points	Team Adjectival Score as a %			Normalized Scores		
		ABC	**XYZ**	**HAL**	**ABC**	**XYZ**	**HAL**
Overall Evaluation	1000				888.51	917.93	918.13
Overall Evaluation Rank					(3)	(2)	(1)
Non-Cost	600				523.8	520.6	518.1
Non-Cost Evaluation Rank					(1)	(2)	(3)
Factor 1 - Technical Approach	275				238.8	238.8	238.8
Rank					(1)	(1)	(1)
Subfactor 1: Enterprise Services	100	85.0%	90.0%	90.0%	85.0	90.0	90.0
Subfactor 2: Transition	100	90.0%	85.0%	85.0%	90.0	85.0	85.0
Subfactor 3: Contractor's Performance Work Statement & WBS	75	85.0%	85.0%	85.0%	63.8	63.8	63.8
Factor 2 - Management	225				195.0	194.4	194.4
Rank					(1)	(2)	(2)
Subfactor 1: Program Leadership	100	90.0%	87.5%	87.5%	90.0	87.5	87.5
Subfactor 2: Subcontractor Management	75	85.0%	82.5%	82.5%	63.8	61.9	61.9
Subfactor 3: Metrics & SLA Reporting & Management	50	82.5%	90.0%	90.0%	41.3	45.0	45.0
Factor 3 - Past Performance	100	90.0%	87.5%	85.0%	90.0	87.5	85.0
Rank					(1)	(2)	(3)
Factor 4 - Price ($M)	400	$12.01	$11.02	$10.95	364.8	397.3	400.0
Rank					(3)	(2)	(1)

FIGURE VII.22

Congratulations! You have now accomplished your first PTW project. Onward to the next one!

Glossary of Terms & Acronyms

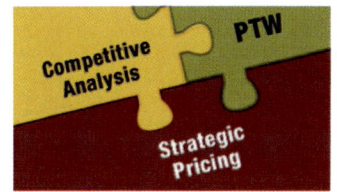

Addressable Budget
The amount of money that a customer has to spend on a contract after deducting expenses needed to support the contract from the requested and approved budget.

Best And Final Offer (BAFO)
The invitation that the customer may give bidders to submit their best prices after a bidder's initial submission has apparently made it into the competitive range by being deemed to be an acceptable offer.

Business Development (BD)
That activity of any business that is devoted to bringing new work to the enterprise.

Black Hat Review
The process through which the Home Team reviews its competitors and their likely teams, solutions, and capture strategies that the competition is likely to propose to beat the Home Team with respect to a specific opportunity. The information derived helps fashion the Home Team's White Hat development of proposal themes and discriminators.

Blanket Purchasing Agreement (BPA)
This is a U.S. General Services Administration (GSA) term that relates to quantity purchases. BPAs are discrete orders that exist under a vendor's GSA Schedule for goods, services, or both.

Bottom Line Up Front (BLUF)
A solution development approach whereby the target price is set up front for solution developers to meet and/or beat.

Basis Of Estimates (BOE)
The model that brings together the Work Breakdown Structure (WBS) and schedules with labor category Levels Of Effort (LOEs) and Other Direct Cost (ODC) quantities (and their unit prices) plus scaling factors to produce a "partially gamed" price.

Bill Of Materials (BOM)
A list of the raw materials, sub assemblies, sub components, components, parts, and the quantities of each required to manufacture and end item (final products).

Compound Annual Growth Rate (CAGR)
A multiplier that is used to predict the effect of, for instance, inflation or deflation, on labor rates and other prices.

Cost As an Independent Variable (CAIV)
An approach to solution design and development that is driven by setting cost targets up front. The affordable cost (price) is determined, then functionality, performance, product design, program schedule, etc., are established as a function of cost (i.e., are driven by cost). The purpose is to contain or reduce cost and succeed in the marketplace—cost can no longer be the product or a dependent variable.

Capture Team
The team established following a "pursue" decision to analyze the customer, the requirement, detail customer issues/considerations related to competitor and internal positioning, and to define strategies, solutions, and approaches to be implemented to guide the capture of a specific opportunity.

Collective Bargaining Agreement (CBA)

These are agreements with unions that apply minimum hourly direct labor and labor fringe to union employees employed under certain contracts entered into by the United States or the District of Columbia.

Competitive Intelligence (CI)

The process of collecting and using information about the nature and activities of one's competitors to support more effective business development.

Contract Line Item Number (CLIN)

As defined in a Draft Request For Proposal (DRFP) or final RFP, each CLIN is defined and described in detail so that both the customer and contractor personnel fully understand the work that each CLIN represents.

Cost Of Living Adjustment (COLA)

A COLA is an adjustment to direct labor costs (e.g., salaries) that is highly dependent on location. (e.g., New York City versus Fairmont, West Virginia).

Commoditization

The process that, over time, turns innovative and "brand name" products into commodities as other manufacturers seek to compete on price.

Corporate Personality

Corporate attributes that provide the PTW practitioner the ability to distinguish and model differences between and among contractors.

Commercial, Off The Shelf (COTS)

A category of ODCs that are available as plug and play items of hardware and/or software.

Contract Year (CY)

A specific year of a contract's duration or period of performance.

Design, Develop & Test (DD&T)

The activities needed to ready a system for acceptance and implementation.

Direct Labor (DL)

An employee's gross salary.

Delta Margin Gaming (DMG)

A CAI/SISCo approach to gaming competitive bids that are quantitatively evaluated as part of a PTW study that seeks to exploit differences in the customer's evaluation quantities and what the various bid teams expect to sell.

Draft Request For Proposal (DRFP)

An initial solicitation document that invites comments from potential bidders to assist the government in developing the highest quality final RFP. Prospective offerors are encouraged to comment on: proposed innovations, improvements, and enhancements to the stated requirements; items that are unclear, ambiguous, or otherwise warrant additional information or clarification; potential impediments to full and open competition or innovative proposals and approaches; perceived risk issues associated with the performance of work; and business concerns such as financial risks, insurance, or indemnification issues.

Design To Cost (DTC)

A process that constrains design options to a fixed cost limit. The cost limit is usually what the buyer can pay or what the marketplace demands. An affordable product is obtained by treating target cost as an independent design parameter that needs to be achieved during the development—also see CAIV.

Engineering Change Proposal (ECP)

A post-award proposal that is typically made to a government customer by a contract awardee to change the scope or other contract detail.

Economic Research Institute (ERI)

A developer of salary and other surveys.

Evaluation Model

The means by which the customer reveals to prospective bidders for an opportunity how they intend to evaluate offers.

Earned Value Management System (EVMS)

A process that monitors a contract as it unfolds to determine the level of value that accrues to the customer.

Firm, Fixed Price (FFP)

A type of contract pricing whereby the prospective contractor has to offer to perform the entirety of the work it proposes for a set price.

Freedom Of Information Act (FOIA)

The U.S. government statute that allows citizens and enterprises to request copies of contracts and other materials from agencies.

Forward Pricing

The process of breaking a product down to its constituent components and then forecasting the likely annual rise/depreciation of each of these components over the contract period to establish a curve for future pricing of the product.

Full Time Equivalent (FTE)

A person or group of persons who individually or severally put in a full year's worth of billable hours.

Fully Gamed Price

The price that PTW develops to represent a competitor's likely bid price designed to Win The Job.

Fiscal Year (FY)

The accounting year that governs customer budgets. For instance, the U.S. federal government's FY is October 1 through the end of September the next year.

General and Administrative Expenses (G&A)

Business operating expenses related to the general operations or overall administration of the business.

Gaming

The practice of, for instance, using the delta between an opportunity's Evaluation Model and a bid team's Reality Model to determine the degree of unreality that is available to support price gaming. See DMG (Delta Margin Gaming).

General Services Administration (GSA) (U.S.)

The U.S. federal agency that maintains pre-negotiated acquisition schedules with suppliers of goods and services to federal and state and local agencies.

Government-Wide Acquisition Contract (GWAC)

A U.S. government contract that is available for use by all agencies.

Home Team

Your firm's capture team/organization.

Hot & Cold Buttons

Hot buttons are important issues or sets of issues that bidders should keep in mind because they are likely to drive customers' buying decisions. Cold buttons are customer prejudices—negative or potentially embarrassing things that bidders should not bring up to the potential customer.

Independent Cost Estimate (ICE)

The customer's estimate of a project's cost that was used to support a budget request.

Infocentricity

A term coined by CAI/SISCo in the 1980s to describe an environment where information is central to the enterprise rather than peripheral.

Integrated Product Team (IPT)

IPTs are established to work together to produce the interdependent elements of an overall solution. Each IPT is comprised of personnel to support product requirements definition, design and development, and undertake any changes over the life of the product. They are empowered to make critical life cycle decisions for the development of the product or system.

Joint Venture (JV)

A corporate vehicle whereby multiple corporate entities form a separate entity for the purpose of bidding a specific job or series of jobs. Rationales for creating such a vehicle include: lowering costs, isolating risk, masking intentions, and so forth.

Labor Model

A model that uses the many facets of Corporate Personality to turn salary data into labor rates.

Life-Cycle Cost (LCC)

The expected total cost of a solution over the entire period of performance of a contract.

Labor Fringe (LF)

Employer cost items, over and above salary, that directly benefit the employee.

Level Of Effort (LOE)
Used to define the amount of work performance within a period of time and measured in person days or hours per day/week/month/year.

Materiality
The PTW practitioner's need to concentrate on issues that provide competitor discriminators and stay away from immaterial issues that don't translate into competitive advantages.

Most Important Requirements (MIR)
Identification of key requirements that can put daylight between bidder solutions that are identified by means of analysis of an RFP's requirements.

Not Invented Here (NIH)
A classic management pathology, in which a team refuses to use information it didn't develop on its own.

Non-Cost Evaluation
Those portions of an RFP evaluation scheme (e.g., technical solution, management approach, staffing plan, past performance, financial stability etc.) that do not relate to proposed pricing.

Net Present Value (NPV)
Net present value results from taking out year discounts and applying them to future prices (in today's currency values) to approximate the future value of a bid.

Non-Recurring Engineering (NRE)
Activity related to the development of a system or capability that occurs once. Contrast this with O&M which is continuous.

Not To Exceed (NTE)
An amount of money that, regardless of need, cannot be exceeded without renegotiation.

Other Direct Costs (ODCs)
Direct and/or indirect non-labor elements of a bid, i.e. costs that do not fit readily into other categories such as radioactive waste disposal, computer time for data analysis, purchased services, etc.

Overhead (OH)
Those additional costs that are directly related to an employee but which don't provide an additional monetary benefit to the employee. If the work is on contractor site, this would include office costs, whereas if the work is on government site, it normally would not.

Operations & Maintenance (O&M)
Post-implementation activities related to a systems life-cycle.

Price As an Independent Variable (PAIV)
See CAIV and substitute Price for Cost. A way of viewing Price To Win (PTW).

Partially Gamed Price
The price that PTW develops to represent a competitor's likely price that is designed to do the job.

Project Management Office (PMO)
The focal point for all contract activity in either the customer's or the contractor's domain.

Provenance
A PTW practitioner's support for a contention or an assumption (i.e., where did you get this?).

Price To Win (PTW)
The process whereby a Capture Team uses the price that competitive bid teams are likely to develop as the price that their solution will have to live within if they are to prevail.

Performance Work Statement (PWS)
Defines specific results or outcomes derived from the commercial activity, including performance measures, standards and timeframes.

Readout
For example, the presentation of Price To Win (PTW) findings at bid team encounters.

Reality Model
Developed by means of research and customer knowledge to determine the most likely quantities of items (being evaluated quantitatively) that the customer is likely to buy, and when.

Request For Proposal (RFP)

An invitation for potential suppliers to submit a proposal on a specific opportunity. These can be highly complex documents that cover all technical, business and evaluation aspects of the bid.

Return On Investment (ROI)

A performance measure used to determine likely investment return.

Rough Order of Magnitude (ROM)

Estimate of costs and time in the early stages of the project.

Service Contract Act (SCA)

This act applies minimum hourly direct labor and labor fringe to non-exempt employees employed under every contract entered into by the United States or the District of Columbia, the principal purpose of which is to furnish services to the United States through the use of service employees.

Section M

Typically the section of a U.S. government RFP that details the proposal evaluation criteria.

Service Level Agreements (SLAs)

Performance standards that contractors offer to meet as part of a proposal or sign up for as part of contract. If SLAs are not met, there is usually a penalty for the contractor. For example, when a piece of hardware malfunctions, a contractor might agree to respond with a technician within two hours of the contractor's Service Desk being informed of the problem.

Subject Matter Expert (SME)

A person who is knowledgeable in a given technical or commercial area.

Snowflakes

Units of intelligence and/or other information that are captured and pre-positioned for possible reuse and used to build support for competitive positioning or other aspects of a PTW analysis.

Service Oriented Architecture (SOA)

A flexible set of design principles used during the phases of systems development and integration in computing. A system based on a SOA will package functionality as a suite of interoperable services that can be used within multiple, separate systems from several business domains.

Statement Of Objectives (SOO)

A government-prepared document that is incorporated into an RFP and states the overall solicitation objectives, but contains little of the specificity that is normally associated with a SOW. SOOs provide each offeror the maximum flexibility to propose an innovative solution.

Statement Of Work (SOW)

A SOW is a formal document that captures and defines the work activities, deliverables, and timeline a vendor will execute against in performance of specified work for a customer. Detailed requirements and pricing are usually included in the SOW, along with standard regulatory and governance terms and conditions.

Source Selection Authority (SSA)

The person who is ultimately responsible for selecting the contractor based on evaluations and recommendations of the SSEB.

Source Selection Evaluation Board (SSEB)

The team tailored for a particular acquisition that includes appropriate contracting, legal, logistics, technical, and other expertise to ensure a comprehensive evaluation of offers.

Strategic Strike Zone (SSZ)

A CAI/SISCo term that plots the Desirability and the Affordability of competing offers in a manner that visually presents their relative merits.

Street Talk

The corpus of information gathered from a variety of interpersonal sources to gain an understanding of competitors, their teams, solutions, etc.

Strengths, Weaknesses, Opportunities and Threats (SWOTs)

Related to a competitive bid team.

Time and Materials (T&M)

A type of contract whereby customer billings are based on the actual quantities of ODCs and/or actual time expended by the contractor at pre-determined labor rates.

Total Cost of Ownership (TCO)

The net cost of a proposed solution that uses "as is" costs that can be avoided and "to be" costs that will be incurred.

Task Order (TO)

An order to perform a discrete set of activities that is issued under an indefinite delivery, indefinite quantity contract.

Unreality

The difference between an RFP's evaluated quantities and a bidder's perception of what they are likely to sell.

Uncompensated Overtime (UOT)

The concept that divides the cost of compensating an individual for a 40 hour work week by a greater number of hours (e.g., 50) to develop a more aggressive labor rate.

Work Breakdown Structure (WBS)

The WBS is used to define and group a project's discrete work elements (or tasks) in a way that helps organize and define the total work scope of the project. A WBS also provides the necessary framework for detailed cost estimating and control along with providing guidance for schedule development and control.

Wrap Rate

Fully loaded labor rate expressed as a multiplier to direct labor costs. A wrap rate of two implies that if the direct labor cost is $1, then the customer will pay $2. The 100% uplift from one to two includes all statutory taxes (e.g., federal and state income taxes) as well as discretionary items (e.g., vacation time) that relate to the "personality" of a specific bidder/bid team.

Index

Bold number refers to definition.

A

ACA. *See* After Contract Award (ACA)
actual cost, 2
Addressable Budget
   about, 11
   defined, **125**
   PTW Framework, 28, 32, 33fII.6, 35fII.7, 36fII.8
   PTW Phase 1, 38–39, 44–48, 51–53, 54fIII.16, 55–57, 57fIII.20
   PTW Phase 2, 61
   PTW Phase 3, 82, 92, 93fV.9
   PTW Problem, 103–5, 105fVII.3, 114fVII.13
adjusted contract value, 49
Administration, 16, 16fI.11
Advanced Research Projects Agency Network (ARPANET), 101
Aerospace Model, 19–20
After Contract Award (ACA), 104
aggregate evaluation points, 50
aggregate prices, 76
allocation realities, 7
APMP. *See* Association of Proposal Management Professionals (APMP)
Apparent Loss, 20, 20fI.14
Apple, 22, 71, xvii
Apple's Hypercard PC database software, xvii
ARPANET. *See* Advanced Research Projects Agency Network (ARPANET)
"As Is" pursuit fund allocations, 18, 18fI.13
Association of Proposal Management Professionals (APMP), 18

B

BAFO. *See* Best And Final Offer (BAFO)
balance of cost, 1
Basic Evaluation Model (BEM)
   PTW Phase 1, 38, 49, 50fIII.10, 52fIII.14, 55, 55fIII.17
Basis Of Estimates (BOE)
   defined, **125**
   PTW Framework, 4, 30, 32–33, 36fII.8
   PTW Phase 2, 76–79
   PTW Problem, 107
Basis Of Estimates (BOE) Model
   PTW Framework, 35fII.7, 36fII.8
   PTW Phase 2, 59–60, 62, 70, 75–77, 77fIV.15, 78
Basis Of Estimates Module, 61, 61fIV.2
BD. *See* Business Development (BD)
BEM. *See* Basic Evaluation Model (BEM)
Best And Final Offer (BAFO)
   defined, **125**
   Food for Thought, 100, 100fVI.2
   PTW Framework, 31
   PTW Phase 3, 87
"best value"
   advantages, 48
   approach, 7, 53fIII.15
   competition, 55
   considerations, 30
   consolidated solution, 104
   example, 50
   issues, 22, 79
   offer, 2
Bid All Options strategy, 100
Bid Analysts, 24
bidder-created unreality, 86
"Bidder from Hell," 59
bidder's corporate risk pool, 33
bidding, 83, 85, 90, 99, 104, 111, 113
Bid Modelers, 24
bid price(s)
   about, xix, xvii
   points, 75
   PTW and, 1, 3–4, 10–12, 14, 17–18, 20, 22

bid price(s) *(continued)*
   PTW Framework, 28-29, 32, 36fII.8
   PTW Phase 1, 38, 42, 46, 48, 50, 55fIII.17
   PTW Phase 2, 59, 75
   PTW Phase 3, 82, 88, 93, 98-99
   PTW Problem, 105fVII.3, 113, 114fVII.13
bid pricing
   about, 7, 20, 20fI.14, 24, xvii
   PTW Phase 1, 67
   PTW Problem, 112
Bid Strategists, 5, 24
bid teams
   about, xvi, xvii, xxi
   Food For Thought, 96, 98-99
   PTW and, 4, 12-13, 20, 24
   PTW Framework, 28, 34, 35fII.7, 36fII.8
   PTW Phase 1, 38, 40, 42, 45, 47, 50-52, 53fIII.15, 54fIII.16, 55-57
   PTW Phase 2, 59-60, 63, 66-67, 69, 71, 75, 78
   PTW Phase 3, 81-82, 87, 89-90, 90fV.6, 91, 93
   PTW Problem, 104, 108-10, 112-13, 115, 119-20
Bid to Addressable Budget, 105
Big Bang theory, 98
Bill Of Materials (BOM)
   defined, **125**
   PTW Framework, 4, 33, 36fII.8
   PTW Phase 2, 61, 78-79, 116, 116fVII.15
   PTW Phase 3, 91, 120, 122, 122fVII.21
   PTW Problem, 107-8, 108fVII.6, 109-10, 110fVII.8, 112-13, 116, 116fVII.15, 118, 118fVII.17, 120, 122, 122fVII.21
Black Hat
   readouts, 13
   Review, 12-13, 13fI.9, 17, **125**
   Statement of Strategic Objectives, 13
   Strategic Platform, 13
   Syndrome, 13
Blanket Purchasing Agreement (BPA), **125**
blogs, 101
blue price points, 75
BLUF. *See* Bottom Line Up Front (BLUF)
BOE. *See* Basis Of Estimates (BOE)
BOM. *See* Bill Of Materials (BOM)
BOM Model, 35fII.7
bottomline risk, 12
Bottom Line Up Front (BLUF), 10, 10fI.7, **125**
Bottoms Up
   BOE, Partially Gamed, 75-77
   estimates, 29
   partially gamed prices, 107
   Partially Gamed PTW, 32, 36fII.7, 77-78, 93, 93fV.9

Bottoms Up *(continued)*
   PTW, Partially Gamed, 27, 31, 56, 77, 89, xix (*See also under* PTW Phase 2)
   PTW details, 91
   PTW errors, 78
   PTW process, 93
   PTW targets, 34
   "should price," 29, 37, 76
BPA. *See* Blanket Purchasing Agreement (BPA)
briefcase brigades, 66
Broker, Trader, Lawyer, Spy: The Secret World of Corporate Espionage (Javer), 41
Brown Bag strategy, 100
budgetary "winds of change," 83
budget constraint forecasts, 83
Business Development (BD), 17fI.12, **125**
Business Development Models, 19-20
Buyers, 71fIV.8

C

CAGR. *See* Compound Annual Growth Rate (CAGR)
CAI/SISC, 1, xvii, xviii fig, xviii-xix
CAI/SISCo
   about, xxi
   Delta Margin Gaming (DMG), 87, 126
   discriminators and MIR analysis, 44
   e-mail contact, 58, 79, 94, xix
   Final, Fully Gamed PTW, 32
   GWAC labor categories, build-ups on, 68
   Infocenter, xxi
   Infocentricity, 127
   Infostructure Consulting, xxi
   LinkedIn "Price To Win" group, xix
   Microsoft Excel spreadsheet models, 58, 79, 94, xix
   mission, xvi
   parametric process, 28
   Pricing Strategies, xxi
   proposal development changes, 18
   PTW analysis, codified approach to, xvii
   PTW Framework, 3-Phase, 10-Step, 1, 27, 29, 32-33, 32fII.5, 33fII.6, 35fII.7
   PTW model suite, 60, 61fIV.2
   PTW practitioners, types of, 24
   PTW training seminars, xviii
   Reality Models, xxi
   Strategic Strike Zone (SSZ), 45, 129
   Subject Matter Experts (SMEs), xxi
CAIV. *See* Cost As an Independent Variable (CAIV)
Capacity Pricing strategy, 100

Index

Capture Activity, 18fI.13
capture campaigns, successful, 2
Capture Manager, 14, 17, 19
Capture Plan Element, 6, 6fI.4
capture strategy, 45, 79, 91
Capture Tactical Plan, 13
Capture Team(s)
    about, 4fI.1, 5, 5fI.2, 13–14, 24
    defined, **125**
    evaluation award points, xv
    job of, 4
    PTW Phase 1, 38–41, 43–44, 46, 56–58
    PTW Phase 2, 60, 76–79
    PTW Phase 3, 82, 91
    PTW Problem, 107
    view of pricing issue, 13–14
CAS. *See* Cost Accounting Standards (CAS)
Cash in Hand strategy, 99
CBA. *See* Collective Bargaining Agreement (CBA)
CDs. *See* compact discs (CDs)
chain of command, 43
CI. *See* Competitive Intelligence (CI)
classic business development model, 5
C-level trench coat, 66
CLIN. *See* Contract Line Item Number (CLIN)
CLIN-level reality quantities, 35fII.7
COLAs. *See* Cost Of Living Adjustments (COLAs)
Collective Bargaining Agreement (CBA), 62, **126**
collective intelligence, 14
Commercial, Off The Shelf (COTS), **126**
Commoditization, 74, **126**
common environmental denominator, 14
compact discs (CDs), 71
company websites, 101
Competition, 5, 5fI.3
competitive
    Bid Teams, 104, xvii
    contract awards, 1, xix, xv, xviii
    contract competitions, 1
    firepower, 2
    information, 12
    opportunity capture campaigns, 1
    pricing analyses, xvii
    situation, 12
    win probabilities (pWins), xviii
Competitive Analysis, 3–4, 4fI.1, 5fI.2
Competitive Analysis/PTW
    about, 18fI.13, 19
    PTW Framework, 29fII.3, 35fII.7
    PTW Phase 1, 37fIII.1
    PTW Phase 2, 59fIV.1

Competitive Analysis/PTW *(continued)*
    PTW Phase 3, 81fV.1
    PTW Problem, 103fVII.1
Competitive Intelligence (CI), 23, 43–44, **126**, xix
competitor past pricing behaviors, 29
competitor's Price To Do the job, 36ffII.8, 76, 87
Competitor Target Pricing Estimates, 38
Compound Annual Growth Rate (CAGR), 110, **125**
Computer Sciences Corporation (CSC), 95
Constable, Anthony C. (author), xvi–xvii
Continuity Of Operations (COOP), 107
Contract Duration, 20fI.14
Contracting Avenues for Acquiring Labor, 95, 95fVI.1
Contract Line Item Number (CLIN)
    CLIN-by-CLIN realities, 83
    defined, **126**
    Deflation Profiles, 72, 73fIV.10
    Food for Thought, 99
    PTW Framework, 30, 36fII.8
    PTW Phase 2, 60, 70, 72
    PTW Phase 3, 81–84, 87
    PTW Problem, 112
    Reality Model, 81
    "Real" opportunity, 84
contractor-addressable budget, 39, 48
contractor-site labor, 68
contractor space, 68
contract sales performance, 12
contract's life cycle, 49
Contract Year (CY), **126**
Contract Year One (CY1)
    PTW Phase 1, 54fIII.16
    PTW Phase 2, 63–64, 68, 70, 74, 79
    PTW Phase 3, 83–84
    PTW Problem, 104, 105fVII.2, 108fVII.6, 109, 109fVII.7, 110, 110fVII.8, 114fVII.12, 116fVII.15, 117fVII.16, 118fVII.17, 121fVII.20, 122fVII.21
Contract Year One (CY2)
    PTW Phase 2, 64–65, 70
    PTW Problem, 104, 105fVII.2, 108fVII.6, 109fVII.7, 110fVII.8, 114, 114fVII.12, 116fVII.15, 117fVII.16, 118fVII.17, 121fVII.20, 122fVII.21
COOP. *See* Continuity Of Operations (COOP)
Corporate Personality, 13, 45, 63, 70–71, 95, **126, 127**
Corporate Profile, 13
Cost Accounting Standards (CAS), 95
Cost As an Independent Variable (CAIV), 7–8, 8fI.5, **125**

cost avoidance potential, 12
cost+-derived solution, 2
Cost Of Living Adjustments (COLAs), 30, 62, 66, 70, **126**
cost of ownership, 1–2. *See also* Total Cost of Ownership (TCO)
cost-plus approach, 11
Cost/Price Take Downs, 61
COTS. *See* Commercial, Off The Shelf (COTS)
critical success factors, 43, 45
CSC. *See* Computer Sciences Corporation (CSC)
Customer Addressable Budget Estimates, 38
customer assets, 30
Customer budget realities, 29
customer environment, xvi
Customer Process, 28
customer's opportunity budget, 44
CY. *See* Contract Year (CY)

D

DD&T. *See* Design, Develop & Test (DD&T)
Deal To Win, 2
Decision Gates, 28
decomposition, 47fIII.7
Defensive Discount, 49, 53
Deflator, 60, 72
Delta Margin Gaming (DMG)
    about, 20, **126,** 127
    PTW Phase 3, 81, 83, 87–90, 93
Demand Elasticity strategy, 100
Design, Develop & Test (DD&T), 46, **126**
Design To Cost (DTC), **126**
Desired Contract Profit Margin, 20fI.14
Direct Labor (DL), **126**
DL. *See* Direct Labor (DL)
DMG. *See* Delta Margin Gaming (DMG)
dogs (customers), 69
DPWS. *See* Draft Performance Work Statement (DPWS)
Draft Performance Work Statement (DPWS), 4. *See also* Performance Work Statement (PWS)
Draft Plans, 21
Draft Request For Proposal (DRFP), 4, **126**
Draft Statement Of Work (DSOW), 4, 50
DRFP. *See* Draft Request For Proposal (DRFP)
DRFP/RFP
    PTW Phase 1, 45, 49
    PTW Phase 2, 61–62, 71
    PTW Phase 3, 82–83
DSOO, 50
DSOW. *See* Draft Statement Of Work (DSOW)

DTC. *See* Design To Cost (DTC)

E

Early PTW analysis, 11
Earned Value Management System (EVMS), 45, **126**
Economic Research Institute (ERI), 62, **126**
ECP. *See* Engineering Change Proposal (ECP)
8 quad core servers, 74
Encounter
    0: PTW Phase 0, 33–34, 35fII.7–35fII.8, 38–39
    1: PTW Phase 1, 31, 34, 35fII.7–35fII.8, 38–40, 46, 57–59, 77, 81
    2: PTW Phase 2, 31, 34, 35fII.7–35fII.8, 56, 60, 78–79
    3: PTW Phase 3, 31, 34, 35fII.7–35fII.8, 56, 82, 91
Engineering Change Proposal (ECP)
    defined, **126**
    PTW Phase 1, 42
    PTW Phase 3, 85–86, 89, 90fV.6
enterprise amnesia, 14
Environmental Protection Agency (EPA), xvi
EPA. *See* Environmental Protection Agency (EPA)
ERI. *See* Economic Research Institute (ERI)
Estimated Reality Sales Value, 88fV.5, 89
Ethics, 24
Evaluated Case, 20
Evaluated Total Price, 88fV.5, 89
Evaluation Model
    Cumulative Profit Margin, 20, 20fI.14
    defined, **126**
    PTW Phase 1, 45, 49, 50fIII.10, 51, 51fIII.11, 52, 52fIII.14, 55–56, 55fIII.17
    PTW Phase 2, 60–61, 78
    PTW Phase 3, 82, 84, 88, 91
    PTW Problem, 105–7, 115, 119, 122
Evaluation Scheme, 30, 44–45, 49–50, 57, 78, 91, 128, xvi
Everything About Everything (Constable), 15, xvii
EVMS. *See* Earned Value Management System (EVMS)
exploitable unreality, 86
Exploitation of Unrealistic Evaluation Quantities strategy, 100

F

facilitator role, 12
FAR. *See* U.S. Federal Acquisition Regulation (FAR)
Federal Telephone Service (FTS), 98

FFP. *See* Firm, Fixed Price (FFP)
Final, Fully Gamed PTW, 32, 93, 99
Final Evaluation Model, 82, 91
Finance, 16, 16fI.11, 17fI.12
Firm, Fixed Price (FFP), 33, 90, 104, **127**
Fiscal Year (FY), **127**
Fixed Cost Allocation strategy, 99
FOC. *See* Fully Operational Capability (FOC)
FOIA. *See* Freedom Of Information Act (FOIA)
Food for Thought
  Best And Final Offer (BAFO), 100, 100fVI.2
  bid teams, 96, 98–99
  consequences, unintended, 101
  Contract Line Item Number (CLIN), 99
  Government Labor Market, 95–96, 95fVI.1
  Home Team, 99
  incumbency tale, cautionary, 98–99
  Other Direct Costs (ODCs), 99–100
  Price To Win (PTW) practitioner, 95–100, 102
  PTW Practitioners, Pricing Strategies for, 99–100
  Public-Private Partnership, 97
  Reality Model, 100
  Request For Proposal (RFP), 100
  research sources, general, 101–2
  Small Business (SB), 104
  Strengths, Weaknesses, Opportunities, and Threats (SWOTs), 97
  Top-Down PTW, 96–97
  U.S. Federal Government Staff Augmentation Marketplace, 97
Forward Pricing, **127**
Freedom Of Information Act (FOIA), **127**
FTE. *See* Full Time Equivalent (FTE)
FTS. *See* Federal Telephone Service (FTS)
FTS2000 berth, 98
Full Time Equivalent (FTE), **127**
Fully Gamed Bottoms Up prices, 91
Fully Gamed Price, **127**
Fully Gamed PTW, 91–93
Fully Operational Capability (FOC), 30
functionality, 1, 129
FY. *See* Fiscal Year (FY)

G

G&A. *See* General and Administrative Expenses (G&A)
Gamed for Price
  bid, 89
  price, 88fV.3, 89
Gamed for Profit
  bid, 89

Gamed for Profit *(continued)*
  price, 88–89, 88fV.5
Game Theory, 11–12, 11fI.8
Gaming, **127**
gaming bid prices, 1
General and Administrative Expenses (G&A), **127**
"get well" plan, 20
global warming, 73
government competitions, 1
government contracting opportunities, xvi
Government Labor Market, 95–96, 95fVI.1
government RFP, 30
Government-Wide Acquisition Contracts (GWAC), 67–68, **127**
Government-Wide acquisition websites, 102
GSA. *See* U.S. General Services Administration (GSA)
GWAC. *See* Government-Wide Acquisition Contracts (GWAC)

H

healthcare costs, 63–65, 65fIV.4, 67
Home Team
  about, 2, 4–5, 8, 11–12, 17–18, 20, 22, xix
  Comfort Factor, 93
  defined, **127**
  Food For Thought, 99
  InfoCenter, 32, 92
  internal Black Hat and Gate, Step, or Milestone review readouts, 39
  PTW Phase 1, 38–39, 41, 44–45, 48, 50–53, 53fIII.15, 55, 55fIII.17, 56–57
  PTW Phase 2, 59–61, 76, 78
  PTW Phase 3, 82, 84–85, 91–93, 93fV.9
  PTW Problem, 103–4, 107, 112, 115, 119, 122
  winning evaluated bid price, 4
hot buttons, 78
Hot & Cold Buttons, **127**
HVAC systems, 74

I

IBM's Lotus Notes, 14
ICE. *See* Independent Cost Estimate (ICE)
IDIQ. *See* Indefinite Delivery, Indefinite Quantity (IDIQ)
incumbent recompetes, 2
Indefinite Delivery, Indefinite Quantity (IDIQ), 35fII.7, 77, 130
Independent Cost Estimate (ICE), **127**
Industry Day, 40

industry events, 101
inflation/deflation profile, 70
Inflators, 72
InfoCenter
   corporate, 15, 79, 91
   corporate database, 58
   "Corporate Memory," xxi
   enterprise's, 43
   Home Team's, 32, 92
Infocentricity
   collective intelligence, 14–15, 15fI.10
   defined, **127,** xvii
   PTW Phase 1, 38–39
information democracy, 23
Information Hounds and Leveragers, 24
Information Technology (IT), 14
Information Technology Infrastructure Library (ITIL), 49
Initial Profit Margin, 20fI.14
"Innovator–Imitator–Idiot" cycle, 22, 45
Input Module, 60, 61fIV.2
In Search of Excellence (Peters and Waterman), xv
insurgent bidder, 21, 75
Integrated Product Team (IPT)
   cost targets, 48
   defined, **127**
   PTW Phase 1, 46–48
Integrator Model, 19
Inter-Exchange Carrier (IXC), 98
Internal Reviews, 28
Internet Protocol version 4 (IPv4), 72
iPod, 22, 71
IPT. *See* Integrated Product Team (IPT)
IPv4. *See* Internet Protocol version 4 (IPv4)
IT. *See* Information Technology (IT)
ITCON. *See* IT Consolidation (ITCON)
IT Consolidation (ITCON)
   Addressable Budget, 105
   BOM Elements, 108fVII.6, 116fVII.15
   competitors, 104
   Labor Categories, 109fVII.7, 117fVII.16, 121fVII.20
   opportunity, 104, 107–8, 112–13
   Phase 1, 106, 115
   Phase 2, 107–11, 113, 116–17, 119
   Phase 3, 112–13, 120–22
   Proposal Evaluation Criteria (PEC), 106fVII.4, 111fVII.9, 115fVII.14, 119fVII.18, 122fVII.22
ITIL. *See* Information Technology Infrastructure Library (ITIL)
IXC. *See* Inter-Exchange Carrier (IXC)

J

Javer, Eamon, 41
Joint Venture (JV), 60, 66–67, 99, **127**

K

key events, 30
Key Personnel, 21
known unknowns, 12

L

Labor, 30
Labor Categories, 30, 77
Labor Fringe (LF), **127**
Labor Level Of Effort (LOE), 120
Labor Model
   about, 35fII.7, **127**
   PTW Phase 2, 62–63, 70, 70fIV.7
Labor Module, 60, 61fIV.2
labor pyramids, 61, 79
Labor Rate Build-Up, 63
Labor Rate Build-up Realities, 63, 63fIV.3
Labor Rate Categories, 95, 95fVI.1
Labor Rate Model, 70
Labor Rates blended to lower Evaluated Prices, 69, 69fIV.6
Labor Rates for CY2 and beyond, 64–65
Labor Rate strategies, 99
Large Business (LB), 104
LCC. *See* Life-Cycle Cost (LCC)
Lease strategy, 100
LEC. *See* local exchange carriers (LEC)
Lego Pricing strategy, 99
Level 0 maturity, 10
Level 1 maturity, 10–11
Level 2 maturity, 11
Level 3 maturity, 11
Levels Of Effort (LOEs)
   about, 4, 30, 33
   defined, **125, 128**
   PTW Phase 2, 61, 75, 78
   PTW Problem, 120
LF. *See* Labor Fringe (LF)
life cycle, 9, 25, 49, 70, 127–28
Life-Cycle Cost (LCC), **127**
life of benefits, 2
Lobbyists, 40–41
local exchange carriers (LEC), 98
LOE. *See* Labor Level Of Effort (LOE)
LOEs. *See* Levels Of Effort (LOEs)
low-priced bidder, 21

M

major milestones, 30
Management Approach, 21
The March Toward Bottom Line Up Front (BLUF), 10fI.7
Martin Marietta, xvi
Materiality, 8, **128**
Maximum Score, 6, 6fI.4
Mercer, 62
Milestone Payment strategy, 99
MIRs. *See* Most Important Requirements (MIRs)
Model. *See also* Basis Of Estimates (BOE) Model
    BOM, 35fII.7
    CLIN Reality, 81
    Final Evaluation, 82, 91
    Labor, 35fII.7
    Labor Rate, 70
Modules
    Basis Of Estimates, 61, 61fIV.2
    Input, 60, 61fIV.2
    Labor, 60, 61fIV.2
    ODC, 60, 61fIV.2
    Reporting, 61, 61fIV.2
    Target-Specific, 60–61, 61fIV.2
monthly recurring charge (MRC), 98
Moore's Law, 100
Most Important Requirements (MIRs), 44, **128**
MP3 digital audio encoding format, 22, 71
MRC. *See* monthly recurring charge (MRC)
"must win" bids, 2
"must win" opportunities, 2

N

National Capital Region (NCR), xvi
NCR. *See* National Capital Region (NCR)
NDA. *See* Non Disclosure Agreement (NDA)
Net Present Value (NPV), **128**
NIH. *See* Not Invented Here (NIH)
Non-Cost Evaluation, **128**
non-cost evaluation
    criterion, 7, 50–51, 55, 115, 119
    issue, 55fIII.18
    scores, 45, 107, 112
Non Disclosure Agreement (NDA), 38
non-incumbent prime, 21
non-labor costs, 30
non-price evaluation criterion, 50
non-price scoring, 45, 53
Non-Recurring Engineering (NRE), 78, 91, 99, **128**
Not Invented Here (NIH), 23, **128**

Not To Exceed (NTE), 42, **128**
NPV. *See* Net Present Value (NPV)
NRE. *See* Non-Recurring Engineering (NRE)
NTE. *See* Not To Exceed (NTE)

O

OCR. *See* Optical Character Recognition (OCR)
ODC Module, 60, 61fIV.2
ODCs. *See* Other Direct Costs (ODCs)
OEs. *See* Operating Environments (OEs)
Office of Management and Budget's (OMB), 86
OH. *See* Overhead (OH)
O&M. *See* Operations & Maintenance (O&M)
OMB. *See* Office of Management and Budget's (OMB)
Open Source information, 41, 86, 101–2
Open Source Snowflakes, 37
Operating Environments (OEs), 104
Operations, 16, 16fI.11, 17fI.12
Operations & Maintenance (O&M), 9, 9fI.6, 46, **128**
Opportunity
    PTW Framework, 29fII.3, 30, 31fII.3
    PTW Phase 1, 37fIII.1
    PTW Phase 2, 59fIV.1, 60, 62
    PTW Phase 3, 81fV.1
    PTW Problem, 103fVII.1
Opportunity Capture Process, 3
opportunity's critical mass, 45
Optical Character Recognition (OCR), 22
Other Direct Costs (ODCs)
    defined, **125, 128**
    Food For Thought, 99–100
    PTW Framework, 30, 36fII.8
    PTW Phase 1, 54fIII.16, 57
    PTW Phase 2, 59–60, 62–63, 70–72, 74–79
    PTW Phase 3, 82, 91
Out Of Hide (OOH) strategy, 100
Overhead (OH), **128**

P

Page Constraints, 21
PAIV. *See* Price As an Independent Variable (PAIV)
Partially Gamed
    Bottoms Up BOE, 75–77
    Bottoms Up PTW, 27, 31, 56, 77, 89, xix (*See also under* PTW Phase 2)
Price, 32, **128**
Price To Do the job PTW, 79

Partially Gamed PTW
  Fully Gamed PTW *vs.*, 31–32, 31fII.4
  PTW Framework, 32–33
  PTW Phase 1, 59, 61
  PTW Phase 2, 76–79
  PTW Phase 3, 87, 89–93
  PTW Problem, 107
PEC. *See* Proposal Evaluation Criteria (PEC)
pent-up demand, 83, xvii
Performance Work Statement (PWS). *See also*
    Draft Performance Work Statement (DPWS)
  defined, **128**
  PTW Phase 1, 42, 46
  PTW Problem, 106fVII.4, 111fVII.9,
    115fVII.14, 119fVII.18, 122fVII.22
Peters, Tom, xv
Phase-In, 21
pipeline value, 7
PMO. *See* Project Management Office (PMO)
Positioning To Win, 2
Post-Award Marketing Plan, 13
Post-Award Operational Plan, 13
Post-mortemists, 24
Potential Competing Bid Team Price Takedowns
  PTW Phase 1, 54fIII.16
  PTW Phase 3, 90fV.6
Prerequisite Pricing strategy, 99
Presenters, 24
price
  erosion curve, 75
  as determinant of competitive contract awards,
    xv
  as significant determinant of competitive
    awards, 1
  point scores, 50
  points post-award, 45
  risk, 44
Price As an Independent Variable (PAIV), 8, **128**
Price Definition, 28
Price Risk Mitigation Zone, 20fI.14
Price Target-Driven Solutions, 10–11, 10fI.7
Price To Win (PTW). *See also* Partially Gamed
    PTW
  about, 1–3
  "Best Value" issue, 22
  Black Hat Review, relationship to, 12–13,
    13fI.9
  Bottoms Up targets, 34
  Business Development Models and, 19–20
  Capture Campaigns, role in shaping successful,
    17
  Capture Process, how PTW changes the, 4–5,
    4fI.1, 5fI.2

Price To Win (PTW) *(continued)*
  Capture Teams, role to fully inform, 13–14
  case study, 25
  competition, shedding light on the, 5, 5fI.3
  concept, xv, xvi
  defined, **128**
  to do or not to do, 23
  Early and/or Late, 18
  Early *vs.* Late, 32
  engagement, first, xvii
  ethics and, 24
  Final, Fully Gamed, 32, 93, 99
  Fully Gamed, 32–33
  function of, 5fI.3
  funded, how it should be, 18–19, 18fI.13
  Game Theory and, 11–12, 11fI.8
  Information Dilemma, 14–16, 15fI.10
  key terms, 7–9, 8fI.5, 9fI.6
  Opportunity Capture Process, 3
  painting by numbers and, 19
  parametric elements, 38, 60, 81
  Partially and Fully Gamed, 31, 31fII.4
  practitioner's role, 3, 5
  Practitioner's view of incumbency, 21
  Price Target-Driven Solutions, 10–11, 10fI.7
  Price To Do the job, 31–33, 31fII.4
  price to win *all things considered,* 17
  Price To Win the job, 31–32, 31fII.4
  readout, 32
  resources, 23–24
  Stakeholders, serves all, 16, 16fI.11
  story it has to tell, 18
  Strategic Bid Pricing 101, 20–21, 20fI.14
  studies, who commissions?, 17
  Team, 11, 11fI.8, 12, 16, 22–23, 25
  Teams, approach advice for, 22–23
  Top Down, 48, 92–93, 96, 103, 105–6
  top down and bottoms up, 3
  Value Proposition of, 12
  way of employing, 16, 17fI.12
  who uses it and why?, 7
  Win Probability (pWin), improving, 6–7, 6fI.4
Price To Win (PTW) Framework
  about, 27
  Addressable Budget, 28, 32, 33fII.6, 35fII.7,
    36fII.8
  Basis Of Estimates (BOE), 4, 30, 32–33, 36fII.8
  Best And Final Offer (BAFO), 31
  bid price(s), 28–29, 32, 36fII.8
  bid teams, 28, 34, 35fII.7, 36fII.8
  Bill Of Materials (BOM), 4, 33, 36fII.8
  BOE Model, 35fII.7, 36fII.8
  CAI/SISCo's, 29, 29fII.3

Price To Win (PTW) Framework *(continued)*
   CAI/SISCo's, other views of, 32–33, 32fII.5, 33fII.6
   Competitive Analysis/PTW, 29fII.3, 35fII.7
   Contract Line Item Number (CLIN), 30, 36fII.8
   in a Nutshell, 36fII.8
   Opportunity, 29fII.3, 30, 31fII.3
   Opportunity defined, 29fII.3, 30, 31fII.3
   Other Direct Costs (ODCs), 30, 36fII.8
   Overall Capture Process, relationship of PTW to, 28, 28fII.1
   Parametric Process, PTW as a, 28–29, 29fII.2
   Partially Gamed PTW, 32–33
   Partially Gamed *vs.* Fully Gamed PTW, 31–32, 31fII.4
   Phase 0, 35fII.7
   Phase 1: *Situational Awareness and the Top Down PTW,* 29fII.3, 31, 31fII.3, 32fII.5, 33fII.6, 35fII.7, 36fII.8
   Phase 2: *The Partially Gamed, Bottoms Up PTW,* 29fII.3, 31, 31fII.3–31fII.4, 32fII.5, 33, 33fII.6, 35fII.7, 36fII.8
   Phase 3: *The Fully Gamed PTW,* 29fII.3, 31, 31fII.3, 32fII.5, 33fII.6, 36fII.8
   Phases, defined, 31, 31fII.3
   PTW Phase 0, 35fII.7
   PTW Team/Capture Team encounters, 33
   Reality Model, 20, 23, 35fII.7, 36fII.8
   target price, 36fII.8
   Tasking to support the, 34, 35fII.7
   Top Down target prices, 36fII.8
   win probabilities (pWins) of 100%, xviii
   Work Breakdown Structure (WBS), 9, 11, 30, 33 31fII.3, 35fII.7, 36fII.8
Price To Win (PTW) Phase 0
   Encounter 0, 33–34, 35fII.7–35fII.8, 38–39
   PTW framework, 35fII.7
Price To Win (PTW) Phase 1: *Situational Awareness and the Top Down PTW*
   Addressable Budget, 38–39, 44–48, 51–53, 54fIII.16, 55–57, 57fIII.20
   Basic Evaluation Model (BEM) (e), 38, 49, 50fIII.10, 52fIII.14, 55, 55fIII.17
   bid price(s), 38, 42, 46, 48, 50, 55fIII.17
   bid pricing, 67
   bid teams, 38, 40, 42, 45, 47, 50–52, 53fIII.15, 54fIII.16, 55–57
   Budget Projection (d), 52
   Budget Realities, 49, 49fIII.9
   Capture Team(s), 38–41, 43–44, 46, 56–58
   Competitive Analysis/PTW, 37fIII.1
   Competitive Intelligence (CI), 43–44

Price To Win (PTW) Phase 1: *(continued)*
   Competitors and the Home Team, 44–45
   Competitor SWOT Summaries (b), 51, 51fIII.12
   Contract Year One (CY1), 54fIII.16
   Customer, understanding the, 43–44
   Customer Requirements, grappling with, 44
   Customer's Cast of Characters, 43, 43fIII.5
   Defensive Discount, 49, 53
   DRFP/RFP, 45, 49
   Encounter 0, 38–39
   Encounter 1, 31, 34, 35fII.7–35fII.8, 38–40, 46, 57–59, 77, 81
   Engineering Change Proposal (ECP), 42
   Evaluation Model, 45, 49, 50fIII.10, 51, 51fIII.11, 52, 52fIII.14, 55–56, 55fIII.17
   Evaluation Models, a word about scoring, 55–56, 55fIII.17
   Home Team, 38–39, 41, 44–45, 48, 50–53, 53fIII.15, 55, 55fIII.17, 56–57
   Incumbent Contractors, 39
   Infocentricity, 38–39
   Integrated Product Team (IPT), 46–48
   Lack of Understanding can really hurt, 42
   Lobbyists, effectiveness of, 40–41
   Non-Cost Evaluation Scoring (b), Color Coding as basis for, 52, 52fIII.13
   Non-Cost Evaluation Scoring (c), Provenance for, 52, 52fIII.14, 53fIII.15
   Opportunity, 37fIII.1
   Opportunity Environment, 38
   Opportunity Understanding, 41–42, 42fIII.4
   Other Direct Costs (ODCs), 54fIII.16, 57
   Partially Gamed PTW, 59, 61
   Performance Work Statement (PWS), 42, 46
   positioning graphic, 42fIII.4
   Potential Competing Bid Team Price Takedowns, 54fIII.16
   Procurement Background, 39
   PTW framework, 29fII.3, 31, 31fII.3, 32fII.5, 33fII.6, 35fII.7, 36fII.8, 37–38, 37fIII.1
   PTW Information, acquiring needed, 41
   PTW practitioner, 39, 41, 44–45, 48–53, 55–56, 58
   PTW Problem, Progressive, 58
   Reality Model, 36fII.8, 49, 54fIII.16
   Request For Proposal (RFP), 42, 45, 50
   Road Map, 39–40, 39fIII.2
   Situational Analysis, developing, 40, 40fIII.3
   SOO-Based Acquisitions and PTW, 42
   Source Selection Authority (SSA), 43
   Statement Of Work (SOW), 42, 46
   Step 1, 48

Price To Win (PTW) Phase 1: *(continued)*
   Step 2 — Evaluation Modeling, 49–51, 50fIII.10, 51, 51fIII.11
   Strategic Pricing Issues, 53, 54fIII.16
   Strategic Strike Zone (SSZ), 45, 56–57, 56fIII.19, 57fIII.20
   Strengths, Weaknesses, Opportunities, and Threats (SWOTs), 38, 40, 51, 51fIII.12, 55, 57
   Takedown Rationale, 53, 54fIII.16
   take-downs, 44, 48–49, 51, 53, 55, 61
   target price, 32, 45–49, 47fIII.8, 53, 57, 57fIII.20
   Teaming Issues to bear in mind, 45
   Top Down Analysis, PTW and WBS for, 46–48, 46fIII.6, 47fIII.7–47fIII.8
   "Top Down" Comparative Evaluation, 55fIII.17
   Top Down Competitor PTW Analysis—Approach 2, 48–49
   Top Down Competitor PTW Analysis—Approach 3, 53, 54fIII.16
   Top Down PTW, 48, 93
   Top Down Strategic Pricing, 53
   Top Down target prices, 32, 36fII.8, 45, 48–49, 53, 57fIII.20, 92
   Top Down target pricing, 48
   Venn-like graphic, 43, 43fIII.5
   Work Breakdown Structure (WBS), 42, 46–48, 57
Price To Win (PTW) Phase 2: *The Partially Gamed, Bottoms Up PTW*
   Addressable Budget, 61
   Basis Of Estimates (BOE), 76–79
   bid price(s), 59, 75
   bid teams, 59–60, 63, 66–67, 69, 71, 75, 78
   Bill Of Materials (BOM), 61, 78–79, 116, 116fVII.15
   BOE, WBS-Level, 76–77, 77fIV.14
   BOE Model, 59–60, 62, 70, 75–77, 77fIV.15, 78
   BOEs, WBS-Based, 76, 76fIV.13
   BOEs and BOMs, 78
   Capture Team(s), 60, 76–79
   change, the only constant, 71–72, 71fIV.8
   commoditization, 74, **126**
   Competitive Analysis/PTW, 59fIV.1
   Contract Line Item Number (CLIN), 60, 70, 72
   Contract Year One (CY1), 63–64, 68, 70, 74, 79
   Contract Year One (CY2), 64–65, 70
   Corporate Personality, 63
   DRFP/RFP, 61–62, 71
   Encounter 2, 31, 34, 35fII.7–35fII.8, 56, 60, 78–79

Price To Win (PTW) Phase 2: *(continued)*
   Evaluation Model, 60–61, 78
   Government-Wide Acquisition Contracts (GWAC), 67–68, **127**
   Healthcare Costs, 63–65, 65fIV.4, 67
   Home Team, 59–61, 76, 78
   Labor Model, 70, 70fIV.7
   labor opportunities, off-site, 68–69
   Labor Rate Build-Up, 63
   Labor Rate Build-up Realities, 63, 63fIV.3
   Labor Rates blended to lower Evaluated Prices, 69, 69fIV.6
   Labor Rates for CY2 and beyond, 64–65
   Levels Of Effort (LOEs), 61, 75, 78
   lower costs, solution development to, 73–74, 73fIV.11
   Modeling Elements, PTW's suite of, 60–61, 61fIV.2
   Non-Wrap Rate Build-Up approaches, 66–67
   ODC discounts and deflators, 72–73, 72fIV.9, 73fIV.10
   Opportunity, 59fIV.1, 60, 62
   Other Direct Costs (ODCs), 59–60, 62–63, 70–72, 74–79
   Overtime, uncompensated, 67, 68fIV.5
   Partially Gamed, Bottoms Up PTW, 27, 31, 56, 77, xix
   Partially Gamed PTW, 76–79
   pricing curves, monitoring and adjusting, 74–75, 75fIV.12
   PTW framework, 29fII.3, 31, 31fII.3–31fII.4, 32fII.5, 33, 33fII.6, 35fII.7, 36fII.8
   PTW practitioner, 60, 62, 64–67, 71–79
   Request For Proposal (RFP), 67
   Small Business (SB), 52fIII.13, 57fIII.20, 67, 70
   Statement Of Work (SOW), 61
   Step 3—WBS for Bottoms Up Analysis, 61–62
   Step 4—Labor Model, 62–63
   Step 5—ODC Model, 70–71
   Step 6—BOE Model, 75
   Step 7—Evaluation Model, 78
   Strategic Strike Zone (SSZ), 61
   Strengths, Weaknesses, Opportunities, and Threats (SWOTs), 60, 79, 82
   take-downs, 72–73
   target price, 61
   Work Breakdown Structure (WBS), 59–62, 75–78, 91
   Wrap Rates, 60, 66–67, 69–70
Price To Win (PTW) Phase 3: *The Fully Gamed PTW*
   Addressable Budget, 82, 92, 93fV.9
   Best And Final Offer (BAFO), 87

Price To Win (PTW) Phase 3: *(continued)*
  bid price(s), 82, 88, 93, 98–99
  bid teams, 81–82, 87, 89–90, 90fV.6, 91, 93
  Bill Of Materials (BOM), 91, 120, 122, 122fVII.21
  Capture Team(s), 82, 91
  Competitive Analysis/PTW, 81fV.1
  Contract Line Item Number (CLIN), 81–84, 87
  Contract Year One (CY1), 83–84
  Delta Margin Gaming (DMG), 81, 83, 87–90, 93
  DRFP/RFP, 82–83
  Encounter 3, 31, 34, 35fII.7–35fII.8, 56, 82, 91
  Engineering Change Proposal (ECP), 85–86, 89, 90fV.6
  Evaluation Model, 82, 84, 88, 91
  Home Team, 82, 84–85, 91–93, 93fV.9
  Opportunity, 81fV.1
  Other Direct Costs (ODCs), 82, 91
  Partially Gamed PTW, 87, 89–93
  Potential Competing Bid Team Price Takedowns, 90fV.6
  PTW framework, 29fII.3, 31, 31fII.3, 32fII.5, 33fII.6, 36fII.8
  PTW practitioner, 82–85, 87, 89–91
  Reality Model, 81–82, 82fV.2, 83–85, 85fV.3, 86, 89, 100
  Request For Proposal (RFP), 83–84, 90fV.6
  Small Business (SB), 101
  Statement Of Work (SOW), 85
  Strengths, Weaknesses, Opportunities, and Threats (SWOTs), 81fV.1, 91
  take-downs, 89–90, 90fV.6, 93
  target price, 92
  Top Down PTW, 92
  Unreality, 82, 82fV.2, 86–87
Price To Win (PTW) Phase Recapitulation, 93fV.9
Price To Win (PTW) practitioner
  about, 28
  Food for Thought, 95–100, 102
  Phase 1: *Situational Awareness and the Top Down PTW,* 39, 41, 44–45, 48–53, 55–56, 58
  Phase 2: *The Partially Gamed, Bottoms Up PTW,* 60, 62, 64–67, 71–79
  Phase 3: *The Fully Gamed PTW,* 82–85, 87, 89–91
  PTW problem, 103, 114
Price To Win (PTW) Problem
  Addressable Budget, 103–5, 105fVII.3, 114fVII.13
  Basis Of Estimates (BOE), 107

Price To Win (PTW) Problem *(continued)*
  bid price(s), 105fVII.3, 113, 114fVII.13
  bid pricing, 112
  bid teams, 104, 108–10, 112–13, 115, 119–20
  Bill Of Materials (BOM), 107–8, 108fVII.6, 109–10, 110fVII.8, 112–13, 116, 116fVII.15, 118, 118fVII.17, 120, 122, 122fVII.21
  Capture Team(s), 107
  Competitive Analysis/PTW, 103fVII.1
  Contract Line Item Number (CLIN), 112
  Contract Year One (CY1), 104, 105fVII.2, 108fVII.6, 109, 109fVII.7, 110, 110fVII.8, 114fVII.12, 116fVII.15, 117fVII.16, 118fVII.17, 121fVII.20, 122fVII.21
  Contract Year One (CY2), 104, 105fVII.2, 108fVII.6, 109fVII.7, 110fVII.8, 114, 114fVII.12, 116fVII.15, 117fVII.16, 118fVII.17, 121fVII.20, 122fVII.21
  Evaluation Model, 105–7, 115, 119, 122
  Home Team, 103–4, 107, 112, 115, 119, 122
  Levels Of Effort (LOEs), 120
  Opportunity, 103fVII.1
  Partially Gamed PTW, 107
  Performance Work Statement (PWS), 106fVII.4, 111fVII.9, 115fVII.14, 119fVII.18, 122fVII.22
  Phase 1 of Progressive PTW Problem, 103–6
  Phase 1 tables, completed, 114–15
  Phase 2 of Progressive PTW Problem, 107–11
  Phase 2 tables, completed, 116–19
  Phase 3 of Progressive PTW Problem, 112–13
  Phase 3 tables, completed, 120–23
  Request For Proposal (RFP), 104
  Small Business (SB), 110, 117
  take-downs, 105, 114, 120
  target price, 103, 105–6
  Top Down PTW, 105–6
  Top Down target prices, 103
  Work Breakdown Structure (WBS), 106fVII.4, 111fVII.9, 115fVII.14, 119fVII.18, 122fVII.22
Pricing Notes strategy, 99
Pricing Strategy, 3, 20, 45, 67, 69, 99, 100fVI.2, 101
Pricing Structure, 30, 83
Procurement Integrity Act, 24
Project Management Office (PMO), 28, 44, 77, 85, 99, **128**
Proposal Evaluation Criteria (PEC)
  IT Consolidation (ITCON), 106fVII.4, 119fVII.18, 122fVII.22
proposal risk, 44

Provenance, 8, **128**
PTW. *See* Price To Win (PTW)
Public Law 108-136, 69
Public-Private Partnership, 97
purchase price, 1
pursuit funds, 7
pWins. *See* win probabilities (pWins)
PWS. *See* Performance Work Statement (PWS)

R

rate cards, 79, 91
Rating (0 through 5), 6, 6fI.4
Readout, **128**
Reality Case, 20
Reality Model
   about, 11, 20, 23, xxi
   defined, 127, **128**
   Food for Thought, 100
   PTW Framework, 20, 23, 35fII.7, 36fII.8
   PTW Phase 1, 36fII.8, 49, 54fIII.16
   PTW Phase 3, 81–82, 82fV.2, 83–85, 85fV.3, 86, 89, 100
Reality Model-Based Price Gaming, 11
Reality Model Cumulative Profit Margin, 20, 20fI.14
"Real" opportunity knowledge, 84
rebalancing, 86
Reporting Modules, 61, 61fIV.2
Request For Proposal (RFP)
   about, 3–4, 7, 10–11, 17, 21–22
   content, 21
   defined, **129**
   Food For Thought, 100
   government, 30
   PTW Phase 1, 42, 45, 50
   PTW Phase 2, 67
   PTW Phase 3, 83–84, 90fV.6
   PTW Problem, 104, 106
Requests For Quotations (RFQs), 3
research sources, general, 101–2
Return On Investment (ROI), **129**
RFP. *See* Request For Proposal (RFP)
RFQs. *See* Requests For Quotations (RFQs)
right sizing, 86
ROI. *See* Return On Investment (ROI)
ROM. *See* Rough Order of Magnitude (ROM)
Rough Order of Magnitude (ROM), 39, **129**

S

Sample Tasks, 21
Sarbanes-Oxley, 16
SATCOM terminals, 15
SB. *See* Small Business (SB)
SCA. *See* Service Contract Act (SCA)
scheduling, 86
SCIP. *See* Strategic & Competitive Intelligence Professionals (SCIP)
Score (Weight * Rating), 6fI.4, 7
scuttlebutt, 38
Section M, **129**
security clearance requirements, xvi
Senior Management, 16, 16fI.11, 17fI.12, 19
Service Contract Act (SCA), 62, **129**
Service Level Agreements (SLAs), 30, 76, 79, **129**, xvi
Service Oriented Architecture (SOA), 18, **129**
share-in-savings approaches, 79
situation's known unknowns, 12
16-bit CPUs, 72
16 quad core servers, 74
64-bit CPUs, 72
64 single core servers, 73
SLAs. *See* Service Level Agreements (SLAs)
Small Business (SB)
   Food For Thought, 104
   PTW Phase 2, 52fIII.13, 57fIII.20, 67, 70
   PTW Phase 3, 101
   PTW Problem, 110, 117
SMEs. *See* Subject Matter Experts (SMEs)
Snowflakes, 9, 23, **129**
SOA. *See* Service Oriented Architecture (SOA)
soft (logical) engineering, 76
Solution Sketchers and Developers, 24
Solution To Win, 2
SOO. *See* Statement Of Objectives (SOO)
Source Selection Authority (SSA), 43, **129**
Source Selection Evaluation Board (SSEB), 39, 43, **129**
SOW. *See* Statement Of Work (SOW)
Specific Experience, 21
SQL-based RDBMS, 14
SSA. *See* Source Selection Authority (SSA)
SSEB. *See* Source Selection Evaluation Board (SSEB)
SSZ. *See* Strategic Strike Zone (SSZ)
Stakeholders, 16, 16fI.11
Statement of Business Solution, 13
Statement Of Objectives (SOO), 30, 42, 85, **129**
Statement of Pricing Solution, 13
Statement of Solution, 13
Statement of Strategic Approach, 13
Statement of Technical Approach, 13
Statement Of Work (SOW)
   about, 9, 30

Index

Statement Of Work (SOW) *(continued)*
   defined, **129**
   PTW Phase 1, 42, 46
   PTW Phase 2, 61
   PTW Phase 3, 85
statutory taxes, 60, 66, 130
Strange Attractor strategy, 99
Strategic & Competitive Intelligence Professionals (SCIP), 24
Strategic Pricing, 3–4, 5fI.2, 18, 20
Strategic Pricing Issues, 53, 54fIII.16
Strategic Strike Zone (SSZ)
   defined, **129**
   PTW Phase 1, 45, 56–57
   PTW Phase 2, 61
Street Talk, 38, **129**
Strengths, Weaknesses, Opportunities, and Threats (SWOTs)
   about, 13, 35fII.7, **130**
   Food for Thought, 97
   PTW Phase 1, 38, 40, 51, 51fIII.12, 55, 57
   PTW Phase 2, 60, 79, 82
   PTW Phase 3, 81fV.1, 91
Subject Matter Experts (SMEs), 12, **129**, xxi
subscription databases, 102
"success multiplier," 12
SWOTs. *See* Strengths, Weaknesses, Opportunities and Threats (SWOTs)
System Warranty and Maintenance strategy, 100

T

take-down prices, 90, 90fV.6
Takedown Rationale
   PTW Phase 1, 53, 54fIII.16
take-downs
   PTW Phase 1, 44, 48–49, 51, 53, 55, 61
   PTW Phase 2, 72–73
   PTW Phase 3, 89–90, 90fV.6, 93
   PTW Problem, 105, 114, 120
talent, 7
target price. *See also* Bottom LIne Up Front (BLUF)
   PTW and, 1, 10–11
   PTW Framework, 36fII.8
   PTW Phase 1, 32, 45–49, 47fIII.8, 53, 57, 57fIII.20
   PTW Phase 2, 61
   PTW Phase 3, 92
   PTW Problem, 103, 105–6
Target-Specific Modules, 60–61, 61fIV.2
Target Team Labor Rate Model, 70
Task Order (TO), 66–67, 99, **130**

TCO. *See* Total Cost of Ownership (TCO)
Technical Approach, 21
technological forecasts, 83
Technology Deflation strategy, 100
"Things We May Have Forgotten," 78
32-bit CPUs, 72
32 dual core servers, 74
Time and Materials (T&M), **130**
T&M. *See* Time and Materials (T&M)
TO. *See* Task Order (TO)
Top Down
   budget-based price target, 50
   Comparative Evaluation, 55fIII.17
   Competitor PTW Analysis, 48–49, 53, 55
   decomposition of the totality of the work, 46fIII.6
   Phase 1 PTW bogey, 77
   price targets, 33, 36fII.8
   "price to beat," 48
   Strategic Pricing, 53
   target pricing, 48
Top Down PTW
   developing a, 96
   History Table, 105, 105fVII.3
   Home Team's, 103
   PTW Phase 1, 48, 93
   PTW Phase 3, 92
   PTW Problem, 105–6
Top Down target price(s)
   PTW Framework, 36fII.8
   PTW Phase 1, 32, 36fII.8, 45, 48–49, 53, 57fIII.20, 92
   PTW Problem, 103
Total Cost of Ownership (TCO)
   about, 9, 9fI.6, 22, **130**
   PTW Phase 1, 49
trade press, 101
Transportation Security Administration (TSA), 96
TSA. *See* Transportation Security Administration (TSA)

U

unblended labor rates, 99
Uncompensated Overtime (UOT), 20, 54fIII.16, 66–67, 99, **130**
Unequal Product Averaging strategy, 100
ungamed bid, 89, 112
Ungamed price, 88, 88fV.5, 110fVII.8
unknown unknowns, 12
Unreality
   defined, **130**
   PTW Phase 3, 82, 82fV.2, 86–87

UOT. *See* Uncompensated Overtime (UOT)
U.S. Army RFP, 7
U.S. Court of Appeals, 22
U.S. Department of Education, 86
U.S. Federal Acquisition Regulation (FAR), 101
U.S. federal government business bid, 22
U.S. federal government marketplace, 95
U.S. Federal Government Staff Augmentation Marketplace, 97
U.S. General Services Administration (GSA), 98, **125**
U.S. Navy Rework Facilities RFP, 84

V

value-for-money, 1
volume usage of an item, 49fIII.9

W

Wall Street Journal article, xv
Warren Buffet's "Innovator–Imitator–Idiot" cycle, 22, 45
Washington Post article, 96–97
Waterman Robert, xv
Wayne Gretzky rule, 67
WBS. *See* Work Breakdown Structure (WBS)
Weight, 6, 6fI.4
weighted allocation, 46
"winner take all," 1
win probabilities (pWins), xviii
Win Probability (pWin), 6–7, 6fI.4
Work Breakdown Structure (WBS)
 defined, **125, 130**
 leaf position activities, 33, 59, 61, 76–77
 PTW Framework, 9, 11, 30, 33 31fII.3, 35fII.7, 36fII.8
 PTW Phase 1, 42, 46–48, 57
 PTW Phase 2, 59–62, 75–78, 91
 PTW Problem, 106fVII.4, 111fVII.9, 115fVII.14, 119fVII.18, 122fVII.22
Wrap Rates
 defined, **130**
 PTW Phase 2, 60, 66–67, 69–70

Made in United States
Orlando, FL
06 March 2024